T0318319

THE ECONOMICS OF THE NEW EUROPE

The European Union is in the process of a great transition. The programme to complete the internal market ended on December 31, 1992, abolishing many of the remaining non-tariff barriers to the free movement of goods, services, labour and capital. The Maastricht Treaty, signed in December 1991, committed the EU to the introduction of a single currency by no later than 1999. Outside the EU, the collapse of communism has added many of the nations of East and Central Europe to the queue of EFTA nations applying for EU membership.

Yet the road to closer economic and monetary integration in Europe is difficult and controversial and many issues remain unresolved. The partial breakdown of the EMS following speculative attacks on weaker currencies, has thrown the timetable for monetary union into disarray. The onset of deep recession across Europe has reignited nationalist and ethnic tensions particularly in eastern Europe, casting doubts on hopes of unified 'family of Europe'.

This book takes a fresh look at the economics of the new Europe. Based on articles by some of the UK's leading economic commentators which were originally published in *Economics and Business Education* (here extensively revised and updated), it remains accessible and lively throughout. Chapter 1 looks at the theory and practice of economic and monetary integration in Europe, giving an overview of the history of the process and providing a lens through which to view the other chapters. Chapters 2 to 6 examine macro issues especially those relating to EMS and EMU, while chapters 7 to 14 examine a whole range of micro and social issues, including the Social Charter, the Common Agricultural Policy and the prospects for future enlargement. The book is supplemented by a useful statistical appendix describing the EU in figures from 1964 to 1994.

Nigel M. Healey is Jean Monnet Professor of European Economic Studies at the University of Leicester and Visiting Lecturer at the University of Gdansk and Kent State University, Ohio.

THE ECONOMICS OF THE NEW EUROPE

From Community to Union

Edited by Nigel M. Healey

Routledge
Taylor & Francis Group

LONDON AND NEW YORK

First published 1995
by Routledge
2 Park Square, Milton Park, Abingdon, Oxon, OX14 4RN

Simultaneously published in the USA and Canada
by Routledge
605 Third Avenue, New York, NY 10017

Routledge is an imprint of the Taylor & Francis Group, an informa business

Typeset in Garamond by
J&L Composition Ltd, Filey, North Yorkshire

British Library Cataloguing in Publication Data
A catalogue record for this book is available from the British
Library

Library of Congress Cataloging in Publication Data
The economics of the new europe: from community to
union / edited by Nigel M. Healey.
p.   cm.
Includes bibliographical references and index.

1. European Economic Community. 2. European
Monetary System (Organization) 3. European Union
countries–Economic policy.
I. Healey, Nige.
HC241.2.C457   1995
337.1'42–dc20   94–39620

ISBN 13: 978-0-415-10875-1 (pbk)
ISBN 13: 978-0-415-10874-4 (hbk)

For Daniel, Jemma and
Nicola

CONTENTS

Part II Microeconomic issues

FIGURES AND TABLES

FIGURES

TABLES

LIST OF CONTRIBUTORS

Robert Ackrill Economics Teaching Fellow, Department of Economics, University of Nottingham, Nottingham.

Harvey W. Armstrong Senior Lecturer in Economics, Department of Economics, The Management School, University of Lancaster, Lancaster.

Michael Artis Professor, Department of Economics, European University Institute, Badia Fiesolana, Via dei Roccettini 9, 1–50016 San Domenico di Fiesole (Fl), Florence, Italy.

Peter Curwen Reader in Economics, Sheffield Business School, Pond Street, Sheffield.

Barry Harrison Senior Lecturer in Economics, Department of Economics and Public Administration, The Nottingham Trent University, Burton Street, Nottingham.

Nigel M. Healey Jean Monnet Chair of European Economic Studies, Department of Economics, University of Leicester, Leicester.

Michael Kitson Fellow, St Catherine's College and Lecturer in Economics, Newnham College, The Judge Institute of Management Studies, University of Cambridge, Fitzwilliam House, 32 Trumpington Street, Cambridge.

Valerio Lintner Principal Lecturer in Economics, Department of Economics, Guildhall University, 84 Moorgate, London.

Frank McDonald   Senior Lecturer in Economics, International Business Unit, The Manchester Metropolitan University, Cavendish Street, Manchester.

Jonathan Michie   Fellow and Director of Studies in Economics, Robinson College, The Judge Institute of Management Studies, University of Cambridge, Fitzwilliam House, 32 Trumpington Street, Cambridge.

Patrick Minford   Edward Gonner Professor of Applied Economics, Department of Economic and Business Studies, University of Liverpool, PO Box 147, Liverpool.

Eleanor J. Morgan   Senior Lecturer in Industrial Economics, School of Management, University of Bath, Claverton Down, Bath.

George Norman   Professor of Economics and Head of Department, Department of Economics, University of Edinburgh, William Robertson Building, 50 George Square, Edinburgh.

David K. Whynes   Reader in Health Economics, Department of Economics, University of Nottingham, University Park, Nottingham.

George Zis   Professor of Economics, Department of Economics, The Manchester Metropolitan University, Cavendish Street, Manchester.

PREFACE

Nigel M. Healey

The European Union (EU) is in a process of rapid transition. The '1992' programme to 'complete the internal market' ended on December 31, 1992, abolishing many of the remaining non-tariff barriers to the free movement of goods, services, labour and capital. The apparent success of the European Monetary System (EMS) during the 1980s inspired the Maastricht Treaty, signed in December 1991, which pledges the EU member states to the introduction of a single currency by no later than 1999. Outside the EU, the collapse of communism added the former Warsaw Pact nations of eastern Europe to the queue of EFTA nations applying for EU membership.

Yet the road to closer economic and monetary integration in Europe is still difficult and controversial. A number of the measures embodied in the 1992 programme remain unresolved. Before the ink on the Maastricht Treaty was dry, the EMS had been buffeted by damaging foreign exchange market volatility, which drove two of the main EU currencies – the pound sterling and the Irish punt – out of the system and forced the survivors to adopt ultra-wide ±15% target bands, setting back the drive for a single currency. And a combination of deep recession and the breakdown of communism in the east during the early 1990s reignited nationalist and ethnic tensions, casting doubt of hopes of a unified 'family of Europe'.

This book, based on articles originally published in *Economics and Business Education* (formerly *Economics*), the quarterly journal of the national Economics and Business Education Association, takes an up-to-date look at the economics of the new Europe. Chapter 1 provides an overview of the theory and practice of economic and monetary integration in Europe, providing both a 'lens' through which to view the following chapters and documenting the main steps along the road to closer European integration. Chapters 2–14, which are written by some of the leading British academic commentators on Europe, explore the changing economic landscape in the EU, reviewing the arguments surrounding monetary union, examining the reasons for the breakdown of the EMS, speculating on the implications of the 'single market' and discussing the operation of regional, social and competition policy in the EU.

All the articles have been thoroughly revised and updated to take account of developments since they first appeared. Thanks are due to all the authors, who skilfully blended new information with their original manuscripts, while tolerating my unhelpful suggestions and editorial changes. For any remaining errors of commission or omission in the revised chapters, I alone am responsible. I would like to thank Emma Dickinson for her invaluable assistance in preparing the final manuscript. Finally, I would like to thank my colleagues and friends at the University of Leicester for their support and the members and officers of the Economics and Business Education Association, (especially the general editor of *Economics and Business Education*, Peter Maunder), without whom this book would not have been possible.

1

FROM THE TREATY OF ROME TO MAASTRICHT

The Theory and Practice of European Integration

Nigel M. Healey

INTRODUCTION

The year 1990 is widely regarded as a high water mark in the history of postwar European integration. During the second half of the 1980s, a combination of special factors coincided to produce a heady, almost euphoric, mood in the 'old world'. The dream of a 'United States of Europe' – a seamless market stretching from Dublin to Bucharest – seemed at last within grasp. The pace of economic integration received its first real boost for a quarter of a century in 1985, with the launch of the single European market (SEM) – or '1992' – programme by the member states of the European Union (EU). Despite two difficult enlargements during the 1980s which brought in the less developed Mediterranean states of Greece (1981) and Spain and Portugal (1986), the SEM remained well on course during the late 1980s. This success, taken together with the demonstrable achievements of the exchange rate mechanism (ERM) in promoting exchange rate and price stability, inspired the EU to go further and plan for the introduction of a single currency. In 1989, the Delors Committee published its blueprint for full economic and monetary union (EMU) in Europe, a plan which was formally adopted with the signing of the Treaty on European Union in 1991 (see Council of Ministers, 1992).

The other states of western Europe, which had previously belonged to a parallel trade grouping known as the European Free Trade Association (EFTA), reacted to the acceleration of the pace of integration within the EU by seeking closer ties with the 'Twelve' (Haaland, 1990; Church, 1991). Although initially confined to a bilateral agreement between EFTA and the EU to jointly adhere to the main provisions of the SEM programme – creating the European Economic Area (EEA), which came into effect in 1994 – almost all the EFTA members had declared their intention to apply for full membership of the EU long before negotiations over the EEA had been concluded.

More dramatically, the late 1980s witnessed the collapse of communism in eastern Europe. During 1989–90, a 'domino effect' rippled through the region as, one by one, the former Soviet satellites rejected central planning and elected democratic governments for the first time in 40 years. The rush to embrace free market capitalism peaked in 1990, with the reunification of Germany symbolising the final end of the 'iron curtain' that had divided east and west Europe. The stage seemed set for the rapid 'marketisation' of eastern Europe, with almost all the states in the region negotiating association agreements with the EU with a view to eventual full membership.

As the new decade progressed, however, the optimism of the late 1980s gradually evaporated. The onset of a deep recession in most of the EU states reignited nationalist and protectionist senti-ments. The Treaty on European Union (more commonly known as the 'Maastricht Treaty') was ratified by member states only after protracted political wrangling, including an initial 'no' vote in the Danish popular referendum. The resulting uncertainties surround-ing the commitment of the member states to EMU contributed to a series of damaging speculative attacks on the ERM. The pound and the lira were forced to withdraw from the system in autumn 1992 and, after repeated devaluations by the weaker currencies, ultra-wide ±15% target bands were introduced in August 1993.

The enthusiasm of certain EFTA members for full EU member-ship began to weaken, with Switzerland abandoning its application and popular hostility to the EU mounting in the Nordic states, notably Norway which ultimately rejected membership in 1994. In eastern Europe, the transition to a market economy proved much more painful than expected, with the region experiencing a cala-mitous collapse in living standards (see Healey, 1994). Without the social control formerly exercised by the communist system, grow-ing poverty, unemployment and social unrest fuelled ethnic and nationalist tensions. The result was widespread inter-communal violence and, *in extremis*, civil war, most horrifically in the former

Yugoslavia. By the mid-1990s, there was a general feeling that the 'grand design' of an integrated pan-European economy had been derailed.

Yet just as the euphoria of the late 1980s was unrealistic, failing to take account of the economic and political difficulties that lay ahead, so the current prevailing mood of 'Euro-pessimism' underestimates the significance of the changes that have already taken place and the momentum that is continuing to take the process forward. European economic integration has never been a linear, incremental process; rather it has been characterised by periods of very rapid advance, followed by episodes of stagnation and backsliding. In the 1970s, for example, little progress was made in a decade plagued by recession and divergent national economic policies. During the long boom of the 1980s, in contrast, when member states enjoyed steady growth and shared a common commitment to fighting inflation, the EU successfully managed two enlargements, completed the internal market and redrafted its constitution in preparation for full monetary union.

The mid-1990s now sees the EU in a state of flux. The legislative and constitutional changes wrought in the 1980s are only now starting to have significant effects and these will continue to build up well into the next century. The 1992 programme, in particular, has set in train a wholesale restructuring of European industry, unleashing a wave of mergers and acquisitions and prompting savage labour-shedding as companies brace themselves for intensified competition. Reforms in the area of social, regional and competition policy promise to reshape the economic environment in the EU, while changes in the Common Agricultural Policy (CAP) have already had a major impact on the farm sector. In other areas, notably monetary and exchange rate policy, the outlook is altogether more uncertain, following the currency instability of the early 1990s. However, even in this sphere, there is a strong political momentum behind monetary unification which has survived the travails of the ERM.

This book is about the changes taking place in the EU economy. Part I focuses on macroeconomic issues, specifically the coordination of exchange rate and monetary policy and the outlook for macroeconomic policy coordination. Part II concentrates on a range of microeconomic issues, examining the implications of further EU enlargements and the reforms that are taking place in the area of social, regional, competition and industrial policy, as well as a comprehensive discussion of the 1992 programme and its likely effects in the years ahead. The purpose of the present chapter is to provide an overview of developments within the EU and thereby provide a context in which to view the other chapters that make up the book. It opens with a discussion of the basic principles underpinning economic integration. It then briefly reviews the present state of the EU, documenting the main historical events since the EU was established in 1958 and outlining the institutional framework within which policy is made. Finally, it offers an introduction to the theory of economic integration.

WHAT IS ECONOMIC INTEGRATION?

The term, 'economic integration', refers to the merging together of national economies and the blurring of the boundaries that separate economic activity in one nation state from another – see El-Agraa (1994) or McDonald and Dearden (1992) for a more detailed discussion. Over the postwar period, the world's economies have become increasingly open and mutually interdependent. Whether they live in Moscow, London or Tokyo, today's teenagers drink Coca-Cola, eat McDonald's hamburgers, wear Levi jeans and listen to the same music on MTV; giant corporations like Ford, Toyota and IBM manufacture and market their products in almost every major economy. The relentless search for new markets and new production locations has led to the so-called 'globalisation of business', as companies restructure their activities across frontiers, weaving national economies ever closer together in the process (Dunning, 1988; Healey, 1991c).

This increasing integration of the world's economies has undoubtedly been accelerated by such 'enabling' technological advances as cheap air travel, computers, telephones, faxes and satellite television, but it has ultimately stemmed from the deliberate trade policies of the main capitalist states. The trade rules negotiated during successive rounds of the General Agreement on Tariffs and Trade (GATT), most recently during the 'Uruguay Round' which ended in 1993, together with the trade liberalisation polices orchestrated by the International Monetary Fund (IMF) and the International Bank for Reconstruction and Development (IBRD or 'World Bank'), have succeeded in eliminating many of

Table 1.1 The dimensions of economic integration

	Free trade between member states?	Common external tariff?	Free movement of factors of production?	Harmonisation of economic policy?	Centralisation of economic and monetary policy?
Free trade area	Yes	No	No	No	No
Customs union	Yes	Yes	No	No	No
Common market	Yes	Yes	Yes	Yes	No
Economic and monetary union	Yes	Yes	Yes	Yes	Yes

the artificial barriers to trade and cross-border investment which plagued the prewar era.

The postwar period has been characterised not just by the steady liberalisation of trade and the globalisation of business, but by the formation of regional trade blocs designed to deepen and widen economic integration between participating member states. Some have simply attempted to free trade in certain designated commodities (e.g., the North American Free Trade Agreement); others have sought to integrate their economies so absolutely that they share a common currency and pool political decision-making across a range of areas (e.g., the monetary union between Belgium and Luxembourg). The EU is, of course, the best known of these regional blocs. It currently offers its member states freedom of movement of goods, services, labour and capital and holds out the promise of a common currency by the end of the decade. The following sub-sections set out the different forms that regional integration may take (see Table 1.1 for a summary).

The free trade area

The 'free trade area' is the weakest form of economic integration. It involves the removal of tariffs and quotas (quantitative restrictions) on trade between member states. The North American Free Trade Agreement (NAFTA) between the United States, Canada and Mexico, formed between 1988 and 1994, and the Association of South East Asian Nations (ASEAN), set up between Indonesia, Brunei, Malaysia, Philippines, Singapore and Thailand in 1967, are contemporary examples of free trade areas. Free trade may be limited to certain sectors, as in the case of EFTA (see above), which initially abolished tariffs and quotas on industrial goods only.

The customs union

One step up from a free trade area is a 'customs union'. It embraces all the provisions of a free trade area – namely, the abolition of restrictions on trade between members – but also obliges member states to pursue a common trade policy in their dealings with the rest of the world (e.g., by adopting a common external tariff). This additional dimension avoids the problem of 'trade deflection', which occurs when goods from the outside world are 'deflected' to whichever country in a free trade area imposes the lowest tariff on imports, before being reshipped (tariff-free) to their ultimate destination elsewhere in the same free trade area.

Trade deflection distorts trade flows and robs high-tariff member states of potential tax revenue on goods arriving from third countries. The disadvantage of coordinating external trade policy to prevent trade deflection – which is the only alternative to complicated 'rules of origin' designed to prevent low-tariff countries re-exporting imported goods to other members tariff-free – is that countries with complex, highly-selective trading arrangements with the outside world (like Britain in the 1950s and the United States today) are forced to conform to a common commercial policy. It is largely for this reason that countries with wider geopolitical interests have typically resisted membership of a customs union.

The common market

A common market encompasses the trade-related provisions of a customs union, together with measures to promote the free movement of factors of production (i.e., labour and capital). Creating a common market in goods, services, labour and capital is, however, a bigger jump up from a common market than simply extending the principles of free trade to cover labour and capital. A customs union (like a free trade area) ensures the free movement of goods and services only in the limited sense that its members abolish explicit, trade-related restrictions on imports from other members of the union. In contrast, a common market implies creating a single, borderless market for products and factors of production (see Nevin, 1990; Healey, 1992b; Vickerman, 1992).

Attaining the goal of a common market requires not just the abolition of explicit controls on trade, immigration and capital movements, but also the harmonisation of government policies in areas like taxation and social security, public procurement and industrial and regional policy to prevent the hidden barriers that would otherwise continue to segment national markets. For example, if governments subsidise domestic steel producers, then allowing in imports from other member states tariff-free is not sufficient to create a common market in steel (see Chapter 13). Instead of a 'level playing field', on which all producers compete openly for business, preferential government policies and inconsistent technical standards would make the pitch so uneven that competition would continue to be stifled.

Economic and monetary union

Economic and monetary union (EMU) is the strongest form of economic integration. Economic union involves making economic policy centrally, rather than seeking to harmonise or coordinate policy as in a common market. The distinction between a common market and an economic union is blurred and essentially one of degree, rather than of kind. The second dimension, namely a monetary union, entails the extension of central policymaking to monetary policy, as well as other areas of economic policy (see Chapters 4–6). To the extent that the fear of exchange rate fluctuations and the transactions costs of switching between national currencies are major factors preventing the cross-border movements of goods, services, labour and capital, it could be argued that monetary union – the move to a single currency issued by a single central bank – is a necessary condition for the attainment of a common market (see Emerson and Huhne, 1991; Artis, 1989). Nevertheless, it is conventional to view the pooling of political sovereignty necessary to achieve economic and monetary union as sufficiently wholesale to make it qualitatively different from the negotiated harmonisation and coordination of policy which characterises a common market.

It is important to recognise that these various stages of economic integration may be viewed either as a process or as alter-

7

native end-points. To paraphrase the comment of a member of the 1985 House of Lords Committee studying European integration,

> just as Dover is a step on the road to Paris, so a customs union is a step on the road to economic and monetary union. But having reached Dover, there is no reason why one cannot choose to stay there and never go to Paris at all. By the same token, one can also decide to stick with a customs union and go no further.

There are many examples of free trade areas (e.g., NAFTA, ASEAN) and customs unions (e.g., the former customs union between Uganda, Kenya and Tanzania) which their members never intended should evolve further. The history of the EU, however, has been characterised by a collective desire for 'an ever closer union', so that there is a strong tendency amongst the member states to view economic integration as an irreversible process which must continue until the ultimate goal of economic and monetary union is achieved (see Chapter 9; Brittan, 1991).

It is useful to conceptualise regional trade blocs as 'zones of differential integration' (or 'concentric circles', as current EU jargon puts it) within the broader framework of global integra-

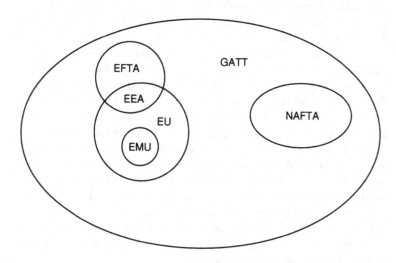

Figure 1.1 Regional trade blocs within the broader framework of global integration

tion, which may overlap to a greater or lesser extent (see Figure 1.1). The figure shows the EU as one trade bloc within the GATT framework, enjoying a special relationship with EFTA (i.e., the overlapping EEA), paralleled by other blocs like NAFTA and embracing a sub-set of member states which may proceed to an exclusive EMU. This approach highlights the fact that economic integration can take place at different rates between different groupings and sub-groupings of countries. Within many EU members, there is undoubtedly a vision of a 'two-speed' Europe – in which a core of states integrates rapidly, while a second tier of more peripheral states integrates more slowly, signing up to certain measures later and phasing them in over longer time periods.

In fact, the existence of the EU has never prevented subsets of its membership accelerating their integration via separate bilateral agreements: for example, the Netherlands and Germany agreed to maintain their ±2.25% exchange rate bands after the European Monetary System moved to ±15% bands in 1993, while nine of the states of the EU have now signed the 1990 Schengen Agreement (eliminating border controls on individuals) outside the framework of the 1992 programme – only Britain, Ireland and Denmark have not yet signed. Moreover, the EU has increasingly recognised the limitations of forcing all member states to integrate at the same pace, allowing so-called 'opt-out' clauses to be written into treaties (e.g., Britain's opt-out from the social chapter of the Maastricht Treaty – see Chapter 10), giving rise to the union's 'variable geometry' (i.e., a union in which different sub-groups of members are integrated to different degrees in different areas).

AN OVERVIEW OF THE EUROPEAN UNION

Table 1.2 provides a brief overview of the twelve member states that presently comprise the EU. It shows that there exist sharp differences both between the relative size of the member states, as measured by their populations, and levels of economic prosperity, as measured by per capita gross domestic product (GDP). In population terms, the EU is dominated by the 'big five' – France, Germany, Italy, Britain and Spain – which together account for approximately 85% of the total population of the EU. In terms of relative living standards, there is an enormous gulf between the rich, northern European states and the poor, southern Mediterranean states. Per capita income in countries

Table 1.2 Population and relative living standards in the EU

	Population (1994)	Per capita GDP (1994) EU average = 100
Belgium	10.1m	110.1
Denmark	5.2m	141.1
Germany	81.6m	126.4
Greece	10.5m	39.0
Spain	39.2m	64.4
France	58.0m	116.4
Ireland	3.6m	71.0
Italy	58.1m	92.7
Luxembourg	0.4m	143.4
The Netherlands	15.4m	109.2
Portugal	9.4m	43.5
Britain	58.2m	91.8
Total EU	349.7m	100.0

Source: European Economy.

like Denmark and Germany is roughly three times higher than in Greece and Portugal. These imbalances raise important questions for the conduct of EU regional policy, while also impacting on social, competition and agricultural policymaking (see Chapters 7–14).

Table 1.3 shows the degree of 'openness' (i.e., the proportion of GDP which is internationally traded) of the EU member states. Unsurprisingly, openness varies inversely with size – larger countries tend to be relatively more self-sufficient than smaller countries. Luxembourg, for example, trades 91.4% of its GDP, in contrast to Germany where trade accounts for only 24.5% of GDP. The table shows that, with the exception of Denmark, the member states of the EU have become increasingly open over the last 35 years. When attention is focused on intra-EU trade (i.e., trade with other member states) rather than total trade, this pattern is even more marked. Again, with the exception of Denmark, trade with other EU partners has increased as a percentage of GDP for all member states, in most cases by proportionately more than total trade. In France, for example, total trade has roughly doubled its share of GDP from 12.4% to 20.4%, while intra-EU trade has increased almost three-fold from 3.6% to 9.7% of GDP. In other words, EU membership has had the effect of accelerating the

Table 1.3 Degree of openness in EU member states[1] (figures in parentheses are for intra-EU trade only)

	1960	1994
Belgium	40.8 (n/a)	67.5 (n/a)
Denmark	33.4 (16.5)	29.4 (12.3)
Germany (West)	16.5 (5.6)	24.5 (11.2)
Greece	16.7 (9.0)	34.4 (20.3)
Spain	7.2 (2.2)	22.0 (11.2)
France	12.4 (3.6)	20.4 (9.7)
Ireland	35.9 (21.9)	56.0 (31.0)
Italy	13.5 (4.4)	20.0 (9.0)
Luxembourg	73.7 (n/a)	91.4 (n/a)
The Netherlands	43.8 (20.6)	47.4 (26.4)
Portugal	23.7 (11.3)	39.0 (26.7)
Britain	22.3 (3.9)	26.2 (10.9)

1. Defined as percentage share of imports in GDP.
Source: European Economy.

opening up of member economies by promoting trade between member states.

Table 1.4 provides a guide to the relative size of the EU, as compared to the other two major economic powers. It shows that in population terms, the EU dwarfs both the United States and Japan with a total population (since German reunification) of 350m. In terms of total GDP, however, the EU is broadly on a par with the United States, reflecting the rather lower per capita income level in the former. Indeed, on this basis, the EU is the poorest of the world's three major trading powers (the so-called 'Triad'), with per capita GDP approximately half that of Japan.

Table 1.4 Population and income in the 'Triad'

	Population (1994)	GDP (1994)	Per capita GDP (1994)
European Union	350m	ECU 5,684bn	ECU 16,240
United States	261m	ECU 5,879bn	ECU 22,524
Japan	125m	ECU 4,065bn	ECU 35,520

Note: ECU 1 = £0.80 approx. (1994).
Source: European Economy.

NIGEL M. HEALEY

A BRIEF HISTORY OF THE EUROPEAN UNION

'Jaw-jaw is better than war-war' – *Winston Churchill*

The formation of the EU must be seen against the backcloth of two catastrophic world wars, both triggered by rivalries between the major European powers. In the immediate aftermath of World War II, the British wartime prime minister, Winston Churchill, floated the idea of a 'United States of Europe', in which he proposed that the national economies of Europe should be fused together into such a complete and mutually interdependent union that war between its member states would be rendered unthinkable. Today such faith in the cohesive power of economic integration has been shaken by the nationalist and ethnic unrest in the former nations of the Soviet Union and Yugoslavia, both of which have been torn asunder since 1989 after decades of economic unification under communist rule. Nevertheless, in the early postwar years, negotiations to build an economic community in Europe were primarily driven by political, rather than economic, considerations (see Lintner and Mazey, 1991). See Table 1.5 for summary of key developments to date.

The concept of a pan-European federation received an early setback with the division of Europe into the (communist) east and (capitalist) west in the late 1940s. A second blow was delivered by the British government which, despite its early enthusiasm for Churchill's vision, withdrew its support as it became clear that closer ties with mainland Europe would entail severing its preferential trading relations with the Commonwealth. Britain came to favour a less comprehensive arrangement, restricted to free trade in industrial goods (see above), and subsequently persuaded the Nordic countries (Finland, Sweden, Norway, Iceland and Denmark), Spain, Portugal, Switzerland and Austria to collaborate in the creation of EFTA, which came into being in 1960. In the event, only six western European states (France, West Germany, Italy, Belgium, the Netherlands and Luxembourg) signed the Treaty of Rome in 1957, the agreement which created the forerunner of today's EU, the European Economic Community (EEC), on January 1, 1958 (see Chapter 9 for a more detailed survey).

The early years of the EU were plagued by internal disputes and wrangles, with the French government becoming increasingly politically isolated over its farm policies and boycotting meetings

12

Table 1.5 Key developments in the history of the EU

1951:	The Treaty of Paris is signed, creating the European Coal and Steel Community (ECSC) which comes into existence on July 23, 1952. Membership comprises West Germany, France, Italy, Belgium, the Netherlands and Luxembourg (the 'Six').
1957:	The Treaty of Rome is signed, creating the European Economic Community (EEC) and Euratom, the European atomic energy agency with effect from January 1, 1958. Membership comprises the Six.
1960:	The European Free Trade Association (EFTA) is established, with membership comprising Britain, Spain, Portugal, Switzerland, Finland, Sweden, Norway, Denmark, Ireland, Iceland and Liechtenstein.
1965:	The Merger Treaty is signed, bringing together the three 'communities' of the ECSC, EEC and Euratom with effect from 1967 and naming the merged grouping the European Community (EC).
1966:	The Luxembourg Compromise is agreed, allowing member states to veto proposals which threaten 'special national interests'.
1973:	Britain, Ireland and Denmark accede to the EC. Norway votes 'No' to membership in a popular referendum.
1979:	The European Monetary System is established. Britain declines to place sterling in the exchange rate mechanism (until October 1990).
1981:	Greece accedes to the EC.
1985:	The White Paper published, setting out the measures necessary for the completion of the internal or 'single' market.
1986:	The Single European Act is signed (taking effect on July 1, 1987); Spain and Portugal accede to the EC.
1989:	The Delors Report is published, setting out a blueprint for economic and monetary union.
1990:	Stage One of the programme for economic and monetary union begins on January 1.
1991:	The Treaty on European Union (the 'Maastricht Treaty') is signed (taking effect following ratification by member states on November 1, 1993). The Maastricht Treaty establishes the EC as one 'pillar' of a new European Union (EU), the other two being a common security/foreign policy and a common internal affairs policy.
1992:	The single market programme is completed on December 31.
1994:	The European Economic Area comes into effect on January 1, extending the main provisions of the single market programme to the members of EFTA. Stage Two of the programme for economic and monetary union begins on January 1; the European Monetary Institute is established in Frankfurt.
1995:	Finland, Sweden and Austria accede to the EU.

in retaliation. The failure of other member states to discipline France led to the 'Luxembourg Compromise' in 1966, an agreement which recognised the inability of a voluntary 'club' like the EU to impose the will of the majority on a reluctant minority by allowing a member state to veto proposals if it felt its 'special national interests' were being threatened. The Luxembourg Compromise meant that all important decisions thereafter were made on a consensus basis. This state of affairs was only altered by the passage of the Single European Act (SEA) in 1986, which restricted the use of the veto to certain areas only (see Chapter 8).

Between 1966 and 1986, the pace of economic integration was relatively sluggish. Since almost any proposal made by the Commission during this period normally involved costs to one or more member states – even though the EU as a whole would have gained – potential losers invariably blocked progress by using their veto. Resistance to change was further strengthened by the fact that all EU countries (except Britain) elect their national governments using a system of proportional representation. This often results in minority governments, which rely for their political survival on support from smaller parties representing particular groups in society (e.g., farmers – see Chapter 11). Such an arrangement gives special interest groups a disproportionate influence in national parliaments which, until the Luxembourg Compromise was partially suspended by the SEA, tended to paralyse decision-making at the EU level as well.

The birth of the 1992 programme

During the early 1980s, frustration with the slow pace of integration within the EU began to mount. There was a growing feeling that the failure to unify its national markets was causing the EU to fall behind its other Triad rivals, the United States and Japan. 'Eurosclerosis' (i.e., economic paralysis) became a popular term. Capital investment within Europe was lagging behind that in the United States and Japan, while unit labour costs (a major component of international competitiveness) had accelerated ahead of costs in the other two Triad members. Superimposed on this deepening sense of economic insecurity in the EU was the strengthening position within key member states of right-wing governments committed to supply-side reform in the early

1980s. Led by the Thatcher government in Britain, but followed closely by, *inter alia*, the Kohl administration in Germany and – after an abrupt U-turn in 1982 – the Mitterand government in France, EU governments came to see free trade and free markets, rather than protectionism and state intervention, as the recipe for economic success.

Against this background of economic stagnation and growing political pressure for supply-side reform, the Commission switched tack in 1985. Instead of proposing new laws and directives one by one as it had done in the past, so ensuring that there was always at least one loser to obstruct the way forward, the Commission outlined all 300 of the measures it deemed necessary to complete the single market in one 'White Paper'. The logic of this change of tactics was to show each member state that the package overall would be to its advantage; hence, each could be induced to accept individual proposals which would damage its national interests in order to guarantee the success of the programme as a whole (see Chapters 7 and 8). Progress could thereafter be made in a giant 'horse-trading' exercise. For example, Britain might accept a standard two-pin plug (incurring the cost of changing from three-pin plugs) if the French agreed to abolish capital controls (so allowing British financial institutions into the hitherto protected French financial market).

The Commission's masterplan for 'completing the internal market' was formally approved and the following year, 1986, the SEA was passed. The SEA pledged the member states to achieving the single market and, more importantly, altered the decision-making processes – limiting the use of the veto (the legacy of the Luxembourg Compromise) to a few key areas – to ensure that the enabling measures could all be voted into EU law by the agreed deadline of December 31, 1992. Despite ongoing disagreement about a limited number of sensitive issues, the necessary legislation was almost entirely adopted by the EU before the self-imposed deadline, creating a unified market in the EU for the first time in 1993.

From the single market to monetary union

Inspired by the revitalisation of the process of economic integration and encouraged by the apparent success of the EMS in promoting 'monetary stability', the European Council (see below) directed the Commission to prepare a blueprint for EMU in 1988. The result was the 'Delors Report', published in 1989, which proposed a radical, three-stage plan (see Chapters 4 and 5). In Stage One, it recommended that all EU currencies should join the ERM 'on equal terms'. In practice, this meant that the currencies outside the system must be incorporated and that, in due course, all members should respect the then mainstream, ±2.25% band (it has since been widened to ±15% – see Chapter 2). Taken in conjunction with the elimination of barriers to the free movement of capital – which under the '1992' programme was to take place in July 1990 – the Delors Plan argued that Stage One would represent a solid foundation on which the EU could build by gradually reducing the width of the target band.

The Delors Plan envisaged that Stage Two would be a transitional phase, during which monetary policy would be increasingly coordinated, thereby allowing the margin for permissible exchange rate fluctuations to be progressively cut to zero and realignments phased out. The report recommended the establishment of a European central bank (ECB), which would supervise and harmonise national monetary policies, although throughout Stage Two, member governments would retain ultimate sovereignty in monetary affairs. Stage Three would involve the move to irrevocably fixed exchange rates and 'the replacement of national currencies by a single [EU] currency . . . as soon as possible after the locking of parities'.

The Council of Ministers (see below) judged that implementation of Stages Two and Three would require institutional changes within the EU which could not be achieved without substantive changes to the Treaty of Rome. To this end, a special intergovernmental committee (IGC) was convened in December 1990, charged with drawing up concrete proposals to turn the Delors Plan into reality. The IGC finally concluded its deliberations in December 1991, when the heads of the twelve member states (the 'European Council' – see below) met in the Dutch town of Maastricht to sign a new Treaty on European Union (see Chapters 4–6 for a discussion of the implications of monetary union). Reflecting concern over the possible costs of EMU to the less-developed, higher-inflation countries of the EU, the treaty envisages that the move to a single currency will depend on certain 'convergence' conditions being fulfilled (e.g., applicants must have inflation and interest rates that are close to the average of the 'best' three states and must not exceed limits on public debt and budget deficits, etc.).

The logic of these conditions is that, if satisfied, the costs of giving up monetary sovereignty will be modest and, by implication, outweighed by the likely benefits (see Chapter 5). If at least seven member states meet all these prerequisites in 1996, this group may set a date for a limited monetary union that – initially at least – will exclude the other EU countries. The remaining states can then join as and when their circumstances allow. Should the 1996 conference fail to set a date for EMU, it will be reconvened in 1998. At this time, if at least five member states meet the prerequisites agreed at Maastricht, those that qualify will automatically adopt a common currency in 1999, leaving the others to apply for membership in due course.

THE INSTITUTIONAL STRUCTURE OF THE EUROPEAN UNION

To achieve the objectives set out in the Treaty of Rome, 'the Six' created four key institutions, whose role and functions have been gradually modified by successive treaty amendments, most recently by the Maastricht Treaty which revised the interrelationship between the Council of Ministers and the European Parliament (see Nicoll and Salmon, 1994, for a more detailed discussion).

The Commission

The Commission is the EU's civil service or executive. It is based in Brussels and has a staff of approximately 17,000 permanent civil servants, of whom approximately 15% are translators. The Commission is structured into 23 departments of state (known as directorate-generals). Its work is overseen by seventeen commissioners, who each control one or more departments of state (e.g., agriculture, economic and financial affairs, etc.). The commissioners are appointed for five-year terms by national governments, but take an oath not to represent their narrow national interests. Germany, France, Italy, Britain and Spain each appoint two commissioners, while the other seven member states each provide one. The Commission has a president (currently the former Luxembourg prime minister, Jacques Santer), who is appointed by the European Council.

In relative terms, the Commission is tiny, employing fewer civil servants than most national ministries. In part, this is possible because much of its day-to-day work is orchestrated via the national departments of its member states. For example, the Ministry of Agriculture carries out the practical business of implementing EU farm policy, acting as the Commission's 'agent' in dealing with British farmers. However, the size of the EU budget is also smaller than popularly believed. Table 1.6 shows the scale and composition of the EU budget for 1993. While national governments spend approximately 40% of GDP in most member states, the total EU budget is less than 2% of the EU's GDP.

The Council of Ministers

The Council of Ministers is the ultimate decision-taking body in the EU, although in certain policy areas it can no longer overrule the European Parliament since the ratification of the Maastricht Treaty (see below). It comprises the ministers of national governments. A meeting dealing with budgetary policy will be attended by the twelve finance or treasury ministers, for example, while a meeting addressing security policy will involve interior (i.e., home) ministers. Of its many guises, 'Ecofin' (the council of

Table 1.6 The EU budget, 1993

	ECU (bn)	Per cent of total
Expenditure		
agricultural policy	35.1	53.4
structural operations	20.7	31.6
external policy	3.0	4.6
research policy	2.2	3.3
administrative expenditure	3.4	5.2
other policies	1.2	1.8
total expenditure	65.5	100.0
Revenue		
agricultural levies	2.2	3.4
customs duties	13.1	20.0
value-added tax	35.7	54.5
additional resources	14.0	21.4
miscellaneous	0.5	0.7
total revenue	65.5	100.0

Source: European Economy.

finance ministers) and the Council of Agricultural Ministers are the most important in the economic sphere, although meetings of foreign affairs ministers frequently warrant the greatest public attention.

The Council of Ministers normally meets in Brussels, where its gatherings are serviced by a secretariat of approximately 2,000 staff, organised into directorates-general which parallel those of the Commission. Each member state holds the 'presidency' of the Council for a revolving six-month term (January–June or July–December), which allows its national representatives to chair meetings, set agendas and generally direct the activities of the Council for the direction of its term.

The deliberations of national ministers are supported by a Committee of Permanent Representatives (COREPER), a group of national civil servants based in Brussels for the purpose of liaising with the Commission and generally assisting their national ministerial representatives to make decisions efficiently. Voting within the Council takes place on a 'qualified majority' basis. Each national minister has an allocated number of votes, depending on the size of his/her state (see Table 1.7). At present, 54 (of the total of 76) votes are needed for a 'yes' vote to be carried. The allocation of votes between member states is to be altered with the accession of the three EFTA states in 1995 and the proposed increase in the number of votes necessary to 'block' a proposal in the Council (presently 23) proved to be a source of some

Table 1.7 Weighted votes in the Council of Ministers, 1994

Belgium	5
Denmark	3
Germany	10
Greece	5
Spain	8
France	10
Ireland	3
Italy	10
Luxembourg	2
The Netherlands	5
Portugal	5
Britain	10
Total	76

Source: EC Commission.

controversy, with Britain in particular opposing what its government saw as an attempt to 'dilute' its voice in the EU.

The council of prime ministers (and heads of state) is known as the 'European Council' and, although it historically has had no clear area of responsibility, it has become the key forum for making major strategic decisions within the EU. The European Council first began meeting in 1974 at the suggestion of the then French president, Giscard d'Estaing, and its role was formally recognised by the SEA in 1986. It comprises the French president and the prime ministers of the other eleven states, together with their foreign ministers and the president and a vice-president of the Commission. The European Council normally meets three times a year, once in each of the countries holding the six-monthly presidency of the Council and once in Brussels.

The European Parliament

Despite recent constitutional reforms, the European Parliament remains a primarily consultative body with limited legislative powers. It essentially discusses EU matters, makes recommendations to the Council of Ministers and the Commission and monitors the execution of EU policy. Its powers were, however, extended by the Maastricht Treaty, which introduced the so-called 'co-decision procedure'. This allows the Parliament to block legislation which has been approved by the Council of Ministers in some fifteen areas of policymaking. The co-decision procedure was first used in 1994 and it remains unclear how much real power this innovation will actually give parliamentarians.

The European Parliament is elected every five years and has 567 members, who arrange themselves into political groupings according to ideology rather than nationality. Following the 1994 elections, the socialists comprise the single largest grouping, with the British Labour Party (which belongs to this group and chairs its meetings) being the largest national party (see Table 1.8). The European Parliament conducts most of its business in Brussels, but once a month it has plenary sessions in Strasbourg, where it is housed in a new purpose-built building.

Seats are allocated to member states on the basis of population, but, as Table 1.9 shows, there is considerable variation in the number of electors per Member of the European Parliament (MEP). This imbalance arises primarily due to the large differ-

Table 1.8 European parliamentary seats by political grouping, June 1994

European Socialist Party	199
European People's Party	148
Independents and Non-attached	96
Liberal, Democratic and Reformist Group	43
European Democratic Alliance	24
Greens	22
European Right	14
Left Unity Group	13
Rainbow Group	8
Total	567

Source: European Parliament.

ences in total population between member states – standardising the number of electors per member of parliament would reduce the representation of the smaller member states to such an extent that their voice would effectively not be heard.

The European Court of Justice

The European Court of Justice rules on interpretations and breaches of EU law. The Court is based in Luxembourg and presently consists of thirteen judges and six advocates-general. It has made a number of important legal rulings which have altered

Table 1.9 National representation in the European Parliament

	Number of MEPs	*Population per MEP*
Belgium	25	403,300
Denmark	16	324,700
Germany	99	819,200
Greece	25	415,600
Spain	64	611,200
France	87	664,400
Ireland	15	238,100
Italy	87	654,700
Luxembourg	6	65,000
The Netherlands	31	495,300
Portugal	25	394,700
Britain	87	669,800
Total	567	—

Source: Eurostat.

the course of European economic integration (for example, by establishing key principles about unfair practices). The famous 'Cassis de Dijon' ruling, for example, outlawed the use of regulations calculated to have the effect of favouring domestic producers over those in other member states, while its rulings on equal pay have had profound effects on the provision of pensions in the EU. However, the Court's relatively small size means that its effectiveness is limited by the number of cases it can process.

THE WELFARE EFFECTS OF ECONOMIC INTEGRATION

In analysing the welfare effects of economic integration, a good starting point is to consider the costs of segmenting national markets by the imposition of various barriers to trade. These barriers can be conveniently represented by a tariff, which increases the market price of imported goods and therefore serves to completely or partially exclude them from the home market. The analysis can, however, be equally applied to less transparent (non-tariff) barriers like discriminatory technical standards, all of which have the ultimate effect of making it more costly for an importer to sell in the home market and thereby protecting local producers from overseas competition. The only difference is that a tariff generates revenue for the government, whereas a non-tariff barrier (NTB) inflates the true opportunity cost of imports and so represents a complete deadweight loss.

The simplest way of analysing the effects of such obstacles to trade is to utilise familiar supply and demand analysis. In Figure 1.2, S_H and D_H represent the domestic supply of, and the domestic demand for, the good being considered. It is conventionally assumed that the country concerned is small, in the sense that its purchases (imports) of the good on the world market have no impact on the world price, P_W. In other words, the country is a 'price-taker', with consumers facing a perfectly elastic world supply curve, S_W, at price P_W.

Trade barriers are intended to restrict imports. In their absence, the effective supply schedule (showing the total amount from all sources supplied to the market at each price) would be ABS_W, which intersects D_H at point E. The market price would be simply the world price, P_W, at which domestic producers would supply Q_1 and consumers would demand Q_4, with the difference between the

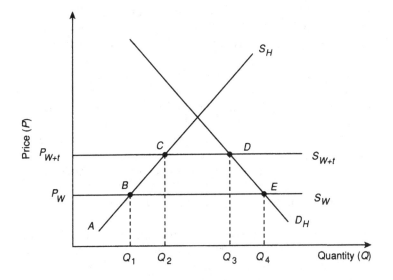

Figure 1.2 The welfare effects of protection

two, $Q_4 - Q_1$, being imported. Suppose the government now introduces the simplest form of trade barrier, a 'specific' tariff – that is, a tariff of a specific amount (e.g., £10) per unit imported.

In Figure 1.2, the imposition of the specific tariff, t, has the effect of shifting the world supply schedule vertically upwards by the amount of the tariff to S_{W+t}, so that the new effective supply schedule becomes ACS_{W+t}. As a result, the market price rises to P_{W+t}. At the higher price of P_{W+t}, domestic producers expand output to Q_2, increasing their profits ('producer surplus') by the area $P_W P_{W+t} CB$. Domestic consumption, conversely, is choked off by the price rise, falling to Q_3. Consumers are now paying more to consume less and the welfare loss they suffer is represented by the reduction in their consumer surplus of area $P_W P_{W+t} DE$. Imports are squeezed by both the increase in domestic production and the decline in demand, falling to $Q_3 - Q_2$. From the government's point of view, the tariff has achieved its objective of reducing imports and boosting domestic production. Bear in mind also that although consumers are now paying P_{W+t}, when they buy imported goods this price includes the tariff, 't', which goes not to overseas producers but to the government. In total, the government raises an amount of tariff revenue given by area *CDFG* (NB, this offsetting welfare gain would be absent in the case of an NTB which raised import costs by an amount *t*).

In net terms – that is, taking the economy as a whole and combining the gains and losses of producers, consumers and government – it is clear that the welfare loss suffered by consumers outweighs the gains enjoyed by the other two groups by an amount *BCG+DFE*. (NB, the larger the tariff, the larger these two 'welfare triangles' and the greater the net loss to society.) Throwing this analysis into reverse and abolishing the tariff implies a net welfare gain to society of *BCG+DFE* (or *BCDE* in the case of an NTB), so providing a neat diagrammatic summary of the economic case for free trade.

Membership of a grouping like the EU does not, however, unambiguously constitute a move to freer trade; rather, it implies a shift to a discriminatory trade policy, in which tariff (and non-tariff) barriers are reduced or eliminated on intra-union trade, while remaining on trade between union members and the outside world. For a country initially protecting its producers against overseas competition, joining the EU thus involves two major changes in trade policy. The first is that it agrees to eliminate tariffs – and other NTBs – against imports from its fellow member countries. The second is that it adopts a discriminatory or preferential trade policy, allowing free access for goods from other EU members, but imposing a common external tariff (CET) against the rest of the world. This latter feature of the EU injects additional distortions into the relative prices faced by domestic consumers (i.e., other EU producers become artificially competitive *vis-à-vis* the rest of the world) and this may, under certain circumstances, cause offsetting welfare losses. It is to a more detailed analysis of these issues that the next section turns (see also Chapter 7).

The welfare effects of the European Union

The analysis of economic integration typically focuses on the effects of forming a customs union and, to the extent that the EU is still in the process of progressing beyond this stage to create a genuine common market, in what follows attention will be focused on the welfare effects of this form of integration. Remember throughout this sub-section that, while the traditional

24

economic analysis examines the effect of switching from a universal to a discriminatory tariff on imports, this framework can also be used to assess the effect of selectively dismantling NTBs (as in the 1992 programme to complete the internal market). As noted above, the only difference is that, in the former case, tariff revenue accrues to the government, whereas in the latter, the true opportunity cost of imports is increased by NTBs.

To further simplify the analysis, consider the formation of a hypothetical customs union between only two countries, H (the 'home' country) and P (the 'partner' country). Assume that both countries initially impose the same tariff on imports, so that the CET levied on imports from the rest of the world after the union is created is the same as the original non-discriminatory tariff. The purpose of this second assumption is to focus attention on the fundamental impact of joining a customs union, namely that imports from the partner country escape the tariff to which they were formerly subject. Any difference between the original tariff and the new CET would simply confuse the issue, since the changes in imports from the outside world it would induce are not a necessary consequence of joining the union; they could equally have been engineered by a unilateral alteration of the original non-discriminatory tariff.

In Figure 1.3a, S_H represents the domestic supply curve and t is both the pre-union tariff (on all imports) and the CET (on imports from the outside world). S_W is the world supply schedule (perfectly elastic as before, since both the home country and the customs union are assumed to be too small to affect the world price, P_W) and S_P represents the supply of goods to the home country market by the partner country. Before the union is formed, when imports from both the outside world and partner country are subject to the same tariff, t, the effective supply schedule is given by ABS_{W+t}. Because S_P is above S_W at every level of output, imports from the partner country are completely excluded from the home market by this tariff.

Once the customs union has been formed, however, imports from the partner country enter tariff-free and compete on equal terms with domestic goods. At any given price, therefore, producers in the customs union collectively supply an amount 'x', of which 'y' is supplied by domestic firms and '$x-y$' by firms from the partner country. The total union supply curve is shown in Figure 1.3b, where S_{CU} is simply the partner's supply, S_P, (horizontally)

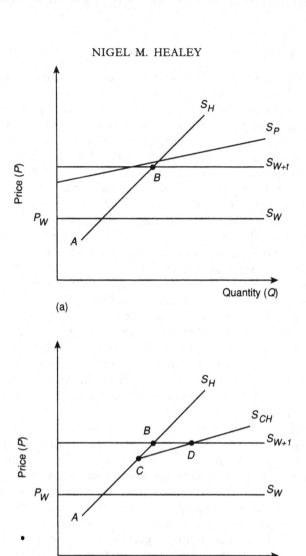

Figure 1.3 Effective supply (a) pre-customs and (b) post-customs union

added to the domestic supply, S_H. The new effective supply curve becomes $ACDS_{W+t}$. The scene is now set to assess the welfare implications of union membership for the home country, which clearly depend on a range of factors, including: the relative

26

competitiveness of the partner's producers *vis-à-vis* the rest of the world; the sizes of the pre-union tariff and the CET; and the relative elasticities of the various supply schedules and domestic demand schedules.

The theoretical analysis of customs unions was pioneered by Viner (1950) and, in what follows, his original terminology will be retained. Figures 1.4a and 1.4b illustrate the two possible extreme outcomes of membership for the home country. In Figure 1.4a, the tariff, tc, is so high that before joining the customs union, the home country imports from neither the partner country nor the outside world. The effective supply schedule is ADS_{W+tc}, which intersects the domestic demand schedule at point D. At price P_1, domestic demand Q_2 is entirely met by domestic producers. After the formation of the union, the effective supply schedule becomes $ABFS_{W+tc}$, since goods from the partner country can now enter the domestic market tariff-free. The new supply schedule cuts the demand schedule at point E. The price falls to P_2, with demand increasing to Q_3 and domestic supply contracting to Q_1. The 'gap' between Q_3 and Q_1 is filled by imports from the relatively more efficient partner country's producers.

In this scenario, the effect of forming the customs union has been to create trade where before there was none. Viner accordingly labelled this 'trade creation' and argued that this was an unambiguously positive result. Although universal free trade would still be the optimal solution (allowing the domestic price to fall to P_W, further increasing both consumption and output by the least-cost producers), trade creation within a customs union nevertheless implies that resources are more efficiently allocated after than before. Focusing on the 'welfare triangles' involved confirms this conclusion. Consumers clearly gain, since they are consuming more ($Q_3 - Q_2$) at a lower price, P_2. Consumer surplus thus increases by the area P_1DEP_2. The losers are domestic producers, suffering a loss of surplus given by the area P_1DCP_2. The net gain to the country as a whole is represented by the triangle CDE.

Joining a customs union will always be trade-creating for the home country provided the pre-union tariff is set at tc or above (so that it initially 'prohibits' all trade). Consider instead the situation illustrated in Figure 1.4b. In this case the tariff is much lower at td. Before joining the customs union, the effective supply schedule is ACS_{W+td} and the domestic price is P_1. At this price, consumers

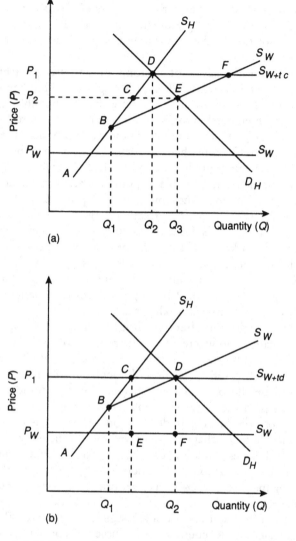

Figure 1.4 (a) Pure trade creation and (b) pure trade diversion in a customs union

demand Q_2, but domestic producers supply only Q_1, leaving the gap to be filled by imports from the outside world. Notice that consumers pay the price P_1 to buy these imports in the shops, although importers only pay P_W to the overseas suppliers. The difference between P_1 and P_W, of course, is simply the tariff, td, which is added on by the government. Area $CDFE$ thus represents the total tariff revenue received by the government on the $Q_2 - Q_1$ imported.

As before, the immediate effect of joining the customs union is that imports from the partner country now enjoy tariff-free access, so that the effective supply schedule becomes $ABDS_{W+td}$. This new supply schedule also cuts the demand schedule at point D, so that there is no change in the domestic price, nor in domestic consumption (which remains at Q_2) and supply (which stays fixed at Q_1). The only difference is that the gap $Q_2 - Q_1$ is now filled by imports from the partner country, which (being tariff-free) can undercut the post-tariff price of imports from the outside world for all quantities up to Q_2.

However, when consumers buy $Q_2 - Q_1$ from the partner country's producers, the price they pay, P_1, is no longer inflated by the government-imposed tariff, but reflects the full opportunity cost of the good. In other words, in Figure 1.4b, the effect of joining the customs union is to *divert* trade patterns away from the cheapest world suppliers towards the relatively less efficient partner country. Far from promoting a more rational allocation of the world's resources, in this latter case the customs union is operating to make matters worse. The negative welfare implications of what Viner dubbed 'trade diversion' can be confirmed by referring to the

Table 1.10 Production costs and market prices in the home country before and after membership of a customs union

Scenario 1	Production costs	Market price before customs union (tariff of 100%)	Market price after customs union (CET of 100%)
Home country	£100	**£100**	£100
Partner country	£80	£160	**£80**
Rest of the world	**£60**	£120	£120

Scenario 2	Production costs	Market price before customs union (tariff of 50%)	Market price after customs union (CET of 50%)
Home country	£100	£100	£100
Partner country	£80	£120	**£80**
Rest of the world	**£60**	**£90**	£90

welfare triangles. Since there is no change in price, neither consumer nor producer surplus is affected; but the tariff revenue formerly accruing to the government, *CDFE*, is now lost to the country, constituting a net welfare loss.

Table 1.10 illustrates the extreme possibilities of trade creation and diversion in simplified numerical form. In Scenario 1, the home country imposes a general, non-discriminatory tariff of 100% before joining the customs union. Consumers are faced with a set of relative prices (column two) which induces them to buy exclusively from domestic suppliers at £100 (i.e., the 100% tariff is 'prohibitive', excluding all imports from the home market). When the home country joins the union, goods from the partner country can now enter the home market unrestricted (see column three). No longer hindered by the tariff, the more efficient producers in the partner country can undercut their home country rivals by £20. Consumers accordingly switch to imports from the new partner country and trade creation takes place. Although goods are still not being bought from the most efficient producers (in the outside world), the formation of the customs union still improves matters, shifting production from less efficient (home country) to more efficient (partner country) producers.

Scenario 2 shows the alternative extreme possibility. Here the pre-union tariff is set at only 50%, which is not high enough to make home producers competitive (see column 2). Consumers therefore buy from world suppliers at £90. Once the union is formed, however, the partner country's producers can undercut the rest of the world by £10, causing consumers to switch from the latter to the former, thus diverting trade from the more to the less efficient source. In this second case, the consequences of the customs union are negative.

In the first scenario, the formation of the customs union results in 'pure' trade creation, turning a hitherto closed economy into an open economy and promoting a more rational allocation of the world's resources. In the second, the union causes pure trade diversion, skewing the trade patterns of an economy already actively engaged in international exchange from lower- to higher-cost producers and worsening the global allocation of resources. In most real-world situations, however, neither one of these extremes is likely to arise. Almost by definition, countries with such high tariff barriers that they have no trade with the outside world are unlikely to be interested in joining a customs union, so that pure

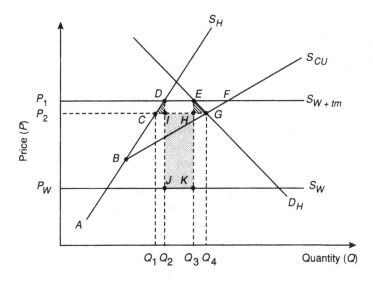

Figure 1.5 Trade creation versus trade diversion in a customs union

trade creation is only a remote possibility. And it would be by coincidence only if the pre- and post-union tariff structures were such that imports from the partner country exactly displaced those from the outside world, giving rise to pure trade diversion. Figure 1.5 sets out a more plausible situation. Here there is trade before entering the union, so that some trade diversion takes place, but the influx of cheaper imports from the partner country also allows some fall in domestic prices, stimulating an expansion of trade as well.

To assess the net impact of union membership on the home country, it is now necessary to set the welfare losses caused by the trade diversion (loss of tariff revenue) against the net gains from trade creation (the increase in consumer surplus less the reduction in producer surplus). Before the union is formed, the effective supply curve is ADS_{W+tm}, the price is P_1 and domestic supply and demand are Q_2 and Q_3 respectively, with the gap $(Q_3 - Q_2)$ being filled by imports from the rest of the world, which yields a tariff revenue to the government of $DEKJ$.

Once the customs union comes into existence, the new effective supply schedule becomes $ABFS_{W+tm}$. The price falls to P_2, increasing consumption to Q_4 (and consumer surplus by

31

P_1EGP_2) and reducing domestic production to Q_1 (and producer surplus by P_1DCP_2). The import gap is larger than before and represents trade creation, the net welfare gain from which is given by the area $DEGC$ ($P_1EGP_2 - P_1DCP_2$). However, because the partner country's producers can now undercut the post-tariff world price, they are also able to seize the share of the home market previously supplied by the rest of the world, giving rise to trade diversion and the loss of the tariff revenue $DEKJ$.

Overall, then, the net welfare effect of joining the customs union is $DEGC - DEKJ$ or, since these areas overlap, the difference between the area of the two hatched triangles ($CDI + EHG$) and that of the shaded rectangle ($IHKJ$). Whether the net result is positive or negative depends on a range of factors. If the tariff levied is high and the partner country only slightly less efficient than the rest of the world, it is likely that the positive, trade-creating benefits will outweigh the negative, trade-diverting costs; and vice versa, if the tariff is low and the partner country much less efficient than the rest of the world.

Tariffs versus non-tariff barriers

As noted above, the welfare effects of NTBs can be analysed using the same tools as tariffs. Inconsistent national technical and safety standards, for example, have the effect of inflating the cost of imports by forcing foreign manufacturers to modify their standard products before they can be shipped. Lengthy frontier delays similarly impose costs on imported goods. From the point of view of overseas producers, NTBs thus raise the selling price of their products in the market in the same way that a tariff would have increased the price of unmodified goods. For this reason, the reduction of NTBs within the EU under the 1992 programme can be expected to have effects on trade patterns which are similar to the earlier reduction in tariffs on intra-EU trade (see Chapters 7 and 8). In some cases, removing NTBs will create intra-EU trade where there was previously none, resulting in an unambiguous welfare improvement. For example, the 1992 programme attacked many state monopolies (e.g., in telecommunications) and so promises to improve the range of services available to EU consumers, while reducing prices.

In other cases, however, scaling down the NTBs previously imposed against other EU producers, while leaving them intact against non-EU competitors, may lead to trade diversion (see Healey, 1992b). In the approach to 1992, foreign companies clearly believed that they would be disadvantaged by the selective removal of NTBs on intra-union trade and fear of a resulting 'Fortress Europe' is widely cited as the main reason for the sharp increase in foreign direct investment in the late 1980s, as US and Japanese companies scrambled to establish new production facilities within the EU (but see Chapter 12). But in terms of the welfare implications for EU members, there is an important difference between the trade diversion that results from the selective removal of tariff as opposed to NTBs. In the former case, the welfare loss is normally dominated by the loss of tariff revenue to the government when trade is diverted from the cheaper world source to the new partner country (see above). In the latter case, there is no tariff revenue. The price paid by consumers includes the non-tariff barrier (NTB) and reflects the full opportunity cost of the goods to the importing country. Thus, when the NTB is removed, the opportunity cost of the goods from the partner country falls below that of the world suppliers. Thus, while trade diversion still represents a reallocation of resources away from the most efficient world suppliers to the partner country, from the point of view of the importing union member, there is a welfare improvement rather than the welfare loss associated with the selective removal of tariffs.

The dynamic benefits of EU membership

Viner's theoretical framework suggests that the benefits (of trade creation) to member states of joining a regional bloc like the EU may be small and possibly outweighed by the negative effects of trade diversion. However, this conclusion is based on 'comparative static' analysis, a technique which allows economists to compare stable or 'static' equilibrium states before and after some event (in this case the formation of a customs union) on the assumption that 'all other things remain equal'. Hence this model ignores the process by which the new equilibrium state is actually achieved and abstracts from complicating issues like changes in capital stocks, industrial concentration, technical innovation, etc., all of which may actually be influenced by the formation of the EU. Many economists stress that it is the very factors which Viner's analysis ignores that give rise to the major benefits of union membership (e.g., Balassa, 1961; Baldwin, 1989; Hughes, 1992). For example, both trade creation and trade diversion imply an expansion of production by the partner country's suppliers. Since many manufacturing industries enjoy declining long-run average cost structures, the resultant economies of scale and experience may, of themselves, yield important welfare gains.

Moreover, both trade creation and trade diversion imply that the formation of a customs union allows the partner country's producers to seize market share, in the former case from home producers and in the latter from the rest of the world. In practice, whichever of the established producer groups is threatened by this new source of competition, it is unlikely to passively allow itself to be squeezed out of the market it hitherto dominated without retaliating in some way. Such competitive retaliation may involve restructuring to lower costs, accepting lower profit margins, investing in new technology and a whole host of other responses which carry with them gains for the consumer. Both by allowing firms within the union to more fully exploit economies of scale and experience and by intensifying internal competitiveness, the EU may therefore generate 'dynamic' ongoing benefits which will, over time, increasingly dwarf the net balance of once-for-all static costs and benefits (Borts and Stein, 1964).

Economies of scale

The welfare benefits that potentially stem from exploiting economies of scale can be explored more formally using the standard tools of the theory of the firm. Figure 1.6 shows the average cost (AC) curves for a declining cost industry. AC_P is below AC_H at every level of output, reflecting the relatively greater efficiency of producers in the partner country, while neither is as cost efficient as the world producers at any level of output (i.e., the world supply schedule, S_W, is below both AC_P and AC_H). For simplicity, demand in the home and partner countries is assumed to be identical, so that $D_{H,P}$ represents the (identical) national demand curves, while D_{H+P} is their combined joint demand curve after the union is formed. Given the shape of the national average cost curves, the only way to protect the domestic industry from overseas competition is to exclude all imports. Before the union, the 'made-to-measure' tariff which achieves this result is JA for the home country (so that home demand, Q_1, is met by home produ-

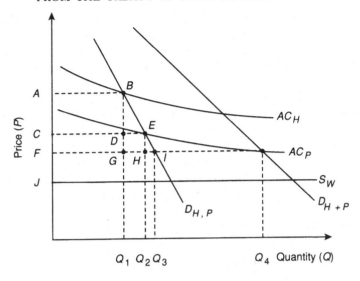

Figure 1.6 Economies of scale in a customs union

cers) and *JC* for the partner country (so that the partner country's demand, Q_2, is satisfied by partner producers).

Note that the marginal cost and revenue curves to which a producer would normally refer in making price and output decisions are ignored in this analysis. This is because, with a horizontal world supply schedule, producers in the home and partner countries effectively face a horizontal demand curve at the tariff-inclusive world price (so that their average and marginal revenues are equal). Moreover, because the marginal cost curve for a declining cost industry is always below average cost, setting marginal cost equal to marginal revenue would (with a horizontal demand curve) lead the monopolist to make a loss, so that the best such a producer can do is to set average cost equal to price and make normal profits; i.e., the average cost curve is the effective supply curve for such an industry.

When the customs union is formed, the more efficient partner producer can supply the entire union market, with the made-to-measure common external tariff now being *JF*. With this tariff, home producers leave the market and the partner producers completely satisfy the joint union demand, D_{H+P}, supplying Q_4. The welfare implications of the union can be calculated in the normal way. The formation of the union has allowed union producers to more fully exploit economies of scale, leading to lower prices (the union-wide price is now F) and higher consumption (Q_4, rather than $Q_1 + Q_2$). The increase in consumer welfare is simply $FABI$ for the home country, plus $FCEI$ for the partner country. The bulk of these welfare gains ($FABG$ for the home country and $FCEH$ for the partner country) are due to the 'dynamic' benefits from exploiting economies of scale and are termed the 'cost reduction' effects. Because average cost always equals average revenue for home and partner producers, there are no welfare implications in terms of changes in producer surplus, although there may, of course, be additional social costs and benefits associated with the closure of the industry in the home country and its expansion in the partner country.

Economies of experience

It has long been observed in industrial economics that average costs depend not just on output per period (i.e., due to economies of scale), but on cumulative output over time. The latter effect is due to the phenomenon known as experience or 'learning' economies, reflecting the role of organisational learning in efficient production. For example, a fast-food company like McDonald's that has cumulatively produced 90bn hamburgers over a 30-year period is likely to be on a completely different (i.e., lower) set of cost curves than a new entrant which tries to break into the market with first-year sales of 3bn units. The incumbent has refined its production, distribution and marketing logistics over three decades in the industry. The new entrant, in contrast, will inevitably make mistakes, suffer bottlenecks and generally find things take time to settle down; all other things equal, therefore, its average costs will initially be much higher than those of its established rival.

The existence of experience economies is one of the main reasons it is so difficult for a new entrant to break into a mass market, unless it has some technological advantage (e.g., access to new plant and equipment, etc.) over the incumbents which will compensate for its cost-increasing lack of experience. Figure 1.7 illustrates a standard experience or learning curve, which can be algebraically represented by:

$$C_n = an^{-b}$$

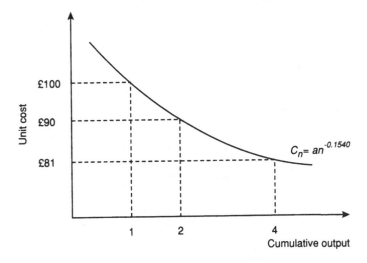

Figure 1.7 The experience curve

where C_n is the cost of nth unit produced, a is the cost of first unit and b is the learning rate. So-called '90%' learning curves are common in many industries. This means that, because of the value of b in the equation above ($b = 0.1540$), unit costs fall 10% with each doubling of cumulative output. For example, if the first unit cost £100 to produce, the second would cost £90 (£100 × 90%), the fourth would cost £81 (£90 × 90%) and so on. While the size of the incremental cost savings from higher cumulative output slowly declines, it nevertheless continues to build up indefinitely over time.

In terms of conventional average cost curve diagrams, this phenomenon implies that as cumulative output increases over time, firms are driven onto ever-lower average cost curves (see Figure 1.8). By allowing the most efficient firms to increase output *per period* – and so the rate at which cumulative output is building up – the formation of a customs union may therefore accelerate the rate at which its producers slide down their learning curves, reducing average costs over time and delivering welfare benefits in a genuinely *dynamic* fashion.

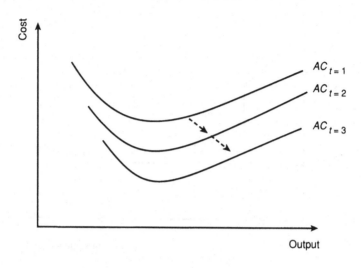

Figure 1.8 Average costs and the experience curve effect

Reduced economic rents and X-inefficiency

A final dynamic benefit concerns the disciplining effect of greater competition within a customs union on national monopolies. When national markets are segmented by the existence of tariffs or other NTBs, the domestic producers accordingly enjoy a degree of monopoly power, allowing them to exploit consumers by restricting output and raising prices, and thereby earning supernormal profits (i.e., economic rent). By opening up national markets to competition from other union producers, a customs union may have the effect of making 'price-takers' of former 'price-makers'.

Figure 1.9 shows a producer in the home country, with a marginal cost curve, MC_H, and average cost curve, AC_H. Before the union is formed, the producer is protected from overseas competition and enjoys a monopoly position in the home market, facing a demand, D_H. The firm sets marginal cost equal to marginal revenue, producing Q_1 at a price A and earning economic rent of $CABD$. When the union is formed, the firm becomes a price-taker in the union-wide market, facing competition from other producers at price, P_{CU}. By setting marginal cost equal to marginal revenue (which, as a price-taker, is equal to the

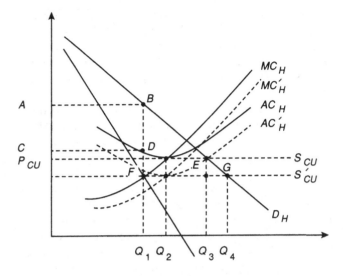

Figure 1.9 The benefits of increased competition and reduced *X*-inefficiency

union price), the firm expands output to Q_2, losing its economic rent and earning only normal profits. Consumers in the home country benefit, with increased consumer surplus equal to the area $P_{CU}ABE$ (n.b., $Q_3 - Q_2$ is imported from the rest of the union).

The effect of the formation of a customs union on *X*-inefficiency can also be shown in the same figure. *X*-inefficiency refers to the tendency of secure monopolies to eschew cost minimisation (profit maximisation) in favour of alternative, non-economic goals. Freed from the need to watch costs in order to survive (or, indeed, the incentive to cut costs in order to grow), the management of a monopoly may engage in grandiose schemes to boost the self-esteem of themselves and their workforce, building expensive, prestigious headquarters and luxurious social facilities, paying inflated salaries and bonuses, tolerating over-manning and wasteful demarcation practices and generally inflating the company's costs in pursuit of an easy life at the expense of their shareholders' profits. The ability of the management of a monopoly to advance its own agenda is limited only by the threat of a shareholder revolt (which ousts the management) or a hostile takeover (which normally has the same effect) which, while not uncommon, is normally significantly blunted by the asymmetry of information available to the two parties involved (i.e., the management and the shareholders). Stripped of the protection afforded by tariff and NTBs, however, the firm will be forced to trim costs to survive.

In Figure 1.9, suppose that the new union supply schedule were represented by the horizontal broken line, S'_{CU}, rather than S_{CU}. The formation of the customs union would drive the union price below P_{CU} to P'_{CU}. If the firm were already operating as cost effectively as possible, it would inevitably go out of business in the long run, since the union price fails to cover its average costs. If, on the other hand, the management had allowed significant X-inefficiency during the days when the firm enjoyed monopoly power, it may be able to cut costs and shift down its costs curves to AC'_H and MC'_H respectively, remaining competitive against its new rivals elsewhere in the union. In the process, consumers would enjoy a further increase in consumer surplus (equal to area $P_{CU}EGP'_{CU}$), providing an additional benefit which stems from the reduction of X-inefficiency.

CONCLUSIONS

The EU is the most integrated of the world's regional trade blocs, with a combined GDP equal to that of the United States. Through a series of treaty revisions, the EU has evolved from a customs union to become a common market and, despite the currency upheavals of the early 1990s, is scheduled to become an EMU by the end of the century. Since its inception in the aftermath of World War II, the motivating force behind integration in the EU has been primarily political rather than economic, with the core member states (notably the original Six) driven by a vision of a supranational 'United States of Europe'. This view of the future shape of the EU has not been shared to the same extent by the newer member states, in particular Britain. Disagreements about the pace and nature of integration have spawned a growing number of opt-outs from joint policy initiatives and the resultant variable geometry has meant that the EU is becoming less uniform, with different sub-groups signing up to different agreements. This pattern looks set to continue for the foreseeable future.

Economic theory suggests that the nature of integration in the

EU to date may give rise to mixed welfare effects. The establishment of the customs union may create genuine new trade between partner states, but it may also displace trade with the outside world. Britain, for example, has undoubtedly suffered to the extent that EU membership diverted agricultural trade away from cheaper Commonwealth sources (e.g., Canada, Australia, New Zealand) towards less efficient producers in continental Europe (e.g., El-Agraa, 1983; Winters, 1987). The elimination of NTBs under the 1992 programme may also be trade-diverting, but the welfare effects are much more positive. In addition, economic integration gives rise to a raft of dynamic benefits, including the fuller exploitation of scale and experience economies and the reduction of economic rents and X-inefficiency.

Part I

MACROECONOMIC PERSPECTIVES

2

THE EUROPEAN MONETARY SYSTEM

Michael Artis and Nigel M. Healey

INTRODUCTION

The European Monetary System (EMS) was established in 1979 after almost a decade of unprecedented exchange rate volatility and rapid global inflation. The objective of member countries was 'to create a zone of monetary stability' within the European Union (EU). By stating their goal in such broad terms, its architects intended to make clear that the aim of the EMS was not just to stabilise exchange rates; in addition, EMS members accepted an obligation to pursue a common, anti-inflationary policy.

This 'twin-track' approach would, the EU hoped, restore both *external* monetary stability (by stabilising exchange rates) and *internal* monetary stability (by curbing inflation) to its member states. In the event, inflation rates across the EU fell sharply during the 1980s, while bilateral exchange rates (i.e., the exchange rates between one member currency and another) became significantly more stable. The apparent success of the EMS on these two, interrelated fronts inspired the EU to consider full European monetary union (EMU) – see Chapters 4 and 5. The fundamental difference between the EMS and EMU is that the latter implies a common inflation rate and the complete fixity of bilateral exchange rates between member countries. This constitutes a stark contrast to the present EMS arrangements, which allow margins within which bilateral rates are allowed to fluctuate and periodic 'realignments' (i.e., devaluations and revaluations of target rates) to neutralise the impact of differential national inflation rates on countries' international competitiveness.

The events of 1992–93, when the EMS came under repeated and sustained attack, resulting in the withdrawal of the pound and the lira (in autumn 1992), a series of devaluations by the weaker currencies and, most damagingly, the abandonment of the long-standing ±2.25% in favour of ultra-wide ±15% target bands in August 1993, are widely regarded as having derailed the move to full monetary union. This chapter examines the history of the EMS, exploring the reasons for its apparent success in the 1980s and its subsequent travails in the early 1990s.

THE BASICS OF EXCHANGE RATE MANAGEMENT

The benefits of exchange rate stabilisation are well known (see, for example, Krugman, 1989; Artus and Young, 1979; Healey, 1988; de Grauwe, 1988). To illustrate the basic principles of an exchange rate arrangement like the EMS, consider Figure 2.1, which shows the supply of, and demand for, sterling against the deutschmark. The vertical axis measures the price of £1 in terms of deutsch-marks, while the horizontal axis measures the quantity of sterling being supplied and demanded. Suppose that, as was the case between October 8, 1990 and September 16, 1992, the British government 'pegs' its exchange rate (i.e., the deutschmark price

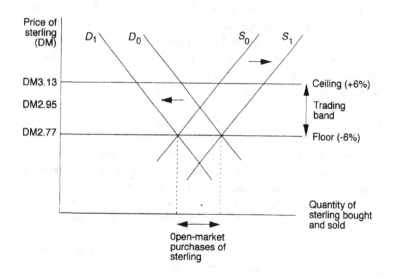

Figure 2.1 The forex market for sterling/deutschmarks

46

of sterling) at a central rate of DM2.95 ±6%. This commitment obliges the Bank of England to ensure that sterling rises to no more than DM3.13 (DM2.95 × 106%) and falls to no less than DM2.77 (DM2.95 × 94%). Maintaining the pound within such narrow bands requires both 'open market operations' in the foreign exchange market – official sales and purchases of sterling – and adjustments in interest rates as necessary.

For example, if sterling were to fall to the floor of its target band (DM2.77), either because the supply of sterling shifted to the right (e.g., from S_0 to S_1) or the demand for sterling shifted to the left (e.g., from D_0 to D_1), the Bank of England would be obliged to buy up the excess supply of sterling, using deutschmarks from its foreign exchange reserves. It could also attempt to lift the pound off its trading floor by raising British interest rates which, all other things equal, would tend to shift the supply of sterling to the left (as holders of sterling find switching into deutschmark assets less attractive) and the demand for sterling to the right (as deutschmark holders are tempted to switch into higher yielding sterling assets). Conversely, if sterling were to rise to its trading ceiling (DM3.13), the Bank of England would be required to satisfy the excess demand for sterling by selling sterling, buying deutschmarks for its foreign exchange reserves. At the same time, it could reduce British interest rates with the aim of boosting the supply of, and curbing the demand for, sterling.

There is clearly an important difference between trying to prop up the pound when it has sunk to its trading floor and trying to 'cap' the rise in sterling when it has appreciated to its trading ceiling. In terms of open market operations, official purchases of sterling when it is weak are limited by the size of the Bank of England's foreign exchange reserves (and whatever it can borrow from other central banks); in contrast, official sales of sterling when it is strong can be made in unlimited amounts, since the Bank of England effectively creates 'new' sterling as it purchases deutschmarks in the market.

THE ROLE OF THE FOREIGN EXCHANGE MARKET

This asymmetry between weak and strong currencies is given a crucial significance by the size of today's foreign exchange market. A recent survey by the Bank of England reported that average daily

Table 2.1 Daily turnover in the major financial centres, 1992

	Daily turnover ($bn)
London	300
New York	192
Tokyo	128
Singapore	74
Zurich	64
Hong Kong	61
Frankfurt	57

Source: Bank of England.

turnover in the London foreign exchange market during the survey period (April 1992) was $300bn (approximately equal to one-third of Britain's annual GDP). Interestingly, the consensus view amongst dealers surveyed was that, during April 1992, business was somewhat lower than normal, suggesting that $300bn may be an *underestimate* of London's daily turnover. Table 2.1 summarises the Bank's findings for the seven largest financial centres. These figures must be set against Britain's official reserves, which averaged roughly $45bn during 1992 – less than one-sixth the daily turnover of the London foreign exchange market. The implication is that the ability of a central bank to mop up the excess supply of a weak currency – once international investors have decided that devaluation is imminent – is very limited.

Once a speculative run against a currency has begun to gather momentum, interest rate increases may also be ineffective. A rise in British interest rates, all other things equal, makes sterling assets more attractive relative to deutschmark assets. But if investors fear a devaluation in sterling, they will have to set against the extra yield on sterling assets the expected fall in the value of the currency in which they are denominated. For example, suppose that investors believe that the probability of a 10% devaluation within the next week is 0.5. The *expected* capital loss on a sterling asset is therefore 5% (i.e., the 10% devaluation multiplied by the probability of devaluation, 0.5). To offset this expected capital loss, the interest rate necessary to induce investors to hold sterling over the following week would have to be 5% over and above the German rate, *per week*; an interest rate differential of 5% per week amounts to an annual interest rate of 1160% above the German rate.

The higher the perceived probability of devaluation, the greater the selling pressure on the weak currency and the larger the required interest rate hike. Because investors know that massive, sustained interest rate increases are likely to be politically unacceptable to the government of the weak currency, a speculative crisis can feed on itself: the larger the interest rate hike needed to stabilise the currency, the less likely it is to take place, so that expectations of a devaluation can get continuously revised upwards (towards a probability of unity) once a crisis is under way, leading to truly massive selling. In terms of Figure 2.1, as investors lose confidence in the currency, the supply and demand schedules move explosively to the right and left respectively, giving rise to an unbridgeable excess of supply over demand. Once a currency has fallen to its trading floor, therefore, central banks may find themselves incapable of arresting the speculative pressure either by open-market purchases or by interest rate hikes. The need to maintain confidence in the declared parities was thus the major task facing the architects of the EMS in 1979 and, during the upheavals of the system in 1992–93, it was the failure to assuage the fears of speculators that led to its near collapse.

THE BACKGROUND TO THE EUROPEAN MONETARY SYSTEM

The attempt to bind the currencies of the EU countries more closely together did not start with the EMS. Indeed, an important part of the background to the establishment of the EMS was the failure of its predecessor, the so-called 'Snake'. The Snake was instituted in April 1972. This came shortly after the demise of the Bretton Woods system and the attempt to resurrect an international monetary system along the same lines in the Smithsonian Agreement reached in Washington in December 1971. In the Smithsonian, margins of fluctuation of the exchange rates against the dollar were widened from the previous ±1% of Bretton Woods to ±2.25%, implying that, against each other, the European currencies could fluctuate by ±4.5%. The European countries felt this to be too large and, in the Snake arrangement, intra-EU parties were to be narrowed to ±2.25%. There were good practical reasons for wanting to maintain a discipline over intra-EU exchange rates. First, the Common Agricultural Policy depended upon setting EU-wide prices for agricultural produce: exchange rate changes could play havoc with these arrangements. They could result in a quite different distribution of incentives to farmers across the member states than that envisaged when the prices were first set (see also Chapter 11). Second, and more generally, the achievements of the EU in removing elements of national protection could be severely compromised by a change in exchange rate parities involving a sharp change in competitiveness. Looking further into the future it was also clear that the desire to create a 'United States of Europe' on the American model would require monetary union – a single currency and a single central bank. This was indeed projected by the Werner Committee, which in 1970 published an ambitious plan for monetary union by the end of the 1970s.

Despite the desirability of greater exchange rate certainty and the long-run attractions of monetary union, the Snake proved in practice a disaster – sterling left the arrangement very early (by June 1972, whereafter sterling floated against all other currencies); the French franc left the Snake in January 1974 and rejoined in July 1975 only to leave it once more in March 1976; Italy did not participate in the system. The arrangement terminated as a grouping of less important currencies – including some non-EU currencies (notably those of the Nordic states) – around the deutschmark in a 'deutschmark zone'. This unhappy experience was to influence the EMS in a number of ways. Besides colouring initial attitudes of scepticism (e.g., no pretensions to monetary union were present in the deliberations leading to the establishment of the system – but see Jenkins, 1978), it bred a determination to avoid a repetition of the mistakes of the Snake and profoundly influenced the precise provisions of the EMS, as detailed below.

THE KEY PROVISIONS OF THE EUROPEAN MONETARY SYSTEM

The EMS began operation on March 13, 1979, its membership comprising all those countries which were then members of the EU, including Britain. It has since been expanded to incorporate Greece, Spain and Portugal. The core of the system, however, consists of those member countries which participate in its exchange rate mechanism (ERM), which Britain declined to do until 1990 (Spain and Portugal both joined within five years of acceding to the EU in 1986). The provisions of the EMS are basically four-fold (see Bank of England, 1990):

1 a set of provisions regarding exchange rates;
2 a supporting set of provisions regarding access to credit facilities;
3 a common currency of denomination, the European Currency Unit (ECU); and
4 special provision for a 'divergence indicator' the purpose of which is to impose a symmetrical adjustment process.

The most important feature of the ERM is that a member should intervene to maintain its currency's bilateral exchange rate against every other country within a target band – ±2.25% of central parity between 1979 and 1993, increased to ±15% in August 1993. This obligation is symmetrical, applying equally to the weak and to the strong currency. Exceptionally, Italy (later to be joined by Spain in 1989 and Britain and Portugal in 1990) negotiated a wider band of fluctuation for its currency of ±6%, which the Italians only ceded for the then regular EMS band in January 1990. The central parities can be renegotiated in realignments, in collaboration with all other ERM members.

As intervention in the foreign exchange markets is obligatory to prevent a currency from breaking through its bands, corresponding credit provisions are also obligatory and the issuer of the hard currency is required to lend – *without limit* – to the issuer of the weak currency for purposes of intervention at the margin. The most important component of the credit mechanism is the so-called Very Short Term Financing Facility (VSTF), repayment under which was initially required within 45 days. Finally, central banks also pool 20% of their gold and foreign exchange reserves in exchange for ECU in a central fund, the European Monetary Cooperation Fund (EMCF), which has been superseded since January 1994 by the Frankfurt-based European Monetary Institute – see Chapters 4 and 5.

The identity of the EMS was enhanced, as contrasted with that of the Snake, by the provision for a common currency, the ECU. The ECU is a literal composite currency, consisting of a fixed quantity of French francs, German deutschmarks and so on. Table 2.2 lists the current currency composition of the ECU after the revisions made to accommodate the new currencies (the peseta and the escudo) in September 1989. (The composition is chosen so that the respective currency weights in the ECU broadly reflect an average of their shares in the EU's GDP and trade.) The ECU is

Table 2.2 The composition of the ECU (since 1989)

Currency	Amount	Weight (%) (in September 1992)
Deutschmark	0.6242	30.1
French franc	1.332	19.0
Sterling	0.08784	13.0
Lira	151.8	10.2
Guilder	0.2198	9.4
Belgian franc	3.301	7.6
Luxembourg franc	0.130	0.3
Peseta	6.885	5.3
Danish krone	0.1976	2.4
Irish punt	0.008552	1.1
Drachma	1.440	0.8
Escudo	1.393	0.8

Source: EC Commission.

used as the currency of denomination for EU transactions (e.g., for the EU Budget, farm support prices, etc.) and the central exchange rates of the ERM currencies are expressed in ECU.

It is easy enough to imagine a set-up in which the central rates for the bilateral parity 'grid' were denominated, not in ECU, but simply in national currencies; but the ECU, or a device like it, is necessary to underpin the divergence indicator. The central function of the divergence indicator is to enforce symmetry in adjustment. Recall that, when originally established, the bilateral limit was set at $\pm2.25\%$. The divergence indicator for a currency is allowed to deviate from all the other currencies by three-quarters of the width of the target band; i.e., $0.75 \times 2.25\% = 1.6875\%$. Because the indicator is dominated in ECU – an artificial currency unit which is composed of the individual EMS currencies – when a currency appreciates (or depreciates) by $x\%$ against the other eleven, its value against the ECU changes by only $(1 - w)x\%$, where w is the currency's weight in the value of the ECU (see Table 2.2). Thus, the divergence indicator will be triggered when a currency's ECU value has moved by more than $(1 - w) \times 1.6875\%$; the larger the currency's weight in the ECU, the smaller the permitted deviation against the ECU (thus the deutschmark's ECU value does not have to move so far from its central parity as, say, the Irish punt, because the weight of the former in the ECU – at around 35% – is much higher than the weight of the latter – at around 1%).

The reason the ECU (or something like it) is essential to the notion of a divergence indicator is simply that some means of 'adding-up' the currencies is necessary to give force to the idea of one currency 'diverging', not simply from some other individual currency, but from all the others together. This concept of singling out a particular currency and forcing the presumption of adjustment upon it whatever the direction of its deviation (i.e., weak or strong) through the device of the divergence indicator was greeted at the time of the inception of the system as a radical new innovation, promising a correction of the bias against weak currency countries which most analysts had come to regard as endemic in fixed exchange rates systems (see especially Chapter 3). More directly, it was an attempt to free the EMS from the dominance of the strong deutschmark which was seen as one of the ingredients of the Snake disaster. Principle and practice are two quite different things however. In some critical ways, the operation of the system as it turned out denied the expectations of its founders. We now turn to discuss the experience of the EMS in practice.

THE EUROPEAN MONETARY SYSTEM AS A CRAWLING PEG, 1979–83

The early years of the EMS featured a number of realignments of central parities. Table 2.3 shows the dates and sizes involved of all the realignments undertaken to date, from which the concentration in the early years is more than obvious. The frequency of the initial realignments was rather unexpected and gave the lie to those who had foreseen that the EMS would be one of rigidly fixed exchange rates. Indeed, the frequency with which realignments occurred provoked the description of the EMS as a mere 'crawling peg'. This was a reference to the concept devised by Williamson (1965) of an exchange rate system in which real rates of exchange (i.e., nominal exchange rates adjusted for differential national inflation rates – see Appendix A) would be kept constant by changing nominal rates in line with inflation differentials (see also Holtham, 1989). Uncovered interest parity (see Appendix B) would imply in such a case that interest rate differentials would match the inflation differentials, which themselves would indicate

Table 2.3 Central rates against the ECU (national currency units per ECU)

	B/L	DK	D	GR[a]	E	F	IRL	I[b]	NL	P[c]	UK[d]
13.3.1979[e]	39.4582	7.08592	2.51064	—	—	5.79831	0.662638	1148.18	2.72077	—	(0.663247)
24.9.1979	39.8456	7.36594	2.48557	—	—	5.85522	0.669141	1159.42	2.74748	—	(0.649821)
30.11.1979	39.7897	7.72336	2.48208	—	—	5.84700	0.668201	1157.79	2.74362	—	(0.648910)
23.3.1981	40.7985	7.91917	2.54502	—	—	5.99526	0.685145	1262.92	2.81318	—	(0.542122)
5.10.1981	40.7572	7.91117	2.40989	—	—	6.17443	0.684452	1300.67	2.66382	—	(0.601048)
22.2.1982	44.6963	8.18382	2.41815	—	—	6.19564	0.686799	1305.13	2.67296	—	(0.557037)
14.6.1982	44.9704	8.23400	2.33379	—	—	6.61387	0.691011	1350.27	2.57971	—	(0.560453)
21.3.1983	44.3662	8.04412	2.21515	—	—	6.79271	0.717050	1386.78	2.49587	—	(0.629848)
18.5.1983	44.9008	8.14104	2.24184	—	—	6.87456	0.725690	1403.49	2.52595	—	(0.587087)
17.9.1984[f]	44.9008	8.14104	2.24184	(87.4813)	—	6.87456	0.725690	1403.49	2.52595	—	(0.585992)
22.7.1985	44.8320	8.12857	2.23840	(100.719)	—	6.86402	0.724578	1520.60	2.52208	—	(0.555312)
7.4.1986	43.6761	7.91896	2.13834	(135.659)	—	6.96280	0.712956	1496.21	2.40935	—	(0.630317)
4.8.1986	43.1139	7.81701	2.11083	(137.049)	—	6.87316	0.764976	1476.95	2.37833	—	(0.679256)
12.1.1987	42.4582	7.85212	2.05853	(150.792)	—	6.90403	0.768411	1483.58	2.31943	—	(0.739615)
19.6.1989	42.4582	7.85212	2.05853	(150.792)	133.804	6.90403	0.768411	1483.58	2.31943	—	(0.739615)
21.9.1989[g]	42.4582	7.85212	2.05853	(150.792)	133.804	6.90403	0.768411	1483.58	2.31943	(172.085)	(0.728627)
8.1.1990[h]	42.1679	7.79845	2.04446	(187.934)	132.889	6.85684	0.763159	1529.70	2.30358	(177.743)	(0.728615)
8.10.1990[i]	42.4032	7.84195	2.05586	(205.311)	133.631	6.89509	0.767417	1538.24	2.31643	(178.735)	0.696904
14.9.1992	42.0639	7.77921	2.03942	(251.202)	132.562	6.83992	0.761276	1636.61	2.29789	177.305	0.691328
17.9.1992[j]	41.9547	7.75901	2.03412	(250.550)	139.176	6.82216	0.759300	(1632.36)	2.29193	176.844	(0.689533)
23.11.1992	40.6304	7.51410	1.96992	(254.254)	143.386	6.60683	0.735334	(1690.76)	2.21958	182.194	(0.805748)
1.2.1993	40.2802	7.44934	1.95294	(259.306)	142.150	6.54988	0.809996	(1796.22)	2.20045	180.624	(0.808431)
14.5.1993	40.2123	7.43679	1.94964	(264.513)	154.250	6.53883	0.808628	(1793.19)	2.19672	192.854	(0.786749)

a. Notional central rates.
b. Temporary notional central rates as from September 17, 1992.
c. Notional central rates until escudo entry into the exchange rate mechanism (ERM) on April 6, 1992.
d. Notional central rates until October 8, 1990 (sterling entry into ERM) and as from September 17, 1992 (suspension of sterling participation in the ERM).
e. Initial parties at the start of the European Monetary System.
f. Revised composition of the ECU and inclusion of the drachma.
g. Revised composition of the ECU and inclusion of the peseta and the Portuguese escudo. The central rate of the Spanish peseta was fixed on June 19, 1989, when it entered the ERM.
h. Accompanied by a narrowing of the Italian lira fluctuation band from 6% to 2.25%.
i. Sterling entry into the ERM with a fluctuation margin of 6%.
j. Accompanied by a suspension of their participation in the ERM by the sterling and the Italian lira.

Source: European Economy.

the expected rates of change of the nominal exchange rates. Such a system would protect countries' competitiveness (their real exchange rates), but would accommodate inflation. At the time, inflation differentials were indeed high and countries found it easy to resort to realignments to ape a crawling peg arrangement.

This phase of the EMS proved temporary as countries began to adopt a more determined counter-inflationary policy stance; but the pace at which countries adopted this new determination varied from one to another, so for the system as a whole, the switch was a gradual one. A more determined counter-inflationary posture implied using a commitment to a fixed exchange rate as a means of taking the steam out of domestic inflationary pressures, losing competitiveness if necessary while these pressures subsided. At the EMS level, this change of emphasis was recognised in the transformation of realignments into multilateral decisions, which for the smaller countries, at least, implied a stronger discipline on devaluationist tendencies; at the country level, the key indicator of the change of emphasis was the decision taken by France early in 1983 to undertake severe measures of retrenchment to squeeze inflation out of the economy. This was quite critical for, at the time, the option of leaving the EMS altogether was a real one for France – one which the Mitterand administration recognised and rejected. But for this decision, the future of the EMS would have been quite different.

THE 'OLD EUROPEAN MONETARY SYSTEM', 1983–88

The end of the 'crawling peg' period – which is difficult to date precisely because of the differing speed at which countries decided to change their policies, but where the momentous French decision of 1983 must stand out as a marker – gave way to a period which we can call the classical 'Old EMS'. It is in this period that the operation of the system as it has come to be generally described settled down.

It is convenient to summarise this period in terms of the following 'stylised facts' concerning its operation. First, realignments became less frequent, so much so that statistical investigations of the behaviour of exchange rates since the beginning of the EMS were able to come to the conclusion that the system had had a stabilising effect; second, member countries consciously used

Table 2.4 Exchange rate variability against ERM currencies (period means)

	1974–79	1979–85	1974–79	1979–85
France	31.6	15.9	16.8	7.6
Germany	29.2	16.3	14.7	7.0
Italy	36.0	19.3	19.3	8.8
Average ERM	28.4	15.1	14.8	7.3
Japan	44.5	48.1	21.1	21.7
Britain	32.7	16.8	20.9	—
United States	34.7	55.7	18.8	27.4
Average non-ERM	34.5	35.9	17.2	17.9

Source: Ungerer *et al.* (1986).

their membership of the EMS as a means of disciplining inflationary expectations and as a reason for taking policy action to reduce inflation; third, the desire to reduce inflation helped to make Germany the centre of the EMS – encapsulated in the suggestion that the system was, in reality, a greater deutschmark zone.

The conclusion that the EMS had a stabilising effect on exchange rates comes from statistical investigations and is one that applies to both nominal and real exchange rates (e.g., see von Hagen and Neumann, 1991). It applies most certainly to intra-EMS rates, less clearly to overall effective rates. A representative sample of results, culled from an authoritative IMF study, is quoted in Table 2.4. This compares measures of exchange rate volatility for the main ERM currencies with similar measures for the non-ERM currencies before and after the establishment of the system. A tendency for volatility within the ERM to decline between 1979 and 1985 is clear. Moreover, whilst results quoted in Table 2.4 only cover the period to the end of 1985, the fact that there were relatively few realignments until 1992 indicates that the stabilising effect of the EMS suggested by the table can only be reinforced if the period 1979–92 is taken as a whole.

The stabilisation of exchange rates was accompanied by a general reduction of inflation towards the German level – a convergence on the 'German standard'. The EMS was seen to be an important component in this achievement, not simply an incidental. The argument draws on the modern theory of 'reputational policy' (e.g., Barro and Gordon, 1983; Backus and Driffill, 1985). According to this theory, a country's ability to reduce its inflation rate and the cost it may have to pay to do so both depend on its ability to establish a good 'reputation'. A government which is credible (i.e., has a good reputation) is able to make announcements about its counter-inflationary intentions which are believed; and, because they are believed, inflationary expectations are reduced and the unemployment-cost of getting inflation down is cut. Because the cost is cut, it is easier to do and more likely to be done (Neumann, 1990). In short, reputation has some very valuable 'virtuous circle' properties. The problem is to see how a reputation can be established (see also Chapter 5). In this respect, it is argued that membership of the EMS may be helpful. Membership implies maintaining an exchange rate which is at least 'fairly-fixed' against low-inflation Germany; this commitment is very visible and easy for people to monitor and understand and, to this extent, a government which participates in the EMS may be well on the way to making a good reputation for itself; i.e. it may be able to 'import' the Bundesbank's reputation. So put, the argument clearly requires the dominance of Germany as the rationale for the system and this invites the familiar description of the EMS as a 'deutschmark zone'.

There are some respects in which this description of the 'Old EMS' seemed well justified. For, although all the formal provisions of the EMS are symmetrical, it was noticeable that Germany sterilised the effect of foreign exchange intervention to a greater extent than other countries, thus pursuing its own independent monetary policy; equally, foreign exchange intervention was itself almost all conducted 'intra-marginally' (i.e., before the exchange rate hit the band) and by countries other than Germany. Germany never devalued against any other currency in any realignment and the divergence indicator fell into disuse (see Bank of England, 1991; Meade, 1990). It is easy to see that when the name of the policy game is the reduction of inflation, the divergence indicator would become useless – it would be inconsistent to ask Germany to raise its inflation rate towards the average in the name of symmetry when the overriding purpose of policy was to cut inflation (Healey, 1993a).

However, as an offset to German dominance in this period countries could recourse to two protective devices. First, they could – within limits, for realignments had become multilateral decisions – realign their currencies. Second, they could rely upon exchange controls over capital flows to permit a degree of decoupling of domestic monetary policy from German monetary policy.

THE 'NEW EMS', 1988–92

It was the decision to remove capital exchange controls under the provisions of the '1992' project (see Chapters 7 and 8) – consciously accepted by 1987 – which, as much as anything, marks the beginning of the 'New EMS'. The removal of these controls, it was felt, would have two effects. First, it would oblige countries to follow the lead of Germany more closely than ever; second, it would make realignments a risky business which could expose the system to destructive speculation. It was not difficult to recall that the end of the Bretton Woods system had been marked by massive speculative capital flows, triggered by expectations of exchange rate realignments.

Recognising these consequences, measures were taken to strengthen the system's ability to deal with speculation in the so-called 'Basle–Nyborg' agreements in 1987, as a result of which the credit provisions – which hitherto had applied only to intervention at the margins – were extended in scope and made to apply also to intra-marginal intervention. Concurrently, the repayment period under the VSTF was extended from 45 to 60 days. At the same time it was resolved that there should be a closer coordination of monetary policies and that realignments, if they occurred, should be small in scope – so that the central rate and the bands could be changed without causing a discrete movement in the market rate.

Such was the early success of these measures that, between 1988 and 1992, the system was widely believed to suffer from a problem of 'excess credibility' (see Davies, 1989). The symptom of this 'problem' was that for much of this period, the strongest currencies in the EMS were the *highest* inflation currencies, notably the Spanish peseta and the Italian lira. Because these member states were attempting to address their inflation problems by deploying high rates of interest and their currencies were seen as less likely to be devalued than under the 'Old EMS', high interest rates forced these currencies towards the top of their bands. This unaccustomed position posed a policy problem. If they were not to allow their currencies to go through the top of the band, the governments of the high inflation countries had either to:

1 relax their fight against inflation; or
2 substitute fiscal for monetary policy; or
3 deliberately create the impression that devaluation might occur; or
4 introduce administrative measures which would deter capital inflows (see van der Ploeg, 1989).

THE CURRENCY UPHEAVALS OF 1992–93

The phenomenon of high inflation countries choosing to follow Germany's anti-inflationary example, rather than devaluing against the deutschmark (or leaving the ERM altogether) became known as 'German policy leadership'. While this feature of the ERM was entirely unintended, by the end of the last decade, it had come to be regarded as the system's greatest attraction. Germany provided a strong, anti-inflationary anchor for Europe. By setting domestic interest rates at whatever level was necessary to maintain their exchange rates within their target bands against the deutschmark, other ERM states could effectively be guaranteed that their inflation rates would come down to low German levels. For countries (like Britain) which had unsuccessfully experimented with monetary targets and were left with no clear guide for monetary policy, ERM membership thus offered the prospect of both greater exchange rate stability *and*, perhaps more importantly, low and stable inflation rates (Healey, 1990).

After the débâcle of the ill-fated 'Lawson boom', when broad monetary growth was allowed to accelerate to almost 25% p.a. and inflation reached 10%, there is no question that a key motive in Britain's entry to the ERM in October 1990 was a desire to bring down inflation. Critics of previous British policy welcomed ERM membership as a transfer of monetary sovereignty to the Bundesbank. The Bundesbank, they argued, was politically independent; ERM membership meant British policy being made by the Bundesbank, which was immune from the pressures that had given rise to Britain's unhappy experience of 'stop–go' policies and a high, underlying rate of inflation.

However, while being one of its most attractive features, the German anti-inflation anchor also created a 'fault-line' in the system (see Healey, 1993a, 1993b). The Bundesbank's known hostility to unlimited intervention in support of weak currencies meant that currencies which fell to their trading floors were vulnerable to speculative attack. In other words, the ERM parities were simply not credible. During the 1980s, German policy leadership became steadily established, but the significance of the fault-line was not fully realised for two reasons. First, until 1990 almost all the ERM members maintained some form of capital controls, which placed legislative restrictions on capital movements and artificially limited the scale of a speculative attack on a weak currency. Second, the business cycles of the EU economies were broadly synchronised during the 1980s, so that the policy adjustments necessary for other countries to follow the German lead and keep comfortably within their target bands against the deutschmark were relatively painless.

Unfortunately, Britain's entry (with a much higher inflation rate than the other ERM states) coincided with both the abolition of capital controls and the reunification of Germany. In order to control mounting inflationary pressures, the Bundesbank was forced to adopt a much tighter monetary stance, at a time when deflationary pressures were already intensifying in other EU states (notably Britain, France and Italy). The protection that capital controls had given to weak currencies was thus removed just as the costs (in terms of higher unemployment and lost output) of following the German policy lead were temporarily increased. Those countries which could not, or would not, continue to match German monetary policy accordingly became increasingly vulnerable to speculative attack, as high German interest rates forced their currencies towards their trading floors. For Britain in particular, international investors watched as growing political pressure to address the recession forced the government into a series of interest rate cuts between October 1990 and September 1992, despite the fact that German rates were rising over the same period. In the immediate run-up to Black Wednesday, clear signals given by the Bundesbank – to the effect that it regarded sterling as over-valued at DM2.95 due to a premature relaxation of British monetary policy – contributed to a massive speculative attack on sterling which (despite a 5% interest rate rise on September 16, 1992) drove the pound below its floor and culminated in its formal suspension from the ERM. The Italian lira was forced out at the same time and a series of devaluations by the remaining weaker currencies failed to settle the financial markets, eventually forcing the EU to introduce ultra-wide ±15% bands in August 1993 to head off a politically embarrassing devaluation of the French franc.

CONCLUSIONS

The Bundesbank's refusal to guarantee unlimited, unsterilised intervention in support of weak currencies meant that the ERM has always been potentially vulnerable to speculative attack. However, during the 1980s, this fault-line was disguised by the presence of capital controls and the synchronisation of business cycles amongst the ERM states. At the same time, the Bundesbank's uncompromising stance provided a valuable anti-inflation anchor for those countries that followed the German policy lead. As more and more member states chose to match Germany's monetary lead rather than opt for devaluation and continuing inflation, Germany became the anchor for the ERM as a whole. This dimension of the ERM was widely regarded as its most attractive feature and was undoubtedly one of the main factors that lay behind Britain's entry in October 1990. In this sense, it was clearly disingenuous for the British government to claim that the ERM is flawed by a fault-line, in the shape of the Bundesbank's unwillingness to aid overvalued currencies, since it was the obverse of this fault-line (i.e., German policy leadership) that induced the government to join in the first place.

On the other hand, developments since 1990, notably the abolition of capital controls and German reunification, have served to make this fault-line in the EMS much more significant. In retrospect, given the inflation rate at which Britain entered the system and the scale of the recession into which the economy was sliding, it is difficult to see that the ERM as it then existed could have managed to embrace sterling for any length of time. In the absence of capital controls and given the scale of international capital movements, orderly devaluations would have proved impractical: after the first, the confidence of the market would have been so severely dented that subsequent speculative attacks would have occurred at any sign of sterling weakness. It is significant in this regard that several of those states (e.g., Spain, Portugal, Ireland) which have devalued within the framework of the ERM since September 1992 have either retained or reimposed capital controls. The importance that the French government ascribed to its '*franc fort*' policy, silencing any serious political talk of devaluation, reflects its view that unless devaluation is regarded as unthinkable, a speculative attack on the franc will be overwhelming.

Against the background of the analysis outlined above, the EU now finds itself in something of a quandary. The ERM's widely acknowledged success in stabilising exchange rates and bringing down inflation in the EU in the 1980s was primarily due to the unplanned emergence of German policy leadership. Yet this feature of the system created a fault-line, which means that weaker currencies will always be vulnerable to irresistible speculative attack. Given that the EU is committed (under both the Treaty of Rome and the Single European Act) to the free movement of capital, which seems to preclude the restoration of widespread capital controls, it is difficult to see how the EU will be able to recreate the 'monetary stability' enjoyed in the late 1980s in the near-to-medium term. It is to be hoped that, as the effects of German reunification slowly dissipate, the business cycles across the EU will move sufficiently into line to make German policy leadership once again acceptable to the higher inflation states. It is to a consideration of the prospects for EMU that Chapters 4–6 turn (see also Temperton, 1993; Currie, 1991; Collignon, 1994).

APPENDIX A: THE REAL EXCHANGE RATE

Economists have several theories to explain the long-run, equilibrium value of a currency, but all are essentially variations on an old theme, namely the concept of purchasing power parity (PPP). In its simplest form, the PPP theory states that, in equilibrium, the purchasing power of £1 in Britain should be equal to that of its deutschmark equivalent in German, its dollar equivalent in the United States and so on. For example, if baked beans were the only commodity purchased in Britain and Germany and the prices in each country were £0.25 and DM0.75 respectively, then the equilibrium exchange rate that ensured PPP would be DM3/£ (i.e., DM0.75/£0.25). At this exchange rate, £1 would buy the same quantity of baked beans (four cans) as its deutschmark equivalent (DM3) in Germany.

At this exchange rate, moreover, producers in Britain and Germany would be equally competitive, with neither having an edge over the other by virtue of an advantageous exchange rate. If the exchange rate were lower than DM3/1, for example, British producers could undercut their German rivals, leading to a current account surplus in Britain; and vice versa. This is a crucial point, for what underpins the PPP theory is the proposition that, in the long run, the current account must be in balance. Countries with overvalued exchange rates cannot finance current account deficits indefinitely by borrowing from overseas and, at some point, their exchange rates must fall to the equilibrium (PPP) value consistent with current account balance.

These same ideas can be expressed with reference to the 'real exchange rate'. As the name suggests, the real exchange rate is the nominal exchange rate (e.g., DM3/£) adjusted for prices in the two countries concerned. The real exchange rate is defined as:

$$ER_r = ER \times P/P^*$$

where ER_r is the real exchange rate, ER is the nominal exchange rate, P is the domestic price level and P^* is the foreign price level. For the simplified, baked beans example used above, the real exchange rate would be:

$$ER_r = DM3.00/£1 \times £0.25/DM0.75$$

$$ER_r = 1.00$$

In other words, when the PPP condition is fulfilled, the real exchange rate is unity. A real exchange rate above one suggests that, given the prevailing price levels in the two countries, the nominal exchange rate is too high; that is, the currency is overvalued, its current account will be in deficit and its exchange rate will tend to fall in the long run; and vice versa for a real exchange rate below one. To give a real-world example, when sterling entered the ERM in October 1990, inflation in Britain was much higher than in Germany. Although the gap subsequently closed, in the interim prices in Britain (expressed at the former DM2.95/£ exchange rate) climbed above those in Germany (and other EU countries). In other words, between entry to the ERM in 1990 and sterling's ultimate withdrawal in 1992, the real exchange rate rose sharply (see Figure 2.2). Evidence that sterling was overvalued at its former ERM parity, in the sense that British producers were finding it increasingly difficult to compete on price with their German (and other European) rivals, was reflected in the trade figures. Despite the severity of the recession, Britain still had a current account deficit of £12bn in 1992.

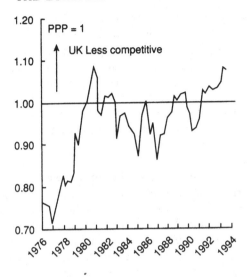

Figure 2.2 Real effective sterling exchange rate
Source: Goldman Sachs.

APPENDIX B: UNCOVERED INTEREST PARITY

PPP considerations play a central role in shaping the foreign exchange market's view of which currencies (like the pound) are overvalued, leading speculators to sell, and which are undervalued and therefore an attractive buy. But PPP is only part of the story. Casual observation reveals that, even when central banks do not intervene to support an overvalued currency (or hold down an undervalued currency) with open-market operations, exchange rates can deviate from their PPP values for long periods. The missing variable in the equation is the interest rate. When currencies are overvalued, rational investors will expect their value to fall over time, resulting in a capital loss. All other things equal, this expectation will lead them to sell the currency until it eventually falls to its PPP value. But suppose the interest rate obtainable on deposits in this currency is higher than those on other currencies. If the interest differential in favour of the overvalued currency is sufficiently high to fully compensate investors for the expected capital loss, the currency will remain at its overvalued exchange rate in the absence of central bank intervention.

The relationship between interest rates and exchange rates can be summarised using a simple example. Suppose an investor has £X to invest. If she invests in a sterling deposit, she will receive £X(1 + r); that is, the principal, £X, plus interest of £Xr, where r is the British rate of interest over the term of the deposit. Alternatively, she might switch the money into deutschmarks at the present exchange rate, ER, and invest in deutschmark deposits which will yield an amount DM(ER × £X)(1 + r*), where DM(ER × £X) is the original deutschmark deposit and DM(ER × £Xr*) is the interest received on the deposit at the German rate of interest, r*.

Whether she believes that the latter option will give her a higher or lower return, *in sterling terms*, depends on the exchange rate she expects to prevail at the time the deutschmark deposit is to be withdrawn and converted back into pounds. Her expectation of the future exchange rate, ER^e, in turn, will be influenced by: (i) the exchange rate consistent with PPP in the long run (which may be above or below the present exchange rate); and (ii) if the exchange rate is being pegged, the perceived likelihood of the government realigning the exchange rate to a level more in line with the PPP rate.

If, for example, there is an interest differential in favour of sterling which exceeds (in percentage terms) the amount by which she expects the pound to fall, she will invest in a sterling deposit. Conversely, if the interest differential is insufficient to compensate the expected capital loss, she will sell sterling and switch into a deutschmark deposit. She will be indifferent between the two options only if:

$$£X(1 + r) = DM(ER × £X)(1 + r*)/ER^e$$

That is, if:

$$ER/ER^e = (1 + r)/(1 + r*)$$

If ER is greater than ER^e, in equilibrium the expected rate of depreciation of the currency, ER/ER^e, must be equal to the interest differential in favour of the currency, $(1 + r)/(1 + r*)$. Investors can profit by switching between currencies whenever this equilibrium condition is not satisfied. However, by so doing, their transactions quickly eliminate the opportunities which initially inspired them. For example, if ER/ER^e were greater than

$(1 + r)/(1 + r^*)$, investors would *en masse* choose to invest in deutschmark rather than sterling deposits. The excess demand for deutschmarks would push down sterling's value, ER, until the expected depreciation, ER/ER^e, fell into line with the interest differential. Conversely, if ER/ER^e were less than $(1 + r)(1 + r^*)$, investors would buy sterling, pushing up the value of sterling until ER/ER^e rose into line with the interest differential.

This review of the role of the rate of interest reveals two key points. First, it illustrates why, if countries run divergent monetary policies that result in different interest rates, currencies may be persistently under- or overvalued. And second, it demonstrates why changes in interest rates exert such a significant and immediate effect on the present exchange rate: in the equation above, any change in either r or r^* will cause an instantaneous change in ER for a given ER^e.

3

FIXED EXCHANGE RATES AND DEFLATION

The European Monetary System and the Gold Standard

Jonathan Michie and Michael Kitson

INTRODUCTION

As noted in Chapter 1, there is now a widespread belief that the 'European project' has been blown off course, if not sunk completely. In light of the apparent divide between Europe's electorate and what might be termed – or what at least gives the impression of being – the political elite, it is interesting to evaluate the economic policy agenda of the past few years, dominated as it has been by the Maastricht Treaty and the unsuccessful attempt to transform the exchange rate mechanism (ERM) into a permanently inflexible system, in light of Keynes's 1925 evaluation of *The Economic Consequences of Mr Churchill*:

> The gold standard, with its dependence on pure chance, its faith in 'automatic adjustments', and its general regardlessness of social detail, is an essential emblem and idol of those who sit in the top tier of the machine. I think that they are immensely rash in their regardlessness, in their vague optimism and comfortable belief that nothing really serious ever happens. Nine times out of ten, nothing really serious does happen – merely a little distress to individuals or to groups. But we run a risk of the tenth time (and are stupid into the bargain), if we continue to apply the principles of an economics, which was worked out on the hypotheses of *laissez-faire* and free competition, to a society which is rapidly abandoning these hypotheses.
>
> (Keynes, 1925)

Certainly, we would argue that the governments of the European Union (EU) *did* pursue deflationary policies in the early years of the 1990s, exacerbated by the operation of the ERM (see also Chapter 2). The resulting unemployment should have come as no surprise. Further, we would argue that these policies were in some respects similar to those pursued under the gold standard of the 1920s, with parallel results in terms of deflationary government economic policies and the creation of mass unemployment. It seems that nothing has been learned. Finally, we argue in this chapter that the world economy only managed to pull itself out of the Great Depression in the 1930s by abandoning fixed exchange rates, cutting interest rates and employing independent national monetary policies.

THE GOLD STANDARD

From the mid-1920s, the cornerstone of international economic management was the gold standard. Founded on the questionable success of the classical gold standard in operation during the quarter-century before World War I, the 1920s' variant was intended to bring stability to international trading relations and increase world prosperity. It failed to achieve these objectives. Its actual effect was to depress real variables such as output and employment and undermine the capacity of individual governments to deal with domestic economic problems.

The adjustment process integral to the gold standard created a severe deflationary bias for the world economy. To capture this bias, the main trading countries can be broadly classified into those 'constrained' and those 'unconstrained' by their trade performance. Those countries that could maintain a sufficient level of exports, relative to imports, at a high level of economic activity were not balance of payments constrained. Such countries could pursue easier monetary policies or could accumulate increased reserves. Conversely, a country that could not maintain balance of payments equilibrium at a high level of economic activity had to reduce domestic demand in order to import only those goods and services which it could afford to finance.

The two key unconstrained countries were France and the United States. France recovered successfully from World War I, with an undervalued exchange rate helping to generate export-led growth. The United States had become the world's leading economy during the late nineteenth century. Its strength was based on huge natural resources of land and minerals, sustained investment which had significantly raised its capital stock, a large internal market and the development of an industrial structure that encouraged research and development and the exploitation of economies of scale.

The two major constrained countries were Britain and Germany, both of which emerged from the aftermath of war with severe economic problems. The British economy had been in relative decline since the 1870s. In addition, the commitment to return to gold necessitated tight monetary policies and the economy suffered a severe slump in 1920–21. The German economy, which had been rapidly expanding from the 1880s, was devastated by World War I. It lost financial and physical assets and reparations constituted a continual drain on its income and wealth. The reconstructed gold standard, therefore, created a fixed exchange rate regime with members at different stages of economic development with different economic structures and different economic problems. Its prospects were not good.

WHAT PRICE AUTOMATIC ADJUSTMENT?

To be effective, the gold standard depended on a process of automatic adjustment to correct payments imbalances. Under this system, the price level would adjust in response to deficits and surpluses on the balance of payments. A deficit would lead to a loss of gold and a contraction in the money supply, leading to a fall in prices, a reduction in the real exchange rate (see Chapter 2, Appendix A) and the eradication of the deficit. Similarly, a surplus would lead to an accumulation of gold, a rise in the money supply and prices and hence a return to a balance of payments equilibrium. But the real world did not work like this. The theory was based on various unrealistic assumptions, including the assumption that all the burden of adjustment would be borne by changes in prices rather than in changes in quantities produced.

As the main trading nations entered the exchange rate system with different initial conditions, it was apparent that the efficacy of the adjustment process would be central to the regime's impact. The option of adjusting the *nominal* exchange rate was effectively precluded. The adjustment of the *real* exchange was slow and erratic. For Britain, most studies indicate a significant average overvaluation of the sterling effective exchange rate in the period

1925–31. Keynes's contemporary estimate of a 10% overvaluation has proved to be a reasonable approximation of recent empirical estimates. The result was lower growth and higher unemployment. Conventionally, it had been assumed that the unravelling of the price-quantity adjustment process would eventually return the economy to its previous position with only a temporary loss of output and jobs. However, the legacy of slow growth in fact lowered the long-run capacity of the economy itself.

The sluggishness of real exchange rate changes left two adjustment alternatives: (i) changes in the level of demand – deflation in constrained countries and reflation in surplus countries; or (ii) the financing of the deficits of constrained countries by capital flows from the unconstrained countries. In fact, the ultimate burden of adjustment was borne by domestic deflation. The surplus countries were reluctant to reflate. The classical adjustment mechanism assumes that gold flows will provide the means of changing the level of demand via prices. But price adjustment was slow, and the reflationary impact of gold flows into France and the United States were negated (i.e., sterilised) by domestic monetary policy. Both countries, which by the late 1920s had between them accumulated 60% of total gold reserves, prevented these reserves from boosting their domestic money supplies. American policymakers were increasingly concerned with curbing stock market speculation, whereas the French were wary of inflation. Deflation was transmitted abroad. Low import demand, particularly in America, led to widening balance of payments deficits in many of the key European economies.

The unconstrained countries' export growth was reasonable and close to the 5.7% growth of world trade. Additionally, due to their reluctance to reflate, they were able to maintain large balance of payments surpluses throughout the 1920s. During 1925–29, France maintained a surplus that averaged over 2% of gross domestic product (GDP), while the US surplus averaged just under 1% of GDP. The US surplus was particularly significant given the size of its economy, averaging 2.5% of world trade compared to 1% for the French. The growth of world trade was therefore limited by the domestic policies of the unconstrained countries. Whereas these nations could choose whether or not to reflate, the constrained countries had no such options. The entire burden of adjustment fell on them – they could either deflate to eradicate balance of payments deficits or they could borrow to fund them. The effective approach of the British economy was the former and Germany the latter.

Deflation could be achieved either through allowing reserves to flow out, depressing the money supply and domestic expenditure – the classical mechanism – or by policies that directly affected the components of demand. In Britain, it was interest rates that acted as the key deflationary tool. From 1923, there was a trend rise in the Bank of England's discount rate as the authorities adopted policies consistent with the return and maintenance of the exchange rate at the prewar parity. At the same time the general trend of other central banks' discount rates was downward. The deflationary impact of such policies helped to keep the overall balance of payments (i.e., on current *and* capital accounts) in surplus and prevented the loss of gold.

The Bank of England also deployed gold market and foreign exchange operations to maintain its stock of international reserves. The impact on the real economy was slow growth, with the economy failing to reap its growth potential (for more detail, see Kitson and Solomou, 1990). Despite the level of GDP in 1924 being below that of 1913, the growth rate of the British economy was significantly below the world average. Unemployment remained persistently high, averaging 7.5% for the period 1924–29.

Unlike Britain, Germany maintained a persistent balance of payments deficit throughout the 1920s. Along with reparations this deficit had to be financed and Germany became heavily reliant on foreign loans, particularly from the United States. Although initially able to attract sizeable capital inflows, the rising debt burden undermined creditworthiness. Germany became increasingly reliant on short-term funds and by 1931 had accumulated net foreign debts equivalent to 25% of GDP. The subsequent concern about the German economy and the collapse of American lending abroad from 1928 led to capital flight, the loss of reserves, a credit squeeze and the raising of interest rates. Germany had been able to cope with its balance of payments constraint in the short term by borrowing; ultimately, however, this only postponed the requirement to deflate.

The asymmetry in the adjustment processes showed in the relative trade performance of the two groups of countries during the 'successful' operation of the gold standard. The trading position of the constrained countries, Britain and Germany, differed significantly to that of the unconstrained countries. Although

Britain managed to maintain a balance of payments surplus, its export performance was poor, exhibiting slow growth and a declining share of world markets. Britain's share of world markets in 1929 was 3.2% below its 1913 level – the result of an average annual decline of 1.6%. The German trading position was also in a precarious position, the deficit on the balance of payments averaging 1.2% of GDP between 1925 and 1929. Germany's export growth was rapid during this period, but this was catching-up from a very low postwar base and was boosted by enforced exports through reparations in kind. Despite this rapid growth, Germany's share of world exports in 1929 was more than 25% below its 1913 level.

THE DEFLATIONARY BIAS OF FIXED EXCHANGE RATE REGIMES

Thus the deflationary bias of the gold standard not only failed to deal with the structural problems of constrained countries, it positively accentuated them. Countries which had entered the system with major structural problems left the system weakened, as they had to bear the burden of adjustment by deflating their domestic economies. This not only lowered growth and raised unemployment; it also hampered long-run competitiveness. The dampening of domestic demand reduced the benefits of mass production and the exploitation of scale economies. Deflation to maintain external equilibrium raised unit costs and generated a further loss of competitiveness and declining shares of world markets. Such a process of cumulative causation led the constrained countries to suffer a vicious cycle of stagnation. Locked into a fixed exchange rate system, there were few policy options to reverse the process.

If the gold standard failed to maximise world growth in the 1920s, its shortcomings were also evident with the onset of the Great Depression. The causes of the Great Depression are subject to continual debate, but key factors were certainly the cumulative impact of structural problems, adverse demand shocks and policy mistakes. One such policy mistake was the constrained countries' adherence to gold. The severity of the Great Depression can certainly be attributed to the operation of the gold standard – the impact of adverse shocks, such as the recession in the United States and the collapse in capital exports, were transmitted to the

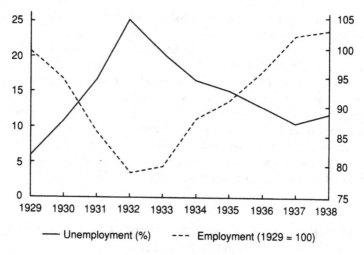

Figure 3.1 World employment and unemployment, 1929–38
Notes: (1) Employment index excludes the USSR. (2) Unemployment
series is the average of two series (A and B) presented in ILO (1940).
Source: ILO (1940) Table 3.

rest of the world through the exchange rate regime. As foreign
loans were called in due to developments in the domestic economy,
the gold flows to the United States increased. The draining of
reserves in the debtor countries accelerated and monetary policy
was tightened to ensure gold convertibility. Thus the deflationary
bias of the gold standard system resulted in a perverse reaction to
adverse demand shocks. Rather than facilitating an expansion of
demand to ameliorate the depression, the system magnified the
problem leading to a collapse in world trade and a sharp rise in
global unemployment (see Figure 3.1).

As countries moved into recession, they needed the capacity to
initiate domestic policies in order to insulate themselves from the
collapse in the world economy. The structure, characteristics and
paths of development of the major economies were different and
thus the timing and the composition of the policy mix required was
also different. The phasing of the depression of the major countries differed: there was approximately a three-year gap between
the onset of decline in Germany and that in Denmark. Yet during
this period, economic policy was constrained by the gold standard,
leaving little flexibility to deal quickly with domestic problems.

The impact of the Great Depression also varied across countries: GDP in the United States collapsed by an annual rate in excess of 10% between 1929 and 1932, whereas other countries such as Denmark and Norway witnessed little or no decline. In part these variations reflected the speed with which countries left gold, although another major factor was the difference in economic structures and institutions. Britain's relatively moderate depression, an annual decline of less than 2% compared to a world average of over 6%, in part reflected the low dependence on agriculture and the stability of its financial institutions. Thus, shocks had different national and sectoral impacts. Binding nations together in a fixed exchange rate regime made no allowance for this.

The interwar gold standard system was structurally flawed. Even if cooperation between countries had managed to limit the deflationary bias, it would most likely have only extended the life of the system rather than preventing its ultimate demise. Indeed, had the system lasted longer, it might have resulted in a greater divergence in growth performance. Reflation in the stronger countries could well have led to faster growth of output and productivity, leading to a virtuous cycle of growth, but with deflation limiting the growth potential of the relatively weaker countries. Also, the system combined together countries with different economic conditions and problems. These problems were not eradicated by the regime; rather they were accentuated. Discretion over the use of monetary, fiscal and exchange rate policy was removed. And finally, the regime was not able to accommodate adverse economic shocks to the system; on the contrary, the operation of the international monetary system magnified the impact of any such recessionary forces. The regime was inappropriate for members with different economic structures and a recession phased differently amongst the international community (see Chapters 4 and 5 for a discussion of the implications of monetary union for countries vulnerable to asymmetric shocks).

The extent and magnitude of the Great Depression put the gold standard regime under severe strain. A series of financial and balance of payments crises ultimately undermined the system, culminating in Britain's decision to abandon the gold standard and devalue in September 1931. This decision marked the effective collapse of the regime. Other countries quickly followed sterling off the gold standard, including most of the dominions

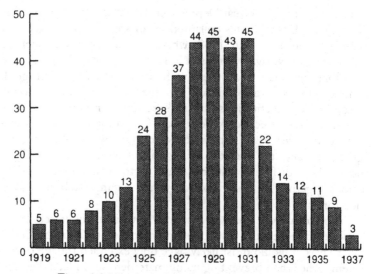

Figure 3.2 Number of countries on gold, 1919–37
Note: The three countries on gold in 1937 were on the 'qualified gold standard'.
Source: Eichengreen (1992) Table 7.1, pp. 188–91.

and Empire, the Scandinavian countries, Canada and Japan. It was not until March 1933 that the United States devalued, while a core of countries including France, Belgium and the Netherlands remained on gold until later in the decade (see Figure 3.2). Devaluation was not the only uncoordinated trade policy implemented; tariffs and quotas were increased while many of the central European countries including Germany and Italy resorted to extensive exchange controls (see Chapter 2).

ECONOMIC RECOVERY IN THE 1930s: THE MECHANISMS

Devaluation can have beneficial impacts through a number of mechanisms. First, it can directly alleviate the balance of payments constraint on growth. Shifts in relative prices and improved competitiveness can raise exports and depress imports. The conventional account of this process is that it is a 'beggar-my-neighbour' policy (see Healey and Levine, 1992a), as the improvement in trade performance is reflected in an improving trade balance for

76

the initiating country and a deteriorating trade balance for trading partners. This account, however, ignores the effects of an independently pursued trade policy on the level of economic activity. Increasing exports and reducing the propensity to import will raise the level of demand in the domestic economy. With unemployment and excess capacity, such a policy initiative will raise output and employment as well as leading to an income-induced increase in imports, so that there need be no change in the actual trade balance. Indeed, this is precisely the reason why, although Britain devalued and adopted widespread protectionism in 1931, the current account deficits persisted throughout the 1930s. If countries get locked into a pattern of trade which constrains domestic expansion, an active and independent trade policy provides one means of overcoming the problem without necessarily affecting adversely other trading partners.

The second benefit of devaluation is that it removes the exchange rate constraint on domestic policy, encouraging expansionist policies. In particular, monetary policy can be relaxed and therefore interest rates can be determined by domestic economic conditions rather than by the need to maintain the exchange rate or by the need to prevent excessive loss of reserves. For instance, Britain's suspension of the gold standard allowed the government to pursue a more expansionist policy after 1932. This 'cheap money' policy has been identified as a permissive policy for economic revival, especially important in stimulating a housing boom. Conversely, the reason that the British Government's claims on September 16, 1992 (that it would remain in the ERM by raising interest rates as far as was necessary) lacked credibility was that raising interest rates by 5% in one day in the midst of the longest economic recession for 60 years was not believed to be a feasible policy option.

Devaluation and the accompanying introduction of other expansionist policies also led to a third, less mechanistic, benefit. Under the prevailing world conditions of uncertainty and monetary and financial turbulence, the reorientation of policy towards the domestic economy improved business confidence. The prospect of a stable and growing economy encourages home producers to increase, or at least bring forward, investment and expand production.

JONATHAN MICHIE AND MICHAEL KITSON

ECONOMIC RECOVERY IN THE 1930s: THE EVIDENCE

Although a wide range of uncoordinated policies were implemented in the 1930s, including devaluation, it is possible to classify the major trading nations into different trade policy regimes (see Kitson and Solomou, 1990):

1 the sterling bloc that devalued with or soon after Britain and linked their currencies to sterling;
2 other countries which also devalued either early (before 1932) or later (1932 and after);
3 the exchange control group, that was reluctant to devalue for fear of inflation; and
4 the gold bloc countries which remained, at least in the short term, committed to the system.

During the 1929–32 depression, 'world' output declined by more than 6% per annum. The sterling bloc exhibited the mildest contraction, with GDP falling by an annual rate of less than 2% per annum, and just 0.5% if Canada is excluded from the sample (Canada was particularly adversely affected by its large agricultural sector and its links with the United States). This suggests that devaluation policies may have helped to mitigate the adverse effects of the depression. Leaving gold provided less help for the 'other devaluers' group although there is evidence that those who devalued early experienced a milder depression than those who delayed and devalued late. Thus, the timing of the policy response was important.

For the period of recovery, from 1932–37, most countries exhibited reasonable cyclical growth. The exception was the gold bloc countries. Constrained by their commitment to their exchange rate parities they had to adopt tight monetary and fiscal policies to maintain internal and external balance. Thus although output was depressed, the French government in the early 1930s adopted contractionary fiscal policies to prevent destabilising exchange rate speculation.

A simple comparison of growth performance during recovery can be misleading, as it will include both a cyclical component (the automatic recovery from a deep depression) and policy induced effects. An alternative is to examine inter-period, peak to peak growth performance. Looking at the change in the annual rate of growth of GDP during 1929–37 relative to 1924–29, the results for the 'world' economy indicate a retardation of the growth path. This is consistent with other findings that the shock of the Great Depression had persistent effects on the level of output. The performance of the different policy regimes, however, provides important contrasts. The countries that devalued, particularly those that devalued early, experienced only a small (or zero) fall in trend growth. Those countries that had the limited benefits of exchange controls experienced a deterioration in annual growth of 3.3%. The poorest performing group was the gold bloc, which had little flexibility to initiate policies for domestic recovery.

Further evidence of the striking contrasts in performance of different policy regimes is shown in figures for annual growth of industrial production. These indicate that those countries which devalued, and to a lesser extent those that introduced exchange controls, had a milder industrial depression, faster recovery and a better inter-period growth performance. Evidence on the unemployment performance of the different policy regimes shows that the high unemployment that developed during the depression persisted throughout the period of recovery. Only for the sterling bloc was there any fall in the unemployment rate; for the other regimes unemployment increased during 1933–37. In part this reflects employment lagging output, plus changing activity rates and demographic shifts. But it is also evidence of the persistent effects of the Great Depression, the long-term unemployed having difficulty re-entering the labour market.

As always, there are some authors (e.g., Beenstock *et al.*, 1984) who argue that it was wage movements that accounted for the cyclical fluctuations in output, both for the Great Depression and the subsequent recovery. It is true that real wages (adjusted for price changes) did move counter-cyclically over the 1929–37 cycle in Britain – rising relative to trend in the recession and then falling relative to trend during the recovery – but the causes of the output fluctuations lay elsewhere, and the timing of the wage fluctuations do not actually fit the claim that recession was caused by wage rises and recovery caused by wage cuts. We have shown elsewhere (Michie, 1987) that this wage–output correlation itself does not, in any case, hold outside those particular years – a finding which reinforces the argument that the output and wage series are independently generated, with output influenced crucially by the level of demand for output and wages by factors such as productivity levels and bargaining strength.

Growth and improved economic performance during the 1930s was dependent on countries untying themselves from the strictures of the gold standard and adopting independent policies, with different exchange rate regimes created and with some countries also reaping the advantages of increased protectionism and fiscal expansion. What is apparent, however, is that the cooperative regime failed and uncoordinated policies were a vast improvement.

The use of uncoordinated policies may have led to some resource misallocation effects. The overriding impact, however, was positive as independent policies overcame the deflationary bias of the gold standard and led to increased resource mobilisation. Despite these economic gains some commentators persist in identifying the 1930s as a period of 'economic nationalism' which helped to usher in totalitarian and fascist political regimes. This is a complete misreading of history. The rise of racism and fascism in the 1920s and 1930s was fuelled by mass unemployment and the destructive economic policies imposed on Germany at Versailles and on the rest of the world by the gold standard. Keynes (1919, 1925) had warned as much in *The Economic Consequences of the Peace* and *The Economic Consequences of Mr Churchill*, but to no avail. Currency stability was, of course, paramount.

CONCLUSIONS

The similar experience of deep slumps and widespread unemployment has led to comparisons between the interwar period and recent economic events, including by analogy between the ERM and the interwar gold standard. Both resemble 'adjustable peg systems' in theory, but proved to be rather less adjustable in practice. Both failed to deal with external shocks. Both suffered adversely from speculative attacks. And both limited the flexibility of domestic policy. As in 1931, Britain disengaged itself from the exchange rate system, allowed the exchange rate to fall, and introduced cheap money. As in 1931, policy initiatives today reflect crisis management rather than any coherent strategy, although the benefits of devaluation were at least more fully discussed 60 years ago than they were prior to September 1992. Similarly, the French 'franc fort' policy of the 1980s and 1990s resembles the ultimately misconceived French commitment to gold in the 1930s (although at least the French now have the flex-ibility to introduce expansionary policies, despite their reluctance to take advantage of this opportunity).

Despite the historical similarities some important differences remain. International capital markets are now more integrated, making it more difficult to engineer unilateral reductions in inter-est rates. The British experience of 1992–93 suggests, however, that such unilateral action is still possible, with the leaving of the ERM allowing interest rate cuts despite claims prior to September 1992 that interest rates would actually have to increase in such circumstances to compensate for loss of confidence and credi-bility. Also, the economic problems faced by European economies in the early 1990s had different causes and different characteristics from the interwar period. For instance, depressed demand in the British economy reflected the high level of debt in the private sector resulting from government policy mismanagement and the impact of financial deregulation in the mid-1980s. However, some important lessons can still be drawn.

First, macroeconomic policies which retard growth may have persistent effects on the real economy. The magnitude of the Great Depression did lasting damage to the level of world GDP. We have yet to observe the long-term impacts of the early-1990s' recession. What is apparent, however, is that governments should react to external shocks quickly by using accommodating monetary and fiscal policies and that internal deflation is an inappropriate tool for permanently reducing inflation.

Second, policies which are based on trying to achieve conver-gence of inflation rates and other monetary and financial indicators can have adverse effects on the real economy. This is particularly so when those policies fail to accommodate different initial con-ditions or when they tend to have a deflationary bias or when they fail to successfully accommodate economic shocks. The experience of the gold standard supports this warning, as does more recent evidence. Thus the notion, for example, that because Germany had a strong economy and a strong currency, imposing a strong currency on Britain would thereby strengthen the domestic econ-omy, was fatally flawed. Causation runs from the real economy to the exchange rate, not vice versa. Britain's decision to join the ERM at DM2.95 in October 1992 served to weaken Britain's trading sector and removed the policy options required to deal with domestic recession.

One of the keys to economic growth during the 1930s was the use of independent and uncoordinated policies. This is not the same as saying that coordination itself is necessarily ineffective: what is ineffective is a coordination based on convergence towards monetary and financial targets which has adverse impacts on the real economies of the participants. During the 1930s, coordination based on structured reflation and the effective redistribution of resources to regions or countries of the world with difficulties would have been appropriate. The limitations of such policy packages is that the level of cooperation required is significant and the rules required are complex and not easily enforced (Levine, 1990). In the absence of such an agreed and enforced policy package, independent policies were the next best option, and as such proved successful during the 1930s. Unless current European economic policy is reoriented towards the objective of full employment, embracing an active industrial and regional policy, rather than with the myopic concern with zero inflation, the route forward must once again be based on independent national growth strategies which would not only allow countries to help themselves, but by doing so would help each other. Competitive deflation is the real 'beggar my neighbour' policy of the 1990s.

And third, despite economic revival in the 1930s, unemployment remained high. It was a constant source of poverty, disease and malnutrition. The implementation of a growth strategy today, whether it be of a national or European variety, is a necessary condition for tackling unemployment, but may not of itself be sufficient. It is important, therefore, first that the pursuit of market flexibility does not further erode the welfare state upon which the basic needs of so many depends; and second that policies for employment are pursued alongside those for economic recovery and growth. These need to include measures such as reducing the length of the working week and year; expanding employment-intensive public services and public works, such as a major environmental programme; and supply-side measures on education and training, and on research, development and design to see through new products and production processes (see Chapter 10).

4

WHITHER EUROPEAN MONETARY UNION?

George Zis

INTRODUCTION

On January 1, 1994, Stage Two of the process towards the complete monetary unification of the European Union (EU) formally came into effect. However, it no longer seems as likely as it did at the time of the signing of the Maastricht Treaty that the EU will, in fact, implement the third and final stage of this process in 1997 or, at the latest, on January 1, 1999, as prescribed by the Treaty. Doubts exist as to whether the European Monetary System (EMS) can provide the policy anchor for the EU member countries during the transition period. Persistent speculative pressures from the summer of 1992 to the end of July 1993 forced Italy and Britain to drop out of the system's exchange rate mechanism (ERM) in September 1992, a series of realignments in intra-EMS exchange rates and, finally, on August 1, 1993, the decision to alter the mechanism's rules for intervention in the foreign exchange markets by widening the permissible band of fluctuation from ±2.25% to ±15% on either side of the agreed central parities. The 1992–93 turmoil has raised doubts not only about the capacity of the EMS to fend off speculative pressures, even when parities are not inconsistent with market fundamentals, but also regarding the *political* commitment of EU member countries to the objective of economic and monetary union (EMU).

Is the balance between the benefits and costs of monetary union such that it can provide a justification for EU member countries to refrain from fully implementing the Maastricht Treaty and instead seek alternative monetary arrangements? Will all EU member countries move at the same pace towards monetary union or are the demands of the transition to such a union likely to result in the emergence of a 'two-speed' Europe? How can the EMS be strengthened so as to ensure that speculative pressures on intra-EMS exchange rates can successfully be contained during Stage Two? In addressing these questions, first, the principal features and alternative forms of monetary union will be outlined. Second, the benefits and costs for countries that enter into a monetary union will be briefly considered. Third, the provisions of the Maastricht Treaty for Stage Two of the transition towards the complete monetary unification of the EU will be discussed. Fourth, the nature and implications of the 1992–93 turmoil will be assessed. Finally, some conclusions will be presented, the principal one being that a 'two-speed' Europe is likely to emerge.

MONETARY UNION: DEFINITION AND ALTERNATIVE FORMS

Monetary union can be defined as a monetary association between countries that results in common inflation and interest rates across all participating member states. The necessary, but not sufficient, conditions for this to occur are:

1 that there exists a fully integrated union financial sector;
2 capital movements are perfectly free within the union; and
3 intra-union exchange rates are either *de facto* or *de jure* irrevocably fixed.

If these conditions were satisfied and there emerged union-wide inflation and interest rates then, necessarily, union member currencies would be perfect substitutes. It follows, therefore, that, in principle, the creation of a monetary union does not necessitate the replacement of union member countries' currencies by a single union currency (see also Healey, 1993c).

Vaubel (1988) in his survey of the literature on monetary integration discusses a number of alternative sets of arrangements which have been perceived to constitute a monetary union. There is, first, the case of currency union which involves union member countries in adopting a single currency. For a currency union to be viable, it is necessary that there exists only one independent supplier of the currency in use in the union; i.e., there must exist a central bank which is responsible for the monetary and exchange rate policies of the union. In a currency union, then, member countries cease to enjoy any degree of monetary autonomy, however limited.

Second, many economists have identified monetary union with exchange rate union. In an exchange rate union, exchange rates are irrevocably fixed and there are no restrictions on the movement of capital across the union's member countries. The Werner Plan, adopted in 1970, envisaged the monetary unification of Europe through 'the irrevocable fixing of parities and the total liberalisation of capital movements' by 1980. Vaubel (1988) emphasises that the crucial distinction between a currency union and an exchange rate union is that the former, in contrast to the latter, involves *no* intra-union exchange rate uncertainty. So long as there exists a number of national currencies, it is always possible for the 'irrevocably' fixed exchange rates to be altered or restrictions on the movement of capital to be imposed. But in a currency union the replacement of union member countries' currencies by a single union currency eliminates the exchange rate uncertainty that would necessarily persist if, instead, these countries were to be members of an exchange rate union.

Third, in a free intercirculation union, member countries' currencies are allowed to circulate freely within the union. In such a union, exchange rates may, but not necessarily, be fixed. Fourth, it is possible to perceive a state of affairs which involves a parallel currency circulating side-by-side with the national currency. Such an arrangement Vaubel (1988) has termed as a parallel currency union. Again, exchange rates between the parallel currency and the national currencies need not be fixed. The parallel currency union resembles the currency union in that both involve a common currency for all union member countries. Similarly, the parallel currency union is like the free intercirculation union in terms of currency competition. In the former, a member country's currency competes with the parallel currency, while in the latter it competes with the other member countries' currencies.

DEGREES OF MONETARY INTEGRATION

Gros (1989) in his assessment of the alternative forms of monetary union observes that they involve different degrees of monetary integration. A currency union necessarily implies perfect monetary integration. However, this is not necessarily the case with the exchange rate union. Gros (1989) draws attention to the differences in interest rates in Germany and the Netherlands, despite the fact that the German deutschmark/Dutch guilder exchange rate has effectively been fixed since 1983, there are no barriers to the movement of capital between the two countries, monetary policies are closely coordinated and the real sectors of the two economies are highly integrated. If the essence of monetary union is that there prevail the same conditions *as if* a single currency exists, then fixity of the deutschmark/guilder exchange rate, perfect capital mobility and monetary policy coordination have not resulted in the *de facto* monetary unification of Germany and the Netherlands. Continuing exchange rate uncertainty, reflected in the persistent interest rate differentials, has impeded the complete monetary integration between these two countries. Thus, a currency union and an exchange rate union involve different degrees of monetary integration.

A second set of issues relates to the process by which monetary union is achieved, whatever its form. A group of countries can decide to adopt any of the four forms of union outlined above as the end-state of the desired degree of monetary integration. However, they also have to decide *how* this end-state is to be reached. Transitional arrangements inevitably depend, at least in part, on the ultimate objective. For example, if an exchange rate union is the eventual target, the introduction of a parallel currency in the transition would not be necessary. Similarly, if a parallel currency union or a free intercirculation union is the ultimate aim, then exchange rates need not be fixed. Again, these forms of monetary union imply different degrees of monetary integration.

It is possible, on the other hand, to perceive a particular form of monetary union facilitating the transition to the ultimately desired degree of monetary integration. For example, a free intercirculation union may serve as the transition stage to currency union. It is, in principle, conceivable that through currency competition the weaker currencies could be driven out of circulation and that eventually one of the member countries' currencies would become the common currency for the whole union. The same is true of the parallel currency union. Under certain assumptions, the parallel currency could displace all national currencies and emerge as the union's only currency. But for this to occur, it is necessary that the parallel currency is *not* a basket of the union member countries' currencies. If it were, there would always be a national currency which is more attractive than the parallel currency. If, however, national currencies were dropped from the basket as they were driven out of circulation, then this process would result in the parallel currency being identical with the 'strongest' national currency.

In summary, there are different forms of monetary union, with each involving a different degree of monetary integration. Currency union implies perfect monetary integration. Depending on the ultimately desired degree of monetary integration, alternative transitional arrangements are feasible. In principle, a free intercirculation or a parallel currency union could serve as the transition stage to currency union. The same is true of the exchange rate union.

THE COSTS AND BENEFITS OF MONETARY UNION

The implications of exchange rate uncertainty feature prominently in the case against flexible exchange rates (see Artus and Young, 1979). Since the breakdown of the Bretton Woods system in March 1973, nominal exchange rate changes have been large and almost entirely unpredictable. As these changes have not tended to offset inflation rate differentials in the short and medium term, the behaviour of real exchange rates has been highly erratic with countries experiencing sharp fluctuations in their competitiveness (see Chapter 2, Appendix A). Exchange rates have substantially deviated from their long-run equilibrium values for significant periods of time. Examples of such exchange rate misalignments are the external values of sterling during 1979–81 and of the dollar during 1981–85. The creation of the EMS partly reflected disillusion with exchange rate flexibility. If the focus were to be the relative merits and disadvantages of flexible exchange rates when assessing the costs and benefits of monetary union, it would, in principle, suffice to consider the case for and against an exchange rate union. But the Maastricht Treaty envisages the creation of a currency union in 1997 or, at the latest, on January 1, 1999. Therefore, for our purposes, it is necessary also to contrast an exchange rate union against a currency union. The case for a currency union rests on a number of arguments (for surveys, see Brociner and Levine, 1992a; Begg, 1991; Goodhart, 1991; Eichengreen, 1990a).

First, it can be maintained that an exchange rate union is

preferable to a system of flexible exchange rates as it encourages trade growth by generating a greater degree of exchange rate predictability. De Grauwe (1988) has presented empirical evidence indicating that intra-EU trade would have grown less than it did during the 1980s had the EMS not been successful in dramatically reducing the unpredictability of intra-EMS exchange rates. But an exchange rate union cannot eliminate exchange rate uncertainty. As Gros (1989) observes, it is not possible to rule out that an exchange rate union member country may not decide to change its exchange rate. Therefore, a currency union is superior to an exchange rate union in its potential to stimulate trade across member countries. The quantitative significance of this advantage of a monetary union, whether in its exchange rate or currency union form, over a regime of flexible exchange rates has been disputed on the grounds that forward exchange markets allow traders to hedge currency risk. However, such hedging does involve a cost and in that sense constitutes an impediment to the growth of international trade (see Artis, 1989).

Second, it may be argued that exchange rate uncertainty discourages international investment. Morsink and Molle (1991) have presented empirical evidence which supports the proposition that exchange rate uncertainty has had a depressing effect on investment among EU member countries. In the case of foreign investment forward exchange markets cannot provide adequate hedging facilities, even at a cost, as agreements involving the forward sale/purchase of currencies rarely cover a period beyond a year – which falls significantly short of the life of plant and equipment. It follows, therefore, that a currency union is superior to an exchange rate union, as it potentially provides a framework conducive to the more efficient allocation of capital across the union member countries.

Third, Sumner and Zis (1982) have argued that the natural rate of unemployment in a country operating flexible exchange rates will be higher than if it pursued fixed exchange rates. They extended Friedman's (1975) argument that the higher the inflation rate is, the more unpredictable it will be. Therefore, prices become less efficient in transmitting information and, as a result, other things equal, the natural rate of unemployment will be higher. Similarly, they argued, the more uncertain the exchange rate is, the less efficient the price mechanism will be. Again, as only in a currency union is exchange rate uncertainty eliminated, this form of monetary union is preferable to an exchange rate union.

Fourth, exchange rate flexibility has an asymmetrical impact on firms. It is significantly more difficult for small and medium-sized firms to absorb the costs of foreign exchange risk management than it is for large corporations. It follows, then, that the bias against the former can only be eliminated under a currency union (see de Grauwe, 1992). Fifth, the existence of national currencies implies, whether exchange rates are fixed or flexible, that economic agents incur costs whenever they exchange their domestic currency for a foreign currency. These transaction costs are less under fixed than flexible exchange rates. But in a currency union they are entirely eliminated.

Sixth, governments often succumb to the temptation of manipulating money supply growth rates for, among other reasons, electoral purposes (see Alesina and Grilli, 1991; Alesina, 1989). This has largely reflected the constitutional status of central banks. Except for Germany, where the Bundesbank is constitutionally independent and responsible for maintaining price stability, central banks in the other EU member countries effectively have to implement government-determined monetary policies. The manipulation of monetary policies for electoral purposes has usually resulted in the generation of increasingly severe inflationary pressures. In an exchange rate union the ability of governments to abuse monetary policy is more limited than under a regime of flexible exchange rates. But in a currency union, with monetary policy being the responsibility of the union central bank, necessarily no member country can manipulate the money supply growth rate (see Chapter 5 for a further discussion of this point).

In a currency union, member countries cannot engage in independent monetary policies or employ exchange rate changes in pursuit of domestic economic objectives. An exchange rate union allows some scope, albeit very limited, for independent monetary policies in the short run while it is always feasible, however politically costly it may be, for a member country to effect an exchange rate change. The implied loss of autonomy in the conduct of monetary and exchange rate policies, relative to alternative regimes involving greater degrees of exchange rate flexibility, is perceived as the principal cost of monetary unions. The question then arises as to how significant this loss of autonomy is, particularly in the context of the EU. It is, however, important to note that it is no longer possible to argue that even complete exchange rate flexibility is sufficient for any individual country to pursue independent policy objectives.

The post-1973 experience has demonstrated that exchange rate flexibility does not, *per se*, insulate economies from external disturbances. Indeed, nominal disturbances have generated prolonged real changes. The correlation between nominal exchange rate changes and inflation rate differentials is weak, particularly in the short and medium term. Further, the increasing tendency for economic agents to hold diversified currency portfolios implies that, for any single country, the control of the money supply growth rate cannot ensure the control of the domestic long-run inflation rate. This line of argument suggests that the potential benefits of monetary policy autonomy are rather limited.

On the other hand, some economists would argue that, contrary to what was originally argued, the natural rate of unemployment is *not* independent of monetary policy. An unanticipated expansionary change in monetary policy, for example, reduces unemployment. This involves newly employed workers acquiring new skills. Some will remain in employment when the economy fully adjusts to the monetary policy change in the long run. The implication of this line of reasoning is that a currency union potentially deprives member countries of their ability to affect unemployment – not only in the short run, but also in the long run. Whether or not monetary policy can have a lasting effect on output and employment is an empirical issue. The extensive statistical investigation of this issue has yet to yield unambiguous evidence regarding the capacity of monetary policy to affect the real economy.

For the sake of argument, however, suppose that monetary policy *is* an effective policy instrument for the purpose of stabilising output and employment. This is not sufficient for asserting that a currency union will necessarily result in significant costs for member countries (see also Healey and Levine, 1992a). It depends on the nature of the shocks to which the union is subjected. If these are country-specific, then the sacrifice of the monetary policy instrument will involve a cost for the affected country. But if disturbances are symmetrical and impact all member countries, no cost need be incurred as the union monetary authorities can appropriately adjust the union's monetary policy. This is an issue which will be considered further in the following sections. For the moment, it may be argued that the proposition that a currency union necessarily implies a potentially significant cost for member countries, because it deprives them of the ability to employ monetary policy to affect output and employment, is less than convincing.

Changes in nominal exchange rates *may* facilitate adjustment to differences among countries with respect to trend developments in real variables which require changes in real exchange rates. By excluding nominal exchange rate changes as a means of adjustment, a monetary union forces the burden of adjustment on other markets which may be less flexible and efficient than the foreign exchange markets. The quantitative significance of the cost thus incurred is highly uncertain. Further, it may be argued that other policies may well be more effective than exchange rate policy for the resolution of adjustment problems arising from differences in the performance of countries' real sectors.

What, then, can be concluded from this discussion? A currency union is superior to an exchange rate union as it involves all the benefits of the latter plus the gains associated with the elimination of exchange rate uncertainty and exchange rate-related transaction costs. Second, there exists now a perception that the benefits of a currency union exceed the costs. This perception rests on disillusion with independently determined monetary policies and the effectiveness of exchange rate policy as an instrument of macroeconomic management.

THE RATIONALE OF THE MAASTRICHT TREATY

On January 1, 1994, Stage Two of the process leading to the monetary unification of the EU began. During the third, and final, stage of this process, envisaged to commence in 1997 or, at the latest, on January 1, 1999, EU national currencies are to be replaced by the new union currency, the ECU; that is, the Maastricht Treaty prescribes the eventual transformation of the EU into a currency union. The decision of EU member countries to opt for a currency union rather than, for example, an exchange rate union or, alternately, perseverance with the EMS exchange rate arrangements, was ultimately dictated by the objectives of the Single European Act (SEA). The SEA provided for the completion of the internal market through the dismantling of all barriers to the movement of goods, services, capital and labour – see Chapters 7 and 8.

The complete integration of the EU member countries' financial sectors is a necessary condition for the completion, consolidation and development of the internal market. First, these sectors are sufficiently significant that without their becoming fully integrated the concept of a single European market is meaningless. Second, the markets for goods and services cannot become completely integrated in the absence of financial integration. The latter is incompatible with member countries operating exchange and capital controls. Thus, the 1988 Directive provided for the abolition of such controls by July 1990, by all EU member countries except Spain, Portugal, Greece and Ireland for which the end of 1992 was specified as the date by which they had to dismantle their exchange and capital controls. In compliance with the 1988 Directive, France and Italy abolished all exchange restrictions and controls on capital movements during the first half of 1990 and Belgium abandoned its dual exchange rate system. But the removal of exchange restrictions and controls on capital movements, though necessary, is not sufficient to ensure the creation of a single European financial market. It cannot eliminate the exchange rate uncertainty which continues to act as a barrier to the complete financial integration of the EU. Thus, the need for the EU to evolve into a monetary union and, more specifically, into a currency union.

There is a second reason why the complete monetary integration of the EU through the replacement of member countries' currencies with a single currency is necessary for the creation, consolidation and development of the single European market. Assume that the EU were to proceed with the dismantling of all barriers to intra-union trade in goods and services and the abolition of all exchange restrictions and controls on capital movements, but persisted with the EMS exchange rate arrangements. National industries would have to adjust to the abolition of barriers to intra-union trade. The EMS, as operated during the 1980s and early 1990s, could not prevent the accumulation of pressures, or the sudden outbreak of severe speculative attacks, on intra-EMS exchange rates. The defence of prevailing parities became more difficult without exchange and capital controls (see Chapter 2). Thus, there would remain the risk that exchange rate changes could be forced on member countries. It follows, then, that national industries would have to adjust not only to the removal of all barriers to intra-EU trade in goods and services, but also to periodic exchange rate changes. Therefore, resistance to the full implementation of the 1992 programme could develop. This would occur especially if the enforced exchange rate realignments were not consistent with market fundamentals, as was the case with the 1992–93 EMS turmoil.

Pressures on governments to reintroduce exchange and capital controls would be generated (indeed, this was precisely what happened during 1992–93). The temptation to delay, or even abandon, the dismantling of barriers to intra-union trade would become increasingly difficult to resist. Ultimately, exchange rate uncertainty and unpredicted exchange rate realignments could force the abandonment of the objective of completing the internal market. In committing member countries to the principle of monetary union, the SEA recognised that the EMS could not provide the monetary framework necessary for the creation of the single European market. The choice, then, that confronted EU member countries was between a currency union and an exchange rate union. But, as already argued, the concept of 'irrevocably' fixed exchange rates, on which the latter rests, lacks credibility. Therefore, only a currency union is consistent with the single European market objective of the SEA. In brief, then, the internal logic of the SEA dictated the Maastricht Treaty prescription that the EU evolves into a currency union.

AN OVERVIEW OF THE MAASTRICHT TREATY

The SEA came into effect in 1987 (see Chapter 8). The following year the Committee for the Study of Economic and Monetary Union, under the chairmanship of the President of the Commission, Jacques Delors, was established. The Delors Report (1989) was presented in April 1989. It recommended a three-stage process leading to the complete monetary integration of the EU through the replacement of member countries' currencies with a single currency. The principal features of the Delors Plan were adopted in principle at the Rome meeting of the European Council in October 1990. In December 1990 an Inter-Governmental Conference (IGC) began deliberations with the view of preparing amendments to the Treaty of Rome on the basis of the Delors Report. The IGC presented its proposals in the form of a Treaty on European Union at the Maastricht meeting of the European Council in December 1991. The Maastricht Treaty was signed in

February 1992 (see Bank of England, 1992, for a useful summary). By the end of October 1993, the Treaty had been ratified by all member countries. Thus the EU came into existence on November 1, 1993 (see Chapter 1).

Artis (1992) in his assessment of the Maastricht Treaty observes that the debate following the publication of the Delors Report centred on the relative merits of a market-driven and an institutionally-driven transition process towards the complete monetary integration of the EU. The proponents of the market approach, with the British government being the principal one, argued for the introduction of a parallel currency (the so-called 'hard ECU' proposal). It was maintained that market forces would eventually force the emergence of the parallel currency as the single EU currency as it would possess better inflation-proofing properties than national currencies. A number of objections were raised against the parallel currency approach. First, even if the parallel currency were superior to national currencies, it is not necessarily the case that it would eventually replace the latter. Second, assuming that such a replacement would occur at some time in the future, the duration of the process through which the introduction of a parallel currency would lead to a currency union would be so long as to jeopardise the creation of the single European market.

Third, there is no reason why the parallel currency would necessarily outperform, in terms of inflation-proofing properties, all national currencies. Fourth, foreign exchange market crises were likely to occur with increasing frequency. Fifth, there would exist a potential for destabilising friction between the EU authority responsible for the parallel currency and the national monetary authorities. Sixth, exchange rate-related transactions costs would increase. This type of consideration led to the Delors Committee to reject the parallel currency approach to the creation of a European currency union. When the British government sought to revive interest in the approach through its 'hard ECU' proposal, it attracted negligible support from the other member countries, particularly when it became evident that the British government had conceived its plan as a means of frustrating the eventual replacement of national currencies by a single EU currency. Thus, the IGC adopted the approach recommended by the Delors Report in the Maastricht Treaty.

The Treaty assumed that Stage One had begun on July 1, 1990 and set January 1, 1994 as the date for the start of Stage Two. The principal feature of this stage is the establishment of the European Monetary Institute (EMI). The EMI, which is based in Frankfurt, commenced operations as the second stage began. The EMI is entrusted with the administration of the EMS. Further, it is responsible for promoting a greater degree of economic policy coordination among member countries. It can comment and advise on national monetary policies, but has no powers to enforce particular directions. National authorities remain responsible for their respective monetary policies. Third, the EMI will prepare the procedures and instruments that will enable the European System of Central Bank (ESCB) to assume control of the EU monetary policy at the start of Stage Three. At the end of Stage Two, the EMI will cease to exist. It is further envisaged that during Stage Two, the barriers to the use of ECU will be abolished, intra-EMS exchange rate changes will become less frequent and member countries will introduce the necessary legal changes to transform their central banks into independent institutions (see Chapter 5).

The Maastricht Treaty prescribes that during 1996 the European Council will meet to determine whether a majority of EU member countries satisfy the specified convergence criteria and, accordingly, set a date for the start of Stage Three. Thus, the final stage could begin as early as January 1997. However, if such a majority cannot be identified and during 1997 no date is set for the start of Stage Three, then the Maastricht Treaty prescribes that the final stage will begin on January 1, 1999 – even if only a minority of member countries meet the criteria for membership of the currency union. At the start of Stage Three, intra-Union exchange rates will be irrevocably fixed and the European Central Bank (ECB), which is to head the ESCB, will commence operations and assume responsibility for the currency union's monetary policy. Member countries will decide the date for the replacement of national currencies with the new union currency, the ECU.

The ESCB will consist of the national central banks with the ECB at its head (see Lomax, 1991; Harden, 1990). The ECB will determine the EU's monetary policy. The Maastricht Treaty defines the maintenance of price stability as 'the primary objective' of the ECB. Further, the ECB has been assigned a significant role in the determination of the currency union's exchange rate policies vis-à-vis non-EU currencies. The Treaty provides for the complete independence of the ECB and of the ESCB from member countries' governments and EU institutions. However, the ECB will be accountable to the European Parliament, the Commission and to the European Council. In summary, the Maastricht Treaty provides a coherent and internally consistent strategy for the transformation of the EU into a currency union.

THE CONVERGENCE CRITERIA

The Maastricht Treaty specifies five criteria that a member country must satisfy in order to qualify for membership of the currency union (see also Chapter 5). First, its rate of inflation during the year immediately before its joining the union must not exceed by more than 1.5% the three lowest rates of inflation in the Union. Second, the country's long-run interest rate during the year before its becoming a member of the union must not exceed by more than 2% the three lowest long-run interest rates in the EU. Third, the country must have participated for at least two years in the 'normal' band of fluctuation of the ERM (currently ±15%, since August 1993), without a devaluation of its currency. Fourth, its budget deficit must not exceed 3% of its GDP and, fifth, the ratio of its national debt to GDP must not exceed 60%.

These convergence criteria, particularly the fiscal ones, have been the subject of intense debate (see Healey and Levine, 1992b; Levine, 1992; Levine and Pearlman, 1992). Some have questioned whether it was at all necessary to require member countries to satisfy well-defined criteria in order to qualify for membership of the currency union. It could have been left up to each country to decide whether or not it was ready to join the union. However, such an approach would have severely complicated the transition period and, ultimately, placed the entire process of monetary unification in jeopardy. To have allowed member countries complete independence in deciding whether or not they were ready to join the currency union would have been inconsistent with the rationale for the complete monetary integration of the EU and could have resulted in a reversal of the significant progress achieved during the 1980s in effecting a substantial reduction in inflation rates under the discipline of the ERM (see Chapter 2). The rationale for the EU evolving into a currency union can be unambiguously sustained only if placed within the context of the monetary conditions that must be generated for the creation, consolidation and development of the single European market to be achieved.

Suppose that a date for the start of Stage Three were set and member countries' governments were allowed to decide immediately prior to that date whether or not they would join the currency union. If that were the case, the individual member country would have an incentive to maximise and fully exploit its economic policy autonomy during the transition period. Thus it could pursue expansionary fiscal policies and monetary policies that resulted in the progressive overvaluation of its currency in the expectation that it would devalue before the start of Stage Three and then would rely on the ECB to effect a reduction in its inflation rate. If that were to occur, it would not be possible to control the timing of the domestic currency's final devaluation prior to its replacement by the EU currency. Indeed, if a number of member countries were to seek to exploit their economic policy autonomy during the transition period, it is likely that foreign exchange market crises would increase in frequency and severity, forcing, perhaps, repeated exchange rate realignments.

At that point, the temptation to reintroduce exchange and capital controls would become increasingly difficult to resist. The completion of the internal market would, at least, be slowed down. But suppose that such difficulties could be overcome. The implication would be that Stage Three would start with prevailing national inflation rates being significantly different. The ECB would then be under pressure to target the EU's monetary policy towards the average of the prevailing inflation rates. Thus countries which pursued cautious monetary policies during the transition period would be penalised. But, perhaps, more significant, the ECB would start its operations under conditions not particularly conducive to it rapidly establishing an anti-inflation reputation.

Thus, though in theory there is no reason why a group of countries need to converge before they form a currency union, given the specific conditions in and characteristics of the EU, the requirement that member countries satisfy a set of criteria in order to qualify for membership of the currency union is well-founded and justifiable. The Maastricht Treaty by prescribing explicit convergence criteria ensures that the transition period has an operational content while national authorities continue to control their respective monetary policies. Second, by seeking to satisfy these criteria, member countries can consolidate their successes in reducing their inflation rates during the 1980s. Third, the convergence criteria provide an explicit incentive for countries like Greece and Italy to improve their performance and reform their highly inefficient fiscal systems. Fourth, they provide the foundations on which the ECB can rapidly establish its credibility. Fifth, their pursuit can serve as a signal of member governments' commitment to the objective of completing the internal market. Sixth, they provide a basis for objective judgements to be made regarding the unsuitability of particular countries to join the currency union from the start, thus maximising the likelihood that the union will yield the desired benefits – even if only for a minority of the EU member countries.

To support the convergence criteria in the Maastricht Treaty is not to deny that their pursuit will not be costly, particularly in the case of the fiscal criteria. Indeed, for some EU member countries it is no longer possible to satisfy these criteria even by 1999 (see Chapter 5). However, as Artis (1992) emphasises, the Treaty perceives these criteria as well-defined 'guidelines', rather than as rules to be rigidly applied when deciding whether or not a member country qualifies for membership of the currency union. The Treaty is unambiguous in that what is significant is the *progress* that a member country achieves towards meeting the fiscal criteria. Thus a member country whose budget deficit and national debt:GDP ratios exceeded the values specified in the Maastricht Treaty could still qualify for membership of the currency union if these ratios were on a clearly established downward trend. If the budget deficit criterion appears not to be satisfied, the Treaty requires the Commission to report and identify whether that particular country's budget deficit exceeds its government's investment expenditure (the so-called 'golden rule'); that is, in judging a country's eligibility to join the currency union the current rather than the overall budget deficit may be used.

Some critics of the fiscal criteria have focused on their implications after the currency union has been formed. Member countries will no longer be able to employ monetary and exchange rate policies in response to asymmetric shocks. In these circumstances fiscal policy autonomy could have a useful role to play. However, countries that become members of the currency union will have their ability to pursue independent fiscal policies severely restricted. This can be justified in terms of the argument that without fiscal discipline as a principal feature of the currency union, a member country could, by abusing its fiscal policy autonomy, ultimately undermine price stability in the union (see Sargent and Wallace, 1981; Healey and Levine, 1992b). It is further maintained that as the completion of the internal market progresses, the likelihood of country-specific shocks occurring will correspondingly diminish. In other words, the potential benefits of member countries retaining fiscal policy autonomy are exaggerated.

In summary, the specification of convergence criteria that EU member countries must satisfy in order to qualify for membership of the projected currency union is justifiable. The fiscal criteria, which have attracted considerable attention, are not as rigid as they have been presented to be. This of course does not imply that their pursuit will not be costly and for some member countries impossible to satisfy even by 1999.

THE MAASTRICHT TREATY: PROSPECTS OF IMPLEMENTATION

The optimism that prevailed at the time the Maastricht Treaty was signed in February 1992 has given way to widely-held doubts as to whether the Treaty will in fact be fully implemented. The climate of opinion changed suddenly and rather rapidly. The initial rejection (subsequently overturned after treaty revisions) of the Treaty in the first Danish referendum in June 1992 can be identified as the turning point. The referendum result and the reaction it provoked in other member countries, and particularly in Britain, generated the suspicion that EU governments' commitment to the objectives of the Treaty could not be sustained and that they would not even be in a position to proceed with the ratification of the Treaty in the face of mounting popular opposition. Indeed, in Britain the Eurosceptics argued that the result of the Danish referendum implied the end of the road for the Treaty and, therefore, that it could not be brought before Parliament for ratification. Under pressure the British government changed the timetable for the discussion of the Treaty in Parliament, thus encouraging the view that it could be forced to abandon the Treaty altogether.

On the other hand, France – in an effort to maintain the momentum in favour of the Maastricht Treaty – announced the day after the Danish referendum that it would hold its own referendum on September 20, 1992. France need not have held a referendum. The decision to do so can be rationalised. What, however, was a serious error of judgement was to set a date so far ahead. The French government was highly unpopular. Inevitably, the campaign focused on the weaknesses of a 'lame duck' government rather than on the Maastricht Treaty. Opposition to the Treaty came to be seen as the best means of expressing dissatisfaction with the government. Thus, gradually the prospect of the French electorate rejecting the Treaty became real. Doubts regarding the ultimate fate of the Treaty increased in severity. The Treaty, all agreed, could not survive a second rejection.

The markets sought to test the EU governments' commitment to the Treaty by challenging their resolve to defend the intra-EMS exchange rates. Following Portugal's decision in April 1992 to participate in the system's ERM, only Greece was not operating the mechanism. There had been no intra-EMS exchange rate realignment since January 1987. The Maastricht Treaty had effectively assigned a new role to the EMS. It was to serve as a policy anchor during the transition towards the complete monetary integration of the EU. Therefore, if governments were not prepared to defend the EMS, this would signal a weakening of their commitment to the objectives of the Maastricht Treaty. Further, it would question their willingness to proceed with the full implementation of the 1992 programme.

The day after the Danish referendum, the Italian lira came under pressure in foreign exchange markets. By July 1992, the increasingly severe turmoil was engulfing sterling. As support for the opponents of the Maastricht Treaty in France gathered momentum, reflecting the ever increasing unpopularity of the incumbent government, the outcome of the French referendum became highly uncertain, despite the fact that all the major parties were campaigning in favour of a vote for the Treaty. This uncertainty further intensified the pressures on the intra-EMS exchange rates. That sterling and the Italian lira were the first currencies to come under sustained pressure was not accidental. Many had argued that Britain had joined the ERM at an unsustainable exchange rate. Similarly, the Italian lira had been judged to have become progressively overvalued. Further, in the spring of 1992, the collapse of Italy's political system had begun. At the same time, the newly elected government in Britain was making no progress in establishing its credibility. Finally, sterling was forced to drop out of the ERM on September 16, 1992, and was followed the next day by the Italian lira. In the following weeks and months the Spanish peseta was devalued three times, the Portuguese escudo twice and the Irish punt once (see Chapter 2).

By the spring of 1993 the pressures on intra-EMS exchange rates had significantly subsided. France had elected a new government. The performance of the German economy was rapidly deteriorating under the impact of the country's reunification. In contrast, the French economy was proving to be highly resilient and emerging as the strongest in the EU. In May 1993, prior to the general election, a politically engineered devaluation was forced on the Spanish government by opposition forces. However, the EMS appeared to have entered a period of tranquillity. But relations between France and Germany were rapidly deteriorating. Suddenly during July 1993 the French franc was subjected to speculative pressures of unprecedented intensity. On August 1, 1993, the EU member countries decided to change the rules of intervention of the ERM but not the prevailing intra-EMS exchange rates. Thus the band of fluctuation was widened from ±2.25% to ±15% on either side of the central parities. Germany and the Netherlands decided to continue with the narrow band of fluctuation. There was no economic justification for the speculative attack on the French franc. In the weeks that followed the broadening of the fluctuation band, the franc's devaluation never exceeded 3% relative to the floor implied by the original narrow band. By the end of 1993, the French currency had climbed back to values within the narrow band.

There is no commonly accepted economic explanation of either the timing or the rapidity with which speculative pressures on intra-EMS exchange rates emerged. It is true that Germany ought to have revalued immediately after unification. But the failure to do so is not sufficient to explain the 1992–93 turmoil. Nor can it be validly argued that any reduction of German interest rates could have prevented the Italian lira or sterling from dropping out of the ERM. The crisis that engulfed the EMS was a crisis of confidence in EU member governments' ability and/or willingness to proceed with the ratification and full implementation of the Maastricht Treaty. In the event, the Treaty was ratified by all EU member countries by the end of October 1993. EU member countries did not rush to take advantage of the broad band of fluctuation and introduce expansionary monetary policies. Thus, since the July 1993 crisis, no evidence had emerged that member countries were in fact abandoning the policies that had resulted in the reduction and convergence of national inflation rates. Artis (1994) identifies two options. Convergence can be further developed while the broad band of fluctuation is retained and, in terms of the Maastricht Treaty, treated as the 'normal' band. However, such a strategy does entail risks. Alternatively, the band of fluctuation could be renarrowed and provide the foundation for countries to proceed to Stage Three. The indications are that the narrow band of fluctuation is unlikely to be restored in the near future.

The most likely outcome is that a 'two-speed' Europe will develop (see also Chapter 5). The Benelux countries, France and Germany are almost certain to proceed to Stage Three. This is also the case with Austria. Denmark is likely to join the core countries. On the other hand, it is difficult to envisage such political developments in Italy as to enable the country to join the currency union from the start. Similarly, it is unlikely that the British government will have the authority to take the country into the currency union. Spain and Ireland are committed to the objectives of the Maastricht Treaty but may not be in a position to be among the first to join the currency union. Greece is unlikely to join the union both for economic and political reasons. Portugal, too, is likely to delay joining the union. Finally, it is difficult to predict the attitudes of Sweden, Finland and Austria, which accede to the EU in 1995.

CONCLUSIONS

A currency union in the EU would unambiguously provide important economic benefits to member states, while the costs are likely to be modest. The Maastricht Treaty provides a well-founded strategy for the complete monetary integration of the EU, which is consistent with the objectives of the SEA. It was designed so as to enable all EU countries to join the proposed currency union. However, political developments since the signing of the Treaty now suggest that the most likely development is the emergence of 'two-speed' Europe, with the core member states pressing ahead with EMU and leaving the peripheral, less integrated states to apply for membership at some later stage.

5

EUROPEAN MONETARY UNION

Progress, Problems and Prospects

Barry Harrison and Nigel M. Healey

INTRODUCTION

The Treaty on European Union signed at Maastricht in December 1991 commits the European Union (EU) to establishing a single currency. Of all EU countries, only Britain has retained the right to opt out of the final destination of economic and monetary union (EMU). Despite the recent tensions within the European Monetary System (EMS), which culminated in the withdrawal of sterling and the Italian lira, the imposition of emergency capital controls in several countries and an increase in the margins of fluctuation within the exchange rate mechanism (ERM) to ±15%, the Maastricht Treaty was successfully ratified and came into effect in November 1993. However, it has now become clear that some countries will be ready for EMU before others (see also Chapter 4). This article reviews the progress that has been made towards EMU, the problems that remain and the prospects for achieving EMU in the foreseeable future.

WHAT IS EMU?

EMU has two dimensions: an economic dimension and a monetary dimension. In brief, economic union implies the creation of a single market without artificial barriers to trade, a union-wide competition policy, a common regional policy and coordination of macroeconomic policymaking. EU members are in agreement about the benefits of economic union and many of the requirements are now in place. By any standards, progress towards economic union has been swift and the single market was completed by January 1, 1993 (see Chapter 7). However, monetary union is more controversial and involves agreeing to irrevocably fixed exchange rates or the establishment of a single currency (see Chapter 4 for a detailed discussion of the alternative forms of monetary union). A country that agrees to either of these (the latter is the preferred option of most EU members) automatically relinquishes any possibility of an independent monetary policy. EU members have accepted the 'principle of parallelism', which implies that economic and monetary union are integral parts of the same ultimate goal.

THE ADVANTAGES OF EMU

The advantages of EMU are well documented and are clearly set out in Goodhart (1991) – see also Chapter 4. In brief, it is argued that by removing barriers to trade and eliminating exchange rate risk, greater specialisation and trade will be encouraged. The elimination of exchange rate risk will also encourage lower interest rates because it will no longer be necessary for them to embody an exchange rate risk premium. As a result, it is argued that economic growth and living standards will improve.

It is further argued that the creation of EMU will lead to real resource savings for the EU. One important source of such savings arises because it will no longer be necessary to exchange currencies to settle debts arising from intra-EU trade. The Commission has estimated that savings on such transaction costs alone will amount to about 4% of the EU's gross domestic product (GDP) per annum (EC Commission, 1990b). In addition, those instruments such as futures, options and swaps, developed to provide a hedge against exchange rate risk, will no longer be required for intra-EU trade. In both cases, the resources released can then be used for purposes which more directly influence living standards than simply eliminating risk (Levine, 1990). Similarly, if the elimination of exchange rate risk within the union makes a reduction in reserves held by central banks possible, this will again free resources which can be put to more productive purposes.

Another potential benefit from the adoption of a single currency is that it will improve efficiency in the allocation of resources. The most obvious way in which this will happen is that capital will be free to move to where returns are greatest. There will also be increased competition in goods markets because any price differentials would be immediately apparent to potential consumers. In addition it is likely that for most member states prices will be more stable and therefore the price mechanism will more accurately convey the 'correct' signals to producers about changes in society's preferences. It is also alleged that low inflation will be achieved at a lower cost in unemployment.

THE DISADVANTAGES OF EMU

Any country which belongs to a monetary union accepts that policy will be dictated from the centre and that, in particular, there will be no possibility of pursuing an independent monetary policy or of adjusting the exchange rate to restore competitiveness. As part of a monetary union with Europe, no country could pursue its own monetary policy any more than Scotland can pursue its own monetary policy *vis-à-vis* the rest of Britain. For each country, therefore, the question to be asked is whether its economic interests are better served *inside* the union or *outside* the union. Different countries will not always give the same answer. For some countries, it might be possible to improve the performance of the economy by increasing money growth at a faster rate than would be possible inside the union – offsetting any loss in competitiveness by adjusting the exchange rate (see Eichengreen, 1990b; Feldstein, 1992). For others, the degree of economic integration might be such that an independent monetary policy is already impossible. In such cases, monetary union might be thought desirable and even inevitable.

THE GROWTH OF INTEREST IN EMU

Interest in EMU is not new. Perlman (1991) has noted that in 1865 France, Belgium, Italy and Switzerland formed a monetary union and in 1867 a conference of twenty nations convened in Paris to explore the 'desire to see the union, as yet restricted to four countries, become the germ of a union more extended, and of the establishment of a general circulation among the civilised nations'. In the event, agreement proved impossible and this early attempt at monetary union collapsed in the 1870s.

In more recent years interest in EMU has grown since the EMS started operating in 1979 with the aim of establishing 'a zone of monetary stability' (see Chapters 2 and 3). However, at its inception there was no agreement that the ultimate aim of the EMS was the creation of EMU. There was simply a desire among participants to ensure that prices and exchange rates were more stable in the future than they had been in the past. To ensure exchange rate stability, the ERM was created and thereafter participating currencies were allowed only to fluctuate within agreed bands around central rates (originally ±2.25% for most participating member states, now ±15%).

In the early years after the EMS was created, there were frequent realignments of currencies, sometimes twice in the same year. No stable equilibrium emerged in this early period. Some realignment of currencies might have been expected because newly-agreed parities inevitably 'locked in' existing price and cost disparities. However, the problem was exacerbated in these early years, because realignment was not accompanied by a comprehensive set of domestic policy measures to ensure the newly-agreed parities were stable. This situation changed decisively in 1983 when the French government shifted the emphasis of economic policy in favour of controlling inflation and away from domestic expansion. As German inflation had traditionally been the lowest in the ERM, the deutschmark became the anchor to which policy was harnessed and the need to maintain a stable exchange rate was used to justify a programme of disinflationary measures. A similar approach was adopted by other participants in the ERM and as a result the number of realignments fell. This was an important milestone on the road to EMU because it marked a fundamental change in the nature of the ERM, which effectively became a deutschmark zone. The ERM subsequently expanded to include the peseta, the escudo and sterling (although the latter's membership, along with the lira, is at present in temporary suspension) and was generally perceived during the 1980s as having been successful in aiding the disinflationary process and stabilising exchange rates.

Two other economic developments led to growing interest in EMU. The decision to create a single market led many to argue that maximum benefit could only be achieved if exchange rates were irrevocably fixed, and increasingly this has been interpreted as the creation of a single currency. The second development was the decision taken in 1988 to eliminate capital controls by 1990. It was argued that, without capital controls, any uncertainty about exchange rates would motivate capital flows on such a scale that either realignment would be necessary or domestic monetary policy would have to be geared to avoiding a capital outflow.

The commitment to fixed exchange rates rules out realignment and this implies that, even in the absence of monetary union, a completely independent monetary policy would cease to be a realistic option. Since policy sovereignty would be lost by choice or design, there is a clear incentive to create monetary union in which capital would be free to move to where returns are greatest without imposing any strain on the exchange rate.

There is also a political momentum towards EMU which has become increasingly important since the reunification of Germany. The reunified Germany now dominates the European economies (see Chapter 1) and EMU is perceived by many states (especially France) as the most effective way of constraining German economic power. In EMU, there would be more pressure on Germany to consider the interests of the rest of the EU in the conduct of economic policy (see Levine, 1990). There is no guarantee that, outside EMU, German economic policy will not operate to the detriment of other EU members.

THE DELORS REPORT

Officially the growth of interest in EMU was recognised at the Hanover Summit of 1988 which set up a committee to be chaired by Jacques Delors, the then President of the Commission, to set out 'concrete stages' which would lead to EMU. The Delors Report identified three preconditions for a monetary union (Delors, 1989):

1 unlimited and irreversible convertibility of all currencies;
2 complete liberalisation of capital flows and full integration of banking and other financial markets; and
3 irrevocably fixed exchange rates and the complete elimination of margins of fluctuation.

These conditions would establish monetary union, but the Delors Report also indicated that the adoption of a common currency, while not strictly necessary for monetary union, might seem 'a natural and desirable further development of the monetary union'. The Report also indicated that the adoption of a single currency should follow as quickly as possible after the establishment of irrevocably fixed exchange rates.

The Delors Report identified three stages that would lead to EMU. Stage One involved completing the internal market, the adoption of measures to reduce regional disparities within the EU, increased macroeconomic policy coordination and surveillance by the Council of Finance Ministers (Ecofin) and the Committee of Central Bank Governors (CCBG), and full participation in the narrow band of the ERM. Stage Two is more controversial, particularly because it calls for the establishment of a European System of Central Banks (ESCB) whose ultimate role would be to design and implement a common monetary policy. In Stage Two, the ESCB would also carry out the tasks of Ecofin and the CCBG. Additionally, exchange rate realignments would only be made during Stage Two in exceptional circumstances and the margins of fluctuation would be reduced. During Stage Three, the Delors Report proposed, the ESCB would assume full responsibility for the conduct of monetary policy within the EU and participating currencies would be irrevocably fixed. At the Madrid Summit of June 1990, the Delors Report was accepted and it was agreed that Stage One should begin in July 1990.

The Delors Report was very clear on the conditions necessary for monetary union but left many points of detail deliberately vague. Stage One is non-controversial. It deals with matters relevant to completing the internal market and simply aims to promote greater convergence between EU members. One problem was to decide when Stages Two and Three should begin and the issue hinged on whether convergence should *precede* moves towards EMU, or whether a more rapid move to EMU through institutional change was preferable, in the hope that this would *force* convergence. Other major problems were to define precisely how the ESCB was to formulate policy and perform its tasks, how to guarantee its independence from official control, how accountable it should be, who would formulate the EU's exchange rate policy, what sort of rules would govern the size of national deficits and so on.

These are major issues. The Rome Summit of 1990 went some way to dealing with the first problem when eleven of the twelve member states (i.e., the twelve excluding Britain) agreed that Stage Two should start in January 1994 and that Stage Three would begin when a sufficient degree of convergence between members had been achieved. However, it did not specify the degree of convergence required to proceed to Stage Three and much was left to the Inter-Governmental Conference (IGC) which convened a few weeks later and which reported to the Maastricht Summit.

THE POLITICAL DIMENSIONS OF EMU

The IGC also spent a considerable time discussing the political dimensions of EMU. In popular discussion about the advantages and disadvantages of EMU, it is often implicitly assumed that member states make domestic monetary policy to maximise national welfare, whereas in the real world, democratically elected governments typically make economic policy with the intention of being re-elected. In multi-party systems with periodic elections and myopic or only partially informed electorates, the policy which maximises the probability of a governing party (or coalition of parties) being re-elected is unlikely to accord precisely with the policy that maximises some broader concept of national welfare. In this context, the constitutional framework within which monetary policy is conducted – notably in the way that it divides policy-making powers between elected governments and unelected central banks – becomes of prime importance. In Britain, for example, the central bank (the Bank of England) is an arm of the government and acts on instructions from the Chancellor of the Exchequer. In Germany, in contrast, the central bank (the Bundesbank) is constitutionally independent of the government and has a statutory duty to use monetary policy to maintain price stability.

It is now well known that the effectiveness of monetary policy depends critically upon the political and institutional context within which policy decisions are formulated and executed (see Currie, 1991). The IGC's discussion of the shape of a future EMU therefore gave great weight to the constitutional framework within which future EU monetary policy is to be made. Modern economic theory suggests that if the ultimate power over monetary policy is vested with democratic governments (or a central EU body representing their interests, like the Council of Ministers), the outcome is likely to be higher inflation (and a higher average rate of unemployment) than if it is delegated to an independent central bank (Kydland and Prescott, 1977; Barro and Gordon, 1983). Consider each constitutional arrangement in turn.

The political appeal of surprise inflation

The difficulty of allowing governments to make monetary policy is most easily illustrated using the familiar expectations-augmented Phillips Curve model. Figure 5.1 shows that in this model, the

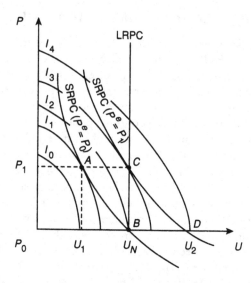

Figure 5.1 Government policy preferences and the Phillips Curve

long-run Phillips Curve, LRPC, is vertical at the natural rate of unemployment, U_N. The short-run Phillips Curves represent the temporary inflation–unemployment trade-offs that exist for a given set of inflationary expectations. For example, SRPC($P^e = P_0$) maps out the relationship between inflation and unemployment when the expected rate of inflation P^e (which is built into wage settlements) is P_0: if actual inflation were to exceed P_0, real wages and so unemployment, U, would fall; and vice versa. In the long run, when expectations have fully adjusted and the actual rate of inflation is completely reflected in wage settlements, the economy will be on its long-run Phillips Curve.

Figure 5.1 also shows a set of indifference curves, I_0–I_4, which represent combinations of inflation and unemployment between which the government is indifferent. They are concave rather than convex because inflation and unemployment are both 'bads' rather than 'goods'; that is, governments prefer less inflation and less unemployment to more. For the same reason, the indifference curves closer to the origin represent higher levels of utility than those further away. Figure 5.1 shows that I_2 is the 'best' indifference curve that the government can attain *in the long run*. In other words, point *B*, which represents zero inflation at the natural rate of unemployment, is the best feasible choice for a government that cares about both inflation and unemployment.

The paradox is that utility-maximising behaviour by the government will inevitably make this outcome unattainable. For example, suppose that the economy were at point B and inflationary expectations were zero. The utility-maximising response of the government would be to adopt a more expansionary monetary policy, because, with expectations of zero inflation, the government can (temporarily) improve its utility by sliding up the short-run Phillips Curve, SRPC($P^e = P_0$) to point A, reaching indifference curve, I_1. In the long run, however, as inflationary expectations adjust, the economy would converge on point C, with inflation entrenched at P_1. Note that, given the shape of the indifference curves in Figure 5.1, there is no temptation for the government to try and move away from point C. Any attempt to push the economy up or down the new, higher short-run Phillips Curve, SRPC($P^e = P_1$), will drive it onto a worse indifference curve. The result is that, if the government tries to maximise its utility each period, the economy will be driven to point C, with equilibrium inflation of P_1 and unemployment at its natural rate.

The case for an independent central bank

The analysis above suggests that vesting control over monetary policy with the government will inevitably lead to persistent inflation. Given the need to face periodic re-election, governments typically act in a short-termist fashion, attempting to maximise their utility period by period. Such behaviour results in an inflationary equilibrium (point C in Figure 5.1). One solution to this impasse is to transfer responsibility for monetary policy to an independent central bank. Because central bankers are normally appointed for long periods and do not have to face re-election in a popular vote, it is argued that they are in a better position than elected governments to take a long-term view. Whereas the temptation for a government to inflate the economy in the run-up to a general election may be irresistible, there exists no equivalent incentive for a central bank to depart from the optimal, long-run goal of price stability.

In terms of the indifference curves set out in Figure 5.1, central banks will thus tend to attach less importance to low unemployment than governments, since there is no electoral advantage to be

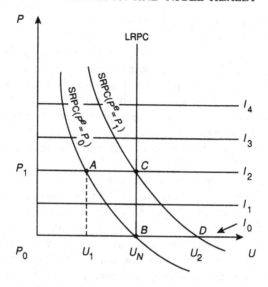

Figure 5.2 Central bank independence and the Phillips Curve

gained. In other words, the indifference curves of an independent central bank are likely to be much flatter than those of a government. The widespread image of central bankers as 'conservative' accords closely with this interpretation of their likely objective function. Moreover, if the central bank were statutorily bound to pursue price stability (and, by implication, give no weight at all to employment and output), it will always pursue the long-run utility-maximising policy. Figure 5.2 shows that, if the central bank were concerned only with inflation (giving no weight to unemployment), its indifference curves would be horizontal. The best indifference curve it could attain would be the one running along the horizontal axis; i.e., I_0.

If the economy were at point B with inflationary expectations equal to P_0, the central bank would (unlike the government) have no incentive to move to a higher inflation rate. And if the economy were at point C, the central bank would move to point D. Although this would cause a temporary increase in unemployment (from U_N to U_2) which would persist until inflationary expectations moderated and thereby shifted the short-run Phillips Curve downwards from SRPC($P^e = P_1$) to SRPC($P^e = P_0$), these costs would be once-for-all and offset by the benefits of price stability which

112

would be sustained over time (but see Rogoff, 1985; Healey *et al.*, 1995).

THE DIMENSIONS OF CENTRAL BANK INDEPENDENCE

There are two dimensions to central bank independence. First, the central bank must be politically independent, in the sense that its decisions should not be subject to the approval or direction of the government. Ideally, the government of the day should not be able to 'rig' the bank's policymaking executive by appointing either the governor or its senior staff. To the extent that the government has the power to make such appointments, the interests of political independence are best served by having lengthy, secure terms of tenure for key executives, which are spread out so that only a small proportion falls due for renewal within the lifetime of any one government. Mandatory government representatives on the bank's executive also militate against political independence.

Second, the central bank should be economically independent, in the sense that it can execute monetary policy without being blown off course by government actions. For example, in many countries, the government has an account with its national central bank, which it can effectively overdraw at will – thereby increasing the money supply. Central banks may also be obliged to buy any issue of government bonds that is not taken up by the general public, with the same effect on the money supply. Under such circumstances, a tight monetary policy could be undermined by an increase in the budget deficit. Some instruments of monetary policy may also be under the control of the government. For example, historically British governments have imposed both qualitative and quantitative controls on commercial bank lending. Tables 5.1 and 5.2 show how the national central banks of the EU member states presently rank on these measures of political and economic independence.

The implications of EMU for public finances

The creation of an independent ECB, with a statutory responsibility for maintaining price stability, will clearly have important implications for the governments of member states. As noted above, it will end the ability of national governments to use

Table 5.1 Measures of political independence

Central bank	1	2	3	4	5	6	7	8	9
Germany		*		*	*	*	*	*	6
The Netherlands		*		*	*	*	*	*	6
Italy	*	*	*		*				4
Denmark		*					*	*	3
Ireland		*				*		*	3
France		*		*					2
Greece			*					*	2
Spain				*	*				2
Belgium				*					1
Portugal					*				1
Britain					*				1

Key:
1. Governor not appointed by government.
2. Governor appointed for 5+ years.
3. Executive not appointed by government.
4. Executive appointed for 5+ years.
5. No mandatory government representative on executive.
6. No government approval of policy decision required.
7. Statutory requirement for central bank to pursue price stability.
8. Explicit conflicts between central bank and government possible.
9. Index of political independence (sum of asterisks in each row).

Source: Alesina and Grilli (1991).

surprise inflation for electoral purposes. But EMU will also affect national public finances in two other ways (see Healey and Levine, 1992b).

First, the right to issue fiat money (i.e., notes and coin) will be transferred from national governments to the ECB, so that 'seigniorage' profits will be lost to member governments (Drazen, 1989; Grilli, 1989). Table 5.3 shows that the southern Mediterranean countries (Greece, Portugal and Spain) will be particularly adversely affected by this change. At present, these countries have relatively undeveloped financial systems, which means that their currency ratios (i.e., currency as a proportion of the money stock) are higher than in northern states. This region also suffers relatively high inflation rates, which continuously erode the real value of currency in circulation, obliging the private sector to hold ever-larger cash balances for transactions purposes. Against the backdrop of inflation, the seigniorage profits from currency issue afford a significant source of revenue for national govern-ments. And the higher the currency ratio and the higher the rate of

Table 5.2 Measures of economic independence

Central bank	1	2	3	4	5	6	7	8	9
Germany	*	*	*	*	*	*	*	*	8
Belgium		*	*	*	*	*		*	6
Britain	*	*	*	*		*	*		6
Denmark		*			*	*	*		4
France				*	*	*	*		4
Ireland		*	*	*		*			4
The Netherlands				*	*	*	*		4
Spain				*	*			*	3
Greece				*		*			2
Portugal				*		*			2
Italy				*					1

Key:
1. Government credit from central bank not automatic.
2. Government credit from central bank at market interest rate.
3. Government credit from central bank for temporary period only.
4. Government credit from central bank limited in amount.
5. Central bank does not take up unsold government bond issues.
6. Discount rate set by central bank.
7. No government qualitative controls on commercial bank lending since 1980.
8. No government quantitative controls on bank lending since 1980.
9. Index of economic independence (sum of asterisks in each row).

Source: Alesina and Grilli (1991).

Table 5.3 Seigniorage revenue as a percentage of national gross domestic product

Country	Seigniorage revenue, 1994
Belgium	0.60
Britain	0.30
Denmark	0.32
France	0.40
Germany	0.57
Greece	1.37
Italy	0.74
Ireland	0.47
Luxembourg	0.16
The Netherlands	0.60
Portugal	1.63
Spain	1.07

Source: Bank for International Settlements.

inflation, the greater the importance of the seigniorage revenue as a means of financing government expenditure.

The second obvious implication of EMU for national public finances is that the requirement of economic independence for the ECB will deny governments the right of automatic, unlimited access to central bank credit (Demopoulos *et al.*, 1987). In contrast to the present arrangements within many member states, national governments will no longer be able to finance budget deficits – or refinance maturing government debt – by selling bonds to their central banks and increasing the money supply. To the extent that both the loss of seigniorage revenues and the ending of automatic credit facilities will make it more difficult for national governments to finance large budget deficits and refinance large national debts (i.e., as fixed-term bonds mature), many economists have argued that member states should have their public finances in order prior to joining EMU.

THE MAASTRICHT TREATY

Reflecting concern over the constitutional status of the new ECB, the Maastricht Treaty requires that the proposed European central banking system will be constitutionally independent of elected governments and legally bound to maintain price stability within the EU. Although collectively termed the ECB, the system will comprise:

1 the ECB, which will have a president and an executive of six members appointed by the European Council for eight-year terms, and a governing council (the executive plus governors of the national central banks from participating member states); plus
2 the European System of Central Banks (ESCB), consisting of participating national central banks, which will act as regional agents in carrying out the policy instructions of the ECB.

To the extent that all the significant decision-making power will reside at the centre with the ECB, the use of the term, ECB, to describe the system as a whole is retained in what follows. Tables 5.4 and 5.5 show that on all indices of political and economic independence the proposed ECB will be identical to the German Bundesbank, which is presently the most independent of all EU central banks (see Tables 5.1 and 5.2).

Table 5.4 Measures of political independence

Central bank	1	2	3	4	5	6	7	8	9
European Central Bank		*		*	*	*	*	*	6
Germany		*		*	*	*	*	*	6

Note: Key as Table 5.1 above.
Source: Alesina and Grilli (1991).

Table 5.5 Measures of economic independence

Central bank	1	2	3	4	5	6	7	8	9
European Central Bank	*	*	*	*	*	*	*	*	8
Germany	*	*	*	*	*	*	*	*	8

Note: Key as Table 5.2 above.
Source: Alesina and Grilli (1991).

Since the ECB will embrace, and operate through, national central banks, the Maastricht Treaty requires that the latter end their present links with their national governments, becoming fully politically and economically independent before they may be admitted to the ESCB. Article 7 of the Treaty, for example, specifically forbids any national central bank in the ESCB seeking or taking instructions from any other EU institution, including its national government (Council of Ministers, 1992).

To minimise the transitional unemployment costs of EMU to the historically high-inflation countries of the EU (e.g., Britain, Italy, Spain, Portugal, Greece), the Treaty envisages that the move to a single currency will depend on the fulfilment of certain 'convergence criteria' (see also Chapter 4). The logic of these conditions is that, if satisfied, the short-run costs of giving up monetary sovereignty will be modest and, by implication, outweighed by the likely benefits. The criteria include three indicators of inflation convergence:

1 successful candidates must have inflation rates no more than 1.5% above the three EU countries with the lowest inflation rates;

2 long-term interest rates should be no more than 2% above the three countries with the lowest rates; and

3 the national currency must not have been devalued and must

have remained within the 'normal' bands of the ERM (currently ±15%) for the previous two years.

With the exception of (2), these three criteria are self-explanatory. The significance of (2) lies in the fact that long-term interest rates provide a guide to the financial markets' expectations of inflation in the longer term. Put simply, today's long-term interest rate is a weighted average of expected future short-term interest rates. If investors expect inflation to be high in the future, they will expect short-term interest rates to be correspondingly high in the future as well. Today's long-term interest rate will accordingly be higher than in a country where inflation is expected to remain low in the future.

There are two further convergence criteria which relate to the ability of member states to bear the fiscal discipline entailed by EMU membership. As noted above, the loss of seigniorage profits and the ending of automatic borrowing facilities will mean that governments will find it harder to finance budget deficits and refinance large public sector debts. The Maastricht Treaty therefore requires limits on both measures of the public finances:

1 national budget deficits must be less than 3% of GDP; and
2 the national debt must be less than 60% of GDP (or at least satisfactorily falling towards this level).

If at least seven member states meet all five prerequisites by the end of 1996, a specially convened IGC may set a date for a more limited EMU that – initially at least – will exclude the other EU countries. The remaining states may then join as and when their circumstances allow. Should the 1996 conference fail to set a date for EMU, it will be reconvened in 1998. At this time, if at least five member states meet the prerequisites agreed at Maastricht, those that qualify will automatically adopt a common currency in 1999, leaving the others to apply for membership in due course.

THE WAY FORWARD

At the end of 1994, only Luxembourg met the five convergence criteria and few of the remaining member states looked like satisfying them by the end of 1996 (see also Chapter 4). Table 5.6 illustrates the convergence criteria as they would have applied had they been in force in 1994, together with the actual economic

Table 5.6 Convergence criteria and out-turns in 1994

Country	Inflation rate 1994 (%)	Long-term interest rate 1994 (%)	Exchange rate criteria met?	Debt ratio 1994 (% GDP)	Budget balance 1994 (% GDP)
1994 limits/criteria	3.8	8.9	±15% EMS band/no devaluation	60.0	−3.0
Belgium	2.6*	7.5*	Yes	142.6	−5.4
Britain	3.5*	8.2*	No	50.3*	−6.0
Denmark	2.0*	8.1*	Yes	82.2	−4.6
Germany	3.0*	6.3*	Yes	53.6*	−3.1
Greece	10.2	n/a	No	154.0	−17.9
Spain	4.8	8.8*	No	61.4	−7.2
France	1.8*	6.9*	Yes	48.1*	−5.6
Ireland	2.8*	7.9	No	93.1	−2.5*
Italy	3.9	9.4	No	123.3	−9.5
Luxembourg	2.9*	6.4*	Yes	7.9*	−0.4*
The Netherlands	2.3*	6.9*	Yes	82.2	−3.6
Portugal	5.6	10.0	No	70.2	−6.2

Note: *denotes convergence criteria met.
Source: *European Economy.*

performance of the EU member states at that time. It shows that, reflecting the severity of the early 1990s' recession in the EU, almost all the member states violated the budget deficit ceiling of 3% of GDP, while only four had debt:GDP ratios below the 60% limit. Moreover, the turmoil in the foreign exchange markets in 1992–93, which led to the withdrawal of sterling and the lira from the EMS and a series of devaluations (despite the enforced widening of the 'normal' target bands from ±2.25% to ±15%), has set back the prospect of the weaker currency states meeting the convergence criteria for exchange rate stability. Although the Edinburgh Summit in December 1992 reaffirmed the commitment of the EU member states to the timetable for EMU embodied in the Maastricht Treaty, the concept of a monetary union embracing all twelve member states (plus those members of the European Free Trade Area which join in 1995) now looks very remote.

A more likely scenario – inspired by, but separate from, the Maastricht Treaty – is the emergence of a 'mini EMU' between

Germany, France, the Benelux countries and (possibly) Denmark. The prospect of a two-speed Europe has always been a possible outcome, given that several of the poorer EU states were unlikely to satisfy the convergence criteria by either 1996 or 1998. But a combination of deepening recession and exchange rate volatility, culminating in Britain and Italy's withdrawal from the ERM and devaluations by the weaker currencies, has seriously weakened the enthusiasm for EMU in the poorer member states and increased the likelihood of an informal mini EMU being established by a core of rich northern European states. The momentum for the 'grand design' envisaged by the Maastricht Treaty may now have been largely lost, at least for the foreseeable future.

A mini EMU would have several important advantages over the model envisaged by the Maastricht Treaty:

1 it need only involve those countries that really want to participate in monetary union (as opposed to those, like Britain, which reluctantly acquiesced in the Maastricht initiative for fear of being left behind);
2 it would follow naturally from economic convergence, rather than forcing convergence on would-be members;
3 the arbitrary convergence criteria set out in the Maastricht Treaty, which if interpreted strictly would permanently exclude members like Belgium on the grounds of its high debt ratio, could be ignored (but see Chapter 4); and
4 it would obviate the need for major institutional changes in the EU, leaving the basic framework of national central banks cooperating within the EMS unchanged.

The shape of a mini EMU

The most probable shape of any mini EMU would be a 'hard' version of the EMS as it presently exists. The central feature of the EMS is, of course, the ERM, an arrangement by which member states undertake to maintain their bilateral exchange rates within narrow margins around predetermined central parities. The width of the official standard band is now ±15%. As noted above, in the absence of capital controls, maintaining exchange rates within these bands requires a high degree of monetary policy coordination (i.e., a significant sacrifice of monetary sovereignty). Higher

Table 5.7 Comparative inflation records, 1979–94

Country	Average inflation rate p.a. (%)
Germany	2.4
France	6.0
Britain	6.8
Italy	8.7

Source: European Economy.

interest rates in one member state imply higher interest rates in all others to preserve the desired pattern of bilateral exchange rates.

In the original design of the EMS, which came into operation in 1979, it was intended that the national central banks of participating states would cooperatively agree a joint monetary stance that maximised collective welfare. In practice, however, the German Bundesbank – an independent central bank charged with a statutory duty to maintain German price stability (see above) – has consistently refused to be tied by such collective decisions, fearing that it might be obliged to adopt a monetary stance that would compromise its domestic inflation objectives (see Chapter 2). The Bundesbank's reluctance is understandable. Its record of low and stable inflation stands in marked contrast to the performance of the other major EU states (see Table 5.7). Accordingly, the Bundesbank continued to set German interest rates exclusively with reference to German economic conditions after 1979, presenting other, more inflation-prone members with a stark choice:

1 either they followed the German lead and adjusted their own interest rates accordingly; or
2 their currencies would depreciate against the deutschmark, eventually forcing them to devalue; or
3 they left the ERM altogether.

While there were, as a direct result of this inherent tension within the EMS, a number of exchange rate realignments during the early years, there was a growing realisation by other EU governments that acceding to so-called 'German policy leadership' – i.e., passively following Germany's monetary stance – might offer a means of achieving greater exchange rate stability (i.e., by reducing the pressure for realignments) and guaranteeing greater domestic price stability. By the mid-1980s, the EMS had grown into a 'deutschmark bloc', with the German Bundesbank setting a common monetary stance for all participating member states. As a monetary arrangement, the EMS offers many of the advantages and disadvantages of EMU:

1 it reduces exchange rate uncertainty;
2 it entails the sacrifice of monetary sovereignty by non-German member states; and
3 at its heart lies the independent Bundesbank, with an established reputation for price stability.

The recent tensions within the EMS have, in turn, largely stemmed from a sharp increase in the perceived costs of sacrificing monetary sovereignty by the weaker member states. As noted above, adhering to a common monetary policy imposes short-run costs on member states unless inflation performance in each is harmonised. The key problem of recent years has been the large economic shock which struck Germany just as the other member states were moving into recession. The impact of German reunification delivered a huge stimulus to the German economy, resulting in strong economic growth during 1990–91 and the build-up of inflationary pressures. The northern European economies (e.g., Denmark, the Benelux countries and, to a lesser extent, France) which are highly integrated with Germany shared some of the fruits of this temporary boom, but for Britain and the poorer southern states, reunification served to desynchronise their business cycles from the cycle in Germany. As the Bundesbank raised interest rates to bear down on German inflation, following the German lead imposed unwelcome and unnecessary deflationary pressure on the weaker member states.

As the recession deepened and unemployment mounted, the calls for governments in countries like Britain to cut interest rates and devalue against the deutschmark mounted. In turn, fear of devaluation generated such intense foreign exchange market speculation that the weaker currencies came under irresistible pressure and, one by one, they were either driven out of the EMS or devalued. For those northern states that remain in the EMS, however, the present arrangements provide the basis for a sustainable mini EMU that could emerge without the need for formal EU approval by all member states. Already Belgium and Luxembourg have a monetary union between their states (i.e., their currencies are interchangeable). These two states, together with the

Netherlands, informally adhere to very narrow target bands *vis-à-vis* each other's currencies and the deutschmark, notwithstanding the EU's decision in August 1993 to officially move to ultra-wide ±15% bands. France and other countries wanting to join the mini EMU (probably only Denmark) could follow suit, steadily reducing the bands for their exchange rate fluctuations until their bilateral rates were irrevocably fixed. All these changes could occur within the present EMS, without the need for fixed timetables or formal treaties. Via this evolutionary approach, a mini EMU might gradually unfold, in which member currencies would be seen as virtually interchangeable – providing many of the benefits of a single currency without actually introducing one.

CONCLUSIONS

Despite the recent upheavals in the currency markets, EU member states remain committed to EMU, and the Maastricht Treaty is an important milestone along the road. It establishes clear and specific criteria to assess whether member states are sufficiently convergent in certain key areas to move to Stage Three and sets a time limit, January 1, 1999, for its commencement. Agreement was also reached on the objectives and independence of the ESCB, though not on the operational procedures it will use to conduct its monetary policy. The task of obtaining agreement on operational procedures is delegated to the European Monetary Institute (see Chapters 4 and 6), which was set up at the commencement of Stage Two in 1994. Although there are several difficult hurdles to clear, such as the way in which the ESCB will operate so as to achieve a uniform interest rate throughout the EU, the reserve ratios it will hold and the extent of prudential supervision it will exercise over the banking system, these problems are not insurmountable. However, it is clear that all member states will not satisfy the convergence criteria and it seems likely that there will be a two-speed approach, with the emergence of a mini EMU taking place – either inside or outside the Maastricht framework.

6

WHAT PRICE EUROPEAN MONETARY UNION?

Patrick Minford

INTRODUCTION

The ratification of the Maastricht Treaty in 1993 led, ironically, to a renewed debate in the European Union (EU) over the future of monetary union. This debate was no longer confined to Britain, but spread to Germany, where there is concern over the premature disappearance of the deutschmark, and to France, where one concern is the potential dominance of Germany in a future European central bank (ECB). In Italy, while there remains enthusiasm for monetary union, there is concern about the Maastricht conditions on public debt and deficits that must be met. This chapter reviews the main issues involved and sets out some new proposals for both the long-term objectives of European monetary union (EMU) and the short-term methods of transition.

THE LONG-TERM CASE FOR EUROPEAN MONETARY UNION: A CRITIQUE

A good starting point for discussing the advantages of a common currency is the report of the EC Commission (1990b), which made an heroic attempt to measure the potential benefits. The report speculates that the efficiency gain from removing currency uncertainty and exchange costs may be worth as much as 10% of the EU's gross domestic product (GDP). Virtually all of this comes from the effect of a supposed reduction in the 'risk premium' on the cost of capital. Various other gains are adduced from the common currency – increased price stability (including through enhanced credibility), more disciplined public finance and greater macroeconomic stability.

However, it is important to note that price stability, on which the report places much emphasis, is attainable *with or without* EMU, as is greater credibility. Whether EMU makes these benefits more easily attainable is a matter of political economy, which is not tackled by the Commission's report. What will the European central bank's powers and incentives be? What legitimacy will be conferred on it by the twelve democratic peoples of the EU? These questions are understandably not addressed in the Commission's report, but merely assumed away.

But even if they were convincingly answered, there would still be the alternative of pursuing price stability credibly by domestic means. Domestic means of commitment exist, and are effectively achieved in many OECD economies such as Germany, the United States and Japan. Essentially they involve some form of domestic nominal target, whether the money supply or nominal income or simply price behaviour, with the commitment penalties supplied by the political process. To put it crudely, governments that fail to deliver acceptable inflation performance lose votes. Ultimately this must be the only effective penalty for macroeconomic mismanagement in a sovereign democracy.

This issue of domestic commitment highlights the difficulties inherent in designing a Europe-wide commitment process for monetary policy. As the Germans have persistently pointed out, there is a 'democratic deficit' in the EU. Without democratic political union, there would indeed be a lack of democratic legitimacy for a European central bank imposing tough monetary policies on twelve (or more) national regions of Europe, some of which may well be suffering from severe recession in spite of an EU-wide inflation. This lack of democratic accountability would also fatally undermine credibility.

If we turn to public finance, the report envisages greater discipline arising from the inability of a national government to raise taxation through printing money ('seigniorage' or the 'inflation tax'); this inability is reinforced by the Maastricht fiscal criteria, designed to limit the risks of country bail-outs (see also Chapter 5). Here a virtue is made of what the literature conventionally regards as a problem, namely making optimal taxation more difficult. However, the Commission's report offers no mechanisms, only pious hopes and peer country pressure, for achieving movement to fiscal balance under EMU. Abolishing seigniorage without an alternative fiscal mechanism for raising revenue hardly seems to constitute a fiscal improvement. The distressing implications are illustrated by the difficulties of Italy, which is unable to raise tax through inflation, while being condemned by the Maastricht criteria to ambitious targets for primary budget surpluses without (judging by its long-standing performance) the political capacity to deliver the necessary taxes or spending cuts.

The large efficiency gain speculated on in the EU report comes from removing the transaction costs of currency exchange and the hedging costs of guarding against currency uncertainty. There are two arguments which suggest its estimate is likely to be well on the high side:

1 currency risk is diversifiable in a world of many currencies and investment vehicles whose risks are correlated with currency risk. Hence the cost of hedging should tend to the premium on specific risk (i.e., zero); and
2 a transaction involving currency exchange should not, on the face of it (given the negligible cost of keying in electronic orders), cost any extra in credit transactions than an ordinary transaction in home currency, other than the cost of hedging net balances in any one currency between clearings.

These considerations suggest that the only saving comes in the exchange of notes and coin. But this is extremely limited. Notes and coin is generally a small percentage of the total money supply (with one or two exceptions such as Italy and Greece) and that part of it which is exchanged for foreign notes and coin is a small percentage of that again.

The Commission's estimate of the transactions cost saving on its own is 0.4% of GDP. This is based on a survey of financial firms' commission charges, and these are applied to estimates of the volume of business attracting these charges. While this is a more believable estimate than the huge aggregate figure, it may still be on the high side. Indeed, the report suggests that it is heavily concentrated among the smaller countries with less sophisticated banking systems (and for a country with a sophisticated system like Britain may be as low as 0.1% of GDP).

We have seen so far that the only firm gain from EMU adduced by the Commission is that connected with transactions costs savings. And this, at 0.1% of GDP for a country like Britain or

126

Germany, is extraordinarily small. Indeed, if the gain were as large as the EU estimate, then other pairs of nations enjoying a similar degree of bilateral trade would have surely actively considered a common currency. Yet the countries of EFTA, of North America, of eastern Europe, to name but a few candidates, have never seemed to put this idea seriously on the treaty agenda.

This last point suggests that, whatever the truth in the Commission's estimate, there must be some key drawback to nations having a common currency. Indeed, the extensive literature on the 'optimum common currency area' (Mundell, 1961) points to just such a drawback. Its thrust is that exchange rate adjustment, because it is more rapid than national wage and price adjustment, is more effective in stabilising an open economy in the face of differential national shocks (an extreme example of which would be German reunification in 1990). This thrust is contrary to the Commission's assertion that EMU would bring greater macroeconomic stability. The optimum currency literature invokes a variety of factors that may improve the stabilising capacity of monetary union – notably, a high degree of labour mobility, and a central budget capable of making large fiscal transfers. But these factors are, as we shall see, absent in the case of the EU.

I wish now to examine how serious a drawback this is for EMU. How damaging is the loss of a flexible exchange rate (and so of flexible national interest rates) in reacting to economic shocks? I shall loosely call this the 'stabilisation' aspect. In order to examine it, I use the method of 'stochastic simulation' on a macroeconomic model of the EU and other G7 economies. This involves peppering the model with a large number of typical economic shocks. The simulated economies' stability with regard to prices and output is then compared under EMU and floating exchange rates. While this method has its weaknesses, which are discussed below, there is no viable alternative. Econometrics cannot disentangle the effects of monetary union from other influences on long-functioning unions such as the United States, and there is no data on the EU. What econometric work exists merely bears on the extent of integration across European countries – for example, Bayoumi and Eichengreen (1992) show that the United States is more integrated than the EU, while de Grauwe and Vanhaverbeke (1991), as well as von Hagen and Neumann (1991), show that the EU is less integrated *across* countries than it is *within* countries.

PATRICK MINFORD

STABILISATION GAINS AND LOSSES OF MONETARY UNION

In evaluating the stabilisation aspect for any given common currency proposal, one must make assumptions about the institutional framework. As noted in Chapter 4, it makes a lot of difference, whether there is a high degree of labour mobility and what the fiscal transfer arrangements are. In the case of the EU, it has been noted by Eichengreen (1990b) that the fiscal offset to any national or regional decline in GDP is less than 1% (as against 30% in the United States, for instance); nor are there any plans to raise this offset coefficient to any number remotely comparable with the US figure. The Delors Committee (Delors, 1989) called for a doubling of EU expenditure, but even that may well not be agreed by the nations that have to double their fiscal contribution to Brussels, still less the much larger amounts suggested as the minimum necessary by MacDougall (1977).

Labour mobility is also limited, for the vast bulk of nationals in the richer countries of the EU. The key reason appears to be language and cultural differences, which make a Frenchman pause before resettling in Frankfurt. What significant migration there is takes place from the poorer countries to the richer, as the immigration controls that normally stop this are gradually dismantled under the 1992 programme (see also Chapter 10). But even this population movement is not great because capital mobility within the free EU market enables workers in poorer countries, such as Spain and parts of Britain and Italy which are on the 'periphery' of the EU, to attract investment and enjoy improved wages without the cost of moving.

We assume that trade is free for our purposes here, even though in reality the full effects of the 1992 programme have not yet fully come through and may not do so until the next century (see Chapter 7). We also assume that capital is perfectly mobile within the EU and that there are no exchange controls. It is obvious, as the optimum currency area literature stresses, that whatever stabilisation task is performed by flexible exchange rates and divergent monetary policy, it can partially be substituted for by either labour mobility or fiscal transfers. To that extent, the EU is handicapped in its bid to be an optimum currency area. Our calculations below reflect this handicap. (If EMU goes ahead regardless, that might

128

well lead to demands for further progress on fiscal policy and labour mobility, but that is another matter.)

Before proceeding, we should note a point frequently made by those in favour of EMU, namely that monetary arrangements as such should not alter the long-run equilibrium state of the real economy, but merely change national price levels. Real business cycle theorists would go further and argue that even the short-run behaviour of real variables should be immune to monetary arrangements, provided that they do not constitute a change in transactions technology. The approach here is straightforward. The models used explicitly assume that real long-run equilibria are immune to monetary arrangements. But these models feature a variety of ways in which short-run behaviour differs under different monetary arrangements, so my position is not that of the real business cycle approach. That approach has not yet come up with a representation of European economies which can rival that produced by more conventional modern models with their stress on nominal contracts, monetary surprises and 'rational' (informationally efficient) expectations.

We still have to answer the question of whether one can properly capture behavioural differences across such different regimes as flexible rates and the totally fixed rates of a common currency. This problem, which was first highlighted by Lucas (1976) – and termed the 'Lucas critique' – is inherent in most pieces of applied work that address issues of policy interest, which usually involve consideration of different policy regimes. Ultimately, there is no satisfactory answer. Either one comes up with a model of stylised consumers and producers whose tastes and technology can be identified and assumed not to change, accepting that such a model will have a poor fit and lack institutional relevance. Or one produces a model of aggregate supplies and demands, as used here, in which the estimates fit reasonably but the estimated coefficients themselves may shift as people change their behaviour in changed environments.

I make use of two multilateral models linking separate models of the major OECD economies: Multimod and Liverpool. Both are reasonably well-known representatives of the class of model described above. The Multimod model (see Masson *et al.*, 1990) estimated conventionally but is a simulation rather than a forecasting model; it assumes fairly long overlapping wage contracts. The Liverpool model (see Minford *et al.*, 1986; Matthews, 1992) is fully estimated. It uses a 'new classical' framework, in which contracts do not overlap but are disturbed by annual monetary surprises. In both models, adjustment costs produce long drawn-out adjustment.

Before embarking on this comparison, it is worth asking what one might expect to find. Holding money supplies of relevant countries constant (as in the 'k-percent rule' suggested by Friedman, 1968), one would observe the relative capacity of the two exchange rate regimes to stabilise shocks, leading to 'model stability'. We have already explained how, following the arguments of the optimum currency area literature, we would expect greater stability under floating exchange rates (with the implied flexibility of national interest rates).

When one turns to the possibilities for active monetary responses to shocks – something that few would wish to rule out, especially when shocks are large and identifiable – there may appear to be a trade-off between the number of independent monetary instruments for dealing with differential national shocks (maximised under floating) and the extent of monetary coordination (which must be total under fully fixed exchange rates). Never-

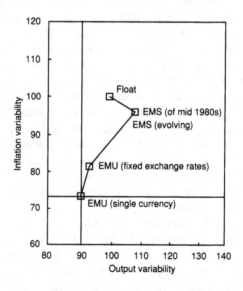

Figure 6.1 Commission estimates (variability measured by standard deviation)

theless, coordination under fixed rates will not imply the same set of monetary policies as coordination under floating rates. It must, in principle, be the case that cooperation using the full scope of independence granted by floating will be optimal. Again, therefore, we would expect floating to have the advantage in this aspect of the competition.

The results of the available studies are summarised in Figures 6.1 to 6.3. Full details of these studies are in EC Commission (1990b), Minford *et al.* (1992), and Masson and Symansky (1992). Both the Commission and Masson and Symansky use Multimod for their stochastic simulations. However, the Commission's study has been criticised by the later studies cited above for two main aspects of its approach. First, it attributes an implausibly high variability to the risk premia on interest differentials between EU currencies (these risks are, of course, eliminated under EMU). Second, it assumes somewhat unusual monetary policy regimes (rules where interest rates vary in response to inflation and output targets). Using these

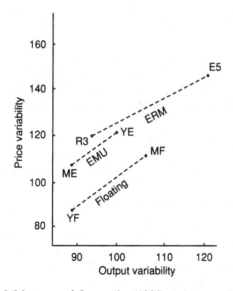

Figure 6.2 Masson and Symansky (1992) estimates with Multimod (variability measured by standard deviation)
Key: R3, 3% bands, real exchange rate trigger for realignment; E5, 5% bands, equilibrium realignment; M(E/F), money target; Y(E/F), nominal income target: E, EMU; F, floating.

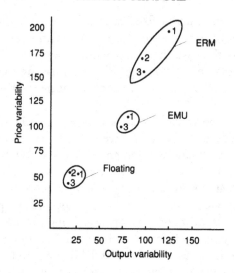

Figure 6.3 Minford *et al.* (1992) estimates on Liverpool model (variability
measured by standard deviation)
Key: 1, money supply fixed; 2, non-cooperative contingent response;
3, cooperative contingent response.

assumptions, the Commission finds that EMU is superior in
stability to floating. When Masson and Symansky allow for plaus-
ibly lower-risk premium variability and for alternative monetary
regimes they obtain results more in line with the prior expectations
described above.

Altering the Commission's simulations for risk premia alone
reduces substantially the 'advantage' it found for EMU. However, this is not the whole story; the monetary policy assumptions
made under the differing exchange rate regimes must also be
appropriate. If a destabilising monetary policy is assumed under
floating, while a stabilising one is assumed under EMU, then the
relative stability of EMU will clearly be biased upwards. In principle, one wishes to assume under each exchange rate regime the
optimal monetary policy within the feasible set: that reveals the best
potential performance of each exchange rate regime. It is also
reasonable to ask how each exchange rate system will perform
under optimal automatic rules for monetary policy. It may be
better for such rules to be embraced by politicians, because of
the difficulties surrounding successful discretionary policy (see

Chapter 5). Again, though, one would wish to choose the best automatic rule for monetary policy under each exchange rate regime.

Masson and Symansky (1992) make two main comparisons: (i) under fixed money supply rules; and (ii) under rules where interest rates target money GDP (or nominal income). Their work makes it possible to put the Multimod simulations alongside those using the Liverpool model produced by Minford *et al.* (1992). These authors looked at a different set of monetary regimes. In respect of regimes with non-automatic responses (discretionary policy in which, however, there is assumed to be no attempted manipulation of expectations by false promises, a phenomenon known as 'time-inconsistency'), they investigated fully optimal monetary policies, both under 'Nash' non-cooperative policies and under EU cooperation. However, among automatic rules, they restricted themselves solely to fixed money supplies.

The main point which emerges from the three sets of results shown in Figures 6.1 to 6.3 is that, whether one uses the Liverpool or the Multimod models, once shocks are put on a comparable basis, then floating gives scope for substantially better stability (provided monetary policies are suitably chosen) than EMU. This result for Multimod is not as strong as for the Liverpool model, which may well reflect the absence of optimisation in the Multimod exercise. However, what emerges overall is essentially the conclusion one would reach from following the logic of the optimum currency area literature in its modern stochastic version.

I have avoided any discussion of the political passions raised by the issue of sovereignty. But, in fact, no nation would be abandoning its sovereignty under the proposals for union so far discussed (see Chapters 4 and 5 for a more detailed discussion). Effectively these have been for little more than totally fixed exchange rates with a single monetary authority. Any country which dislikes the result could, in principle, leave it and issue its own currency again, supposing this to have been merged without trace. This is not, in fact, proposed, given the intentions to allow member states to issue nationally distinct ECU notes – for example, in Britain, future ECU notes may have the monarch's head on one side.

It is this very lack of a political dimension (and so lack of a serious central budget, as well as limited labour mobility) that loads the dice against macroeconomic stability, besides raising the problem of legitimacy. Yet, as is widely conceded, it is totally unrealistic to discuss any political dimension. In these circumstances, one can perhaps discuss the merits of a move to total exchange fixity in purely economic terms. If the economic gains were great then a treaty – reversible, like all treaties – acquiring them could be worthwhile, even though there would still be inevitable doubts about the practical problems of reversibility and the resulting political hostage to fortune. In this sense, political doubts over sovereignty place the burden of proof on EMU.

THE TRANSITION TO MONETARY UNION

The macroeconomic instability likely to be caused by EMU at the present stage of economic integration in the EU, when set against the small gain in transactions costs discussed earlier, seems to make a strong case against moving to a common currency. This is not to say that increasing integration (that is, greater intra-EU trade in goods, services and factors of production, which is nothing whatever to do with the 'convergence' hitherto discussed in Chapters 4 and 5) will not eventually push the calculation the other way, for a gradually increasing set of nations (giving rise to 'variable geometry' or an '*n*-tier' union). Increasing integration both raises the gain from transactions costs and reduces the loss from instability (as shocks become more similar across member states in nature and impact). So there is a need for a transitional regime which both permits this evolving union to occur at the appropriate moments and works effectively for the united as well as the not-so-united member states.

So far, I have not commented on the results for the exchange rate mechanism (ERM) in Figures 6.1 to 6.3. They are palpably worse than for EMU, illustrating the generally appreciated feature that the ERM creates a degree of fixity without full credibility or ultimate policy commitment. This gives the worst of both worlds and accounts for the one element of agreement on all sides – that the system should move either to complete fixity (and so EMU) or back to floating.

There is, however, one regime which gives both good results and achieves the sort of cooperation that has been one of the proclaimed aims of those who set up the ERM. The cooperation that it involves between central banks should also smooth the path to monetary union as and when appropriate. At such a moment, the cooperation would become a lockstep by agreement. The regime in question is illustrated in Figure 6.3 for the Liverpool results (unfortunately it is not available for Multimod) and entails 'co-operative floating', numbered 3 among the floating regimes. This regime, of course, achieves the best of both worlds, exploiting the 'degrees of freedom' in floating, while enjoying the cooperation intended by the ERM.

There are those who argue that such cooperation is inconceivable within Europe, without the rules of an exchange rate arrangement like the ERM. Yet in game-theoretic terms, cooperative equilibrium (which respects individual country interests, but arranges mutually improving policy trades) is a dominant one when players can communicate, since they have a joint interest in achieving it. Hence, the argument can be turned on its head. It is unlikely that, in the absence of the sub-optimal constraints of the ERM, central banks which are used to communicating with each other would abstain from such a cooperative equilibrium. Politically, too, the arrangement would be attractive, given the concerns mentioned at the start of this chapter.

In short, what I am proposing is a reformed Stage Two, in which the European Monetary Institute could take on the role of a coordinating forum in which the twelve governments, represented by their central banks under whatever national controls are desired, could meet regularly and share their monetary plans. All exchange rate bands and intervention targets would be abandoned. The central banks would set monetary targets, both for suitable money supply measures and for operating instruments, especially interest rates. They would also design their own detailed rules and operating procedures for achieving this cooperative equilibrium in everyday practice.

CONCLUSIONS

It is widely believed that the currency upheavals of 1992–93 have derailed the Maastricht route to EMU. However, while the political feasibility of EMU is now in doubt, the idea that, if achieved, EMU would generate major benefits for the EU member states in terms of reduced transactions costs and greater monetary stability is well established. This chapter challenges this received wisdom, testing the EMU proposals against alternative monetary regimes and showing that cooperative floating is the optimal arrangement. It proposes a route out of the present monetary impasse in Europe, where there is little enthusiasm (rightly on the view here) for EMU and yet substantial – and again justified – dissatisfaction with the current ERM. The proposed route is an evolving structure of central bank cooperation that exploits the full stabilising potential of floating exchange rates.

Part II

MICROECONOMIC ISSUES

7

COMPLETING THE INTERNAL MARKET IN THE EUROPEAN UNION

Frank McDonald

INTRODUCTION

It is somewhat ironic that in the 1970s and 1980s the European Union (EU) was often referred to as the 'common market'. For in this period, the EU had not created the conditions which are necessary for a common market to exist (see Chapter 1). The Treaty of Rome called for the creation of a customs union and a common market. These objectives are clearly outlined in Article 3 of the Treaty of Rome. Indeed, many of the articles of the Treaty are concerned with establishing the so-called 'four freedoms' – that is, freedom of movement of goods, services, capital and labour. Yet in spite of this commitment, the EU had not created a common market by the 1980s.

However, in 1987 the Single European Act (SEA) was agreed and it committed all the member states to the creation of a common market by the end of 1992. A legislative programme with a detailed timetable had been published in the 1985 White Paper, *Completing the Internal Market* (EC Commission, 1985). This programme acquired many different names: the 'internal market', the '1992 programme' and the 'single market' or the 'single European market' (SEM). This chapter provides an overview of the 1992 programme, including an assessment of its likely effects (see also Cecchini, 1988; EC Commission, 1988b; Healey, 1992b).

THE ECONOMIC RATIONALE FOR THE SINGLE EUROPEAN MARKET

When the SEA was signed, the EU had achieved a customs union of sorts, with some minor exceptions that related to Spain and

Portugal. The customs union had only been completed in terms of the elimination of tariffs and quotas and by the erection of a Common External Tariff. However, the Treaty of Rome required the removal of 'customs duties and of quantitative restrictions on the import and export of goods, and of all other measures having like effect' (Article 3a). Customs duties and quantitative restrictions refer to tariffs and quotas while other measures can be summed up by use of the term, 'non-tariff barriers' (NTBs). Any measures that act in a similar manner to tariffs and quotas can be classified as NTBs. These include the laws, regulations and policies of national governments that limit or prevent international trade.

The welfare effects of tariffs, quotas and non-tariff barriers

In what follows, it will be assumed that trade is conducted in an environment of perfect competition and that any tariffs or NTBs do not alter prices in international markets. In Figure 7.1, the effects of a tariff are illustrated (see Chapter 1 for a fuller discussion of the welfare effects of protectionism). In this figure, D_H represents domestic demand, S_H is domestic supply, S_W is world supply, P_W is the price in the world market and P_{W+t} is price plus the amount of the tariff (assumed to be a lump-sum tariff). Before

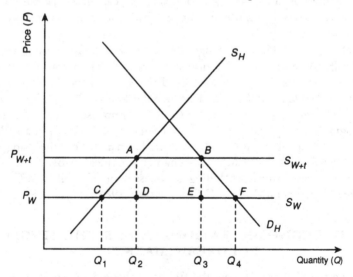

Figure 7.1 The welfare effects of protection revisited

the implementation of the tariff, demand at price P_W would be Q_4, domestic supply would be Q_1 and consequently the difference, $Q_4 - Q_1$, would be imports. If a tariff, t, was imposed, the domestic price would rise by the amount of the tariff, that is, to P_{W+t}, domestic demand would contract to Q_3, domestic supply would increase to Q_2 and the level of imports would fall to $Q_3 - Q_2$.

The welfare effects of this can be measured using the concept of consumer surplus. As a result of the tariff-induced price rise, there would be a fall in consumer surplus shown by the area $P_W P_{W+t} BF$. Of this loss, $P_W P_{W+t} AD$ would be transferred to domestic suppliers in order to obtain the increase in domestic supply. The area CAD indicates the extra cost of supplying the increased domestic output. This is a net welfare loss to society because it is the cost incurred as a result of the increase in domestic supply. Of the remaining consumer surplus loss of $ABFD$, an amount equal to the level of imports times the size of the tariff would be transferred to the government as revenue from the tariff; that is, area $ABED$. The remaining consumer surplus loss, shown by the area BFE, arises from the reduction in domestic demand that results from the tariff. This is a net welfare loss to society resulting from the imposition of the tariff. The effect of the tariff is to transfer income from consumers to producers and the government and there is also a net welfare loss to society equal to the sum of areas CAD and BFE.

If a quota of $Q_3 - Q_2$ was used instead of a tariff, the net welfare loss would be the same, because the quota would push the price up to P_{W+t}, demand would fall to Q_3 and domestic supply would rise to Q_2. The major difference is that the government would not receive any revenue from the quota. In these circumstances, the area $ABED$ accrues to the importers of the good.

The use of an *NTB* would have a very similar effect to that of a quota. Suppose that in order to sell good X, the exporter must comply with the national regulations which govern the sale of that good in the country to which they wish to sell. As the exporter has to comply with the regulations, he or she would face an additional cost which is assumed to be equivalent to the tariff, t, in Figure 7.1. In this case, the effect of the NTB would be to push the domestic price to P_{W+t}, leading to the same welfare effects as a quota of $Q_3 - Q_2$. The difference is that, instead of accruing to the importer as profit, the area $ABED$ would represent the oppor-

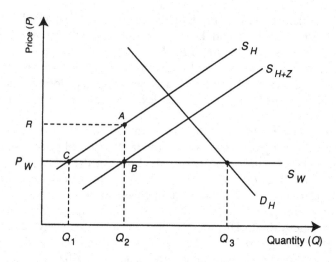

Figure 7.2 The welfare effects of subsidies to domestic producers

tunity cost of supplying the modified products to the domestic market. If the cost of complying with the NTB rose high enough, the exporter would be excluded from the market.

There are other forms of NTBs, such as subsidisation of domestic producers. These can take many forms, for example, subsidies, preferential loans, grants and tax concessions (see Chapter 13). In EU terminology, such practices are called 'state aids'. The welfare effects of such state aids are illustrated in Figure 7.2.

The symbols in Figure 7.2 have the same meanings as in Figure 7.1. The amount of the subsidy is shown by Z; $S_H + Z$ is domestic supply after allowing for the subsidy and the price plus the subsidy would be R. Before the imposition of the subsidy, demand at price P_W would be Q_3, domestic supply would be Q_1 and the level of imports would be $Q_3 - Q_1$. If a subsidy of Z were introduced, domestic supply would increase to Q_2 and imports would fall to $Q_3 - Q_2$. No consumer surplus loss would result from the subsidy because the domestic price remains at P_W. There is a cost to the government of $P_W RAB$ (the cost of the subsidy) of which ABC is a net welfare loss due to the opportunity cost of producing the extra domestic output. This method of protection can be less costly than tariffs, quotas or different national regulations. It does lead to a net welfare loss to society, but this is of a lower magnitude than the other methods of protection (as there is no consumer surplus loss). However, the subsidy would cause welfare losses due to the distortions caused by the taxes necessary to finance this method of protection.

The above analysis ignores the fact that the customs union and the common market of the EU exclude non-members. It also only considers static welfare effects; that is, the effects with a given quantity and quality of resources. Furthermore, the analysis is concerned with trade in goods and services. A common market, however, also requires free movement of capital and labour. The exclusion of non-members from the trade liberalisation measures of the EU can lead to welfare losses if the excluded countries are lower-cost suppliers of goods and services than the member states of the EU. In these circumstances, trade liberalisation within the EU could lead to a shift to higher-cost suppliers. This would result in net welfare losses because the EU would not reap the full benefits of comparative advantage. Such an outcome is referred to by the term, 'trade diversion'. Conversely, if trade liberalisation by the EU led to 'trade creation' (when the member states include the lowest-cost producers) the members of the EU would reap all the benefits of comparative advantage. The concepts of trade creation and diversion are explained in more detail in Chapter 1 (see also McDonald and Dearden, 1994).

Over a period of time, trade liberalisation should lead to a reallocation of resources as a result of companies responding to the new opportunities for trade and to the increase in competition which arise from the removal of trade barriers. This results in dynamic welfare effects (see Chapter 1; Emerson, 1988). The main factors that lead to such dynamic welfare effects are:

1 economies of scale;
2 reductions in supernormal profits;
3 decreases in the level of X-inefficiency;
4 improvements in the qualities of goods and services; and
5 changes to the logistical systems of companies.

The removal of trade barriers induces some companies to expand their output levels in order to supply expanding or new export markets. This expansion of output results in the reaping of economies of scale for those companies which are operating on the declining portion of their average cost curve. If the subsequent reduction in cost is passed on to consumers by a decrease in price a

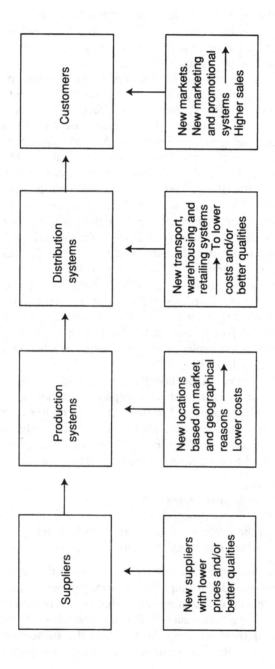

Figure 7.3 A schematic logistics chain

consumer surplus gain would arise and thereby welfare gains would become possible.

The creation of a common market results in an increase in competition by inducing companies to expand sales or enter markets that had previously been protected by trade barriers. This can lead to reductions in supernormal profits and levels of X-inefficiency and possibly in prices as companies seek to improve their competitive position. These changes in the competitive situation can also stimulate non-price competition factors such as improvements in the qualities and characteristics of goods and services. Such improvements can provide benefits to consumers because they enhance the value which buyers place on products. Providing that these enhanced values are not fully matched by increases in prices, a gain of consumer surplus would arise.

The increase in competition resulting from the removal of NTBs may also induce companies to modify their logistical systems; that is, the chain of activities ranging from the determining of sources for inputs through to production processes and distribution procedures. A schematic logistics chain, with indications of possible cost-reducing measures resulting from the removal of NTBs, is shown in Figure 7.3. Restructuring of the logistics chains of companies could lead to lower-cost production and better quality goods and services. Such changes should provide welfare gains by inducing reductions in price and also by releasing resources which could be used more effectively in other economic activities.

Welfare gains would also arise from the removal of NTBs that prevent the free movement of capital and labour and from those that distort the allocation of these resources. These gains would arise from the downward pressure (for the common market as a whole) on the price of capital and labour and by allowing for a more efficient allocation of factors of production (see El-Agraa, 1994).

Theory thus suggests that the creation of a common market should lead to welfare gains that would be largely brought about by reductions in the price of goods, services, capital and labour and by the releasing of factors of production for use in areas where the country has a comparative advantage. However, these benefits can only be secured by changing trade patterns and by restructuring the business activities of companies. These adjustments can lead to costs in terms of unemployment and redundant capital equipment if the workers and owners of capital that are affected by such company restructuring are unable to fully redeploy their resources.

THE PROPOSAL TO CREATE A COMMON MARKET

The 1985 White Paper identified three main types of barriers which had to be removed if a common market were to be created (see Table 7.1 for a summary of the range of measures involved):

1 physical barriers;
2 technical barriers; and
3 fiscal barriers.

Physical barriers

These barriers refer to customs formalities at national frontiers. They affect foreign trade by interrupting the flow of traded commodities to allow for the checks and form-filling necessary to ensure adherence to national indirect taxation systems and the various technical regulations of importing countries. These customs formalities lead to costs for companies in that they have to complete paperwork and submit to inspections at frontiers. The White Paper proposed that indirect taxation systems and the national frameworks for technical regulations should be harmo-

Table 7.1 Proposals presented to the Council of Ministers, 1992

NTBs at which proposals aimed	No. of proposals
Technical barriers and harmonisation	78
Veterinary and phytosanitary	83
Financial services and capital market controls	26
Free movement of persons	21
Control of goods	10
Transport	11
Indirect taxation	22
Public procurement	6
Telecommunications	5
Intellectual property	8
Company law	12
Total	282

Source: EC Commission.

nised, so that the need for such frontier controls would be eliminated. Consequently, the removal of physical barriers depended on the removal of technical and fiscal barriers.

Technical barriers

The free movement of goods and services can be hampered by technical regulations, such as differences in health/safety rules and laws governing the technical specifications of products; for example, French law required yellow headlights for all cars sold in France. Trade in services within the EU was also hampered by diverse and often contradictory legal frameworks. Cross-frontier trade in areas such as insurance, banking, transport and other types of services were rendered very difficult due to these diverse legal frameworks. These differences in technical regulations led to increased costs for companies as they had to modify their standard products to enable them to meet the technical regulations of importing countries. In some cases the differences in regulations could prevent cross-frontier trade (for example, trade in banking and insurance services). The White Paper proposed to eliminate these barriers by use of mutual recognition of technical regulations with selective harmonisation of essential factors. Mutual recognition requires member states to accept the technical regulations of all members of the EU providing that traded products fulfil any technical regulations which exist at EU level. Such EU level technical regulations were to be restricted to essential factors in areas connected to technical compatibility and health and safety.

Free movement of labour was restricted by nationality requirements for some public sector jobs, difference in taxation and social security systems, and incompatible education and vocational training and qualifications. These barriers were also to be removed by the use of mutual recognition and selective harmonisation.

Free movement of capital was restricted by exchange controls, barriers to the free movement of financial services and distortions caused by exchange rate fluctuations. The elimination of exchange controls together with EU laws to enable free movement of financial services along with participation in the exchange rate mechanism of the European Monetary System (EMS) were regarded as the appropriate methods of creating the conditions for the free movement of capital (see also Chapters 4–6).

The White Paper identified public procurement practices and the use of state aids as barriers to free movement in a competitive market setting. Public procurement contracts were often explicitly or implicitly restricted to domestic suppliers by the use of laws or by specifying that public sector contracts must comply with national standards. This meant that a large amount of potential trade was hampered by these procurement policies. The White Paper proposed new laws to ensure that most public procurement contracts would be open to tender from any company which was based in the EU. The widespread use of state aids by national governments to protect domestic industries were also regarded as a major impediment to the completion of the SEM (see Chapter 13). The White Paper proposed that the competition policy of the EU should be vigorously applied to eliminate those state aids that were deemed to reduce competition.

Fiscal barriers

Differences in national taxation systems can cause price distortions which may result in obstacles to the reaping of comparative advantage. If goods are exported with VAT and excise duties which prevail in the exporting country, with no adjustment at borders, the price of such goods in the importing country would reflect the rates of tax levied in the supplying country. In cases where there were significant differences in taxation systems, in terms of coverage (i.e., goods' and services' liability to tax) and tax rates, the price of traded goods would be subject to taxation-induced distortions. This problem did not occur in any major way in the EU before the SEM programme because exports were subject to zero rating for VAT and excise duties when they crossed frontiers. In order to operate this system of tax adjustment, it was necessary to have frontier controls to check the claims for refunds of VAT when goods were exported at zero rate and to ensure goods subject to excise duties were indeed exported and therefore were no longer subject to such duties.

The problem of cross-border shopping (buying goods in member states with lower rates of VAT and/or excise duties) was controlled by specifying limits on personal imports and policing this by frontier controls. However, the removal of frontier controls would make this system of adjustment for taxation differences impossible to operate (see Table 7.2 for a summary of VAT differences prevailing the year before the 1992 programme ended).

Table 7.2 VAT rates in the EU, pre-1992

	Standard VAT rate (1991)	*Luxury VAT rate (1991)*
Ireland	23%	—
Denmark	22%	—
Italy	19%	38%
Belgium	19%	25%
France	18.6%	22%
The Netherlands	18.5%	—
Greece	18%	36%
Britain	17.5%	—
Portugal	17%	30%
Germany	14%	—
Spain	12%	33%
Luxumbourg	12%	—

Source: HM Treasury.

The White Paper proposed to eliminate these fiscal barriers by ending the zero rating of VAT on exports and by introducing a system of bonded warehouses with a marking procedure for goods subject to excise duties; therefore, these goods could only be legally sold in the country which imposed the excise duty. Importers would pay VAT at the rate imposed by the exporting country, then they would reclaim the VAT they had paid from their national taxation authorities when they sold the goods. This system would have required an international clearing-house arrangement because some countries in the EU are net importers and/or have lower than average rates of VAT. In these circumstances such countries would refund more VAT on imports than they would receive from VAT on exports. In order to allow this system to operate it was deemed to be necessary to harmonise both the coverage and rates of indirect tax. This was seen to be necessary to avoid problems of cross-border shopping both by personal visits to countries with lower rates of indirect tax and by the use of mail ordering from such countries.

THE CECCHINI REPORT

A report on the economic implications of completing the SEM was published in 1988. This report is commonly called the Cecchini Report. Summaries of this report can be found in Cecchini (1988) and Emerson (1988), while the full report was published by the EC

Table 7.3 The main results of the Cecchini Report

Microeconomic benefits	ECU (bn)	Per cent of GDP	
Removal of frontier controls	9	0.3	
Removal of technical barriers	71	2.4	
Economies of scale	61	2.1	
Reductions in monopoly rents	46	1.6	
Total	187	6.4	
Macroeconomic benefits	GDP (%)	Prices (%)	Employment (m)
Without other measures[a]	4.5	−6.1	1.8
With other measures[b]	7.5	−4.3	5.7

a. Assuming no accompanying macroeconomic measures.
b. Assuming expansion of public investment and/or reductions in taxation made possible because of the savings in the costs of procuring goods and services by governments and the increase in taxation revenues from the growth in GDP which results from the SEM programme. The microeconomic benefits are based on the original six member states plus the UK, at 1985 prices. The macroeconomic benefits are for all 12 member states; 6 years after the full implementation of the SEM programme (assumed to be 1 January 1993). These estimates are subject to a margin of error of ± 30%.

Source: EC Commission (1988b).

Commission (1988b). In order to identify the net benefits that could be expected from the removal of NTBs, the Cecchini Report utilised theoretical schemes somewhat similar, but more complex, to those outlined above. These net benefits were then estimated by use of surveys and also by statistical/econometric estimation. Some rather strong assumptions had to be made about the significance of these NTBs and on the likely impact of removing them. Estimates of the gains from removing NTBs were made for the main sectors in the major member states and then the results were aggregated and extrapolated to provide estimates for the EU as a whole (see also EC Commission, 1990c). The main results of the Cecchini Report are presented in Table 7.3.

The Cecchini Report has been subject to widespread criticism for failing to accurately estimate the net benefits of creating the SEM. The report is accused of being over-optimistic with respect to the possible benefits which are available from economies of scale. This criticism arises from scepticism about the potential for reaping economies of scale from the removal of NTBs and also with regard to the scope for companies to achieve such scale effects. These issues are examined in Figure 7.4.

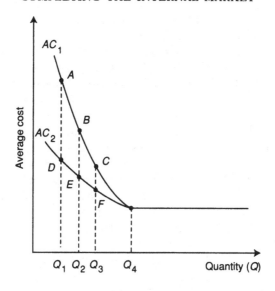

Figure 7.4 Economies of scale under pessimistic and optimistic
assumptions

In Figure 7.4, two possible long-run average cost (AC) curves
are shown: AC_1 and AC_2. The former illustrates, relative to AC_2, a
larger fall in average cost as output is expanded. The output level,
Q_1, refers to the level of sales before the removal of NTBs. Q_2 and
Q_3 refer, respectively, to pessimistic and optimistic estimates of
output after the removal of NTBs and Q_4 indicates the minimum
efficiency scale; that is, the point at which the average cost reaches
its minimum point. If it is assumed that the plant is operating on
AC_1, and the optimistic expansion of output is realised, a reduction
in cost of A to C will be possible; the pessimistic outcome would
lead to a cost reduction equal to A to B. However, if the plant was
operating on AC_2, the reduction in cost would be considerably
lower – from D to F or D to E. If the plant were operating at or
above the output level, Q_4, there would be no cost advantage from
expanding output.

There has also been criticism that the report failed to assess
properly the costs of the restructuring process that would be
induced by the SEM programme. It was assumed that over a
period of six years the unemployed resources would be fully re-
employed in areas where the countries had comparative advantage.

Indeed, Baldwin (1989) has suggested that the restructuring process could result in an increase in the long-run trend rate of growth of the EU. In other words, the SEM programme can be regarded as more than a one-off supply-side boost to the economy. This view is implicitly taken in the Cecchini Report. However, some economists, for example Grahl and Teague (1990) and Culter et al. (1989), have expressed the opinion that, at least for some parts of the EU, the SEM programme could lead to a downward spiral in employment as some companies in the less competitive regions lose market share to more efficient producers in the heartland of the EU (see Chapter 14). If such regions cannot develop new markets they would suffer a decline in income. If labour mobility out of these regions was not sufficient to solve the unemployment created by this process, permanent damage would be inflicted on these regions. The Cecchini Report tends to ignore this 'regional effect' of the SEM programme. This issue is more fully examined in Vickerman (1992).

In general, the report assumed that the SEM programme would be sufficient to ensure the removal of most NTBs and that this process would automatically lead to large-scale changes in trade patterns and, subsequently, to the reconstruction of the economies of the member states. Critical evaluations of the Cecchini Report can be found in Culter et al. (1989), Davies et al. (1989), McKenzie and Venables (1991), McDonald and Dearden (1994) and Swann (1992).

THE POSITION POST-1992

In principle, the SEM programme was technically 'completed' on January 1, 1993. Frontier controls were abolished and most of the proposed legislative changes had by then been adopted by the Council of Ministers. However, in some areas, notably financial services, some major pieces of legislation have not yet been adopted. For example, a directive to allow for cross-frontier trade in life insurance did not come into effect until July 1994. Awareness campaigns have brought the challenges and opportunities of the SEM to the attention of companies. Many companies have responded to this by constructing new strategic plans and some have altered their operational activities and organisational structures by the use of mergers and acquisitions and strategic alliances and by changing their production, marketing and distribution systems (see, for example, Prescott and Welford, 1992; Preston, 1992).

However, the legislative programme is not yet complete and a report by the Commission – the Sutherland Report (see below) – suggests that there may have to be another batch of new legislation before the legal conditions are right for the effective operation of the SEM. Fiscal barriers have not been fully eliminated and the wave of company restructuring was connected to a wide range of factors and the SEM programme may have played only a small part in this process.

The Sutherland Report

This report found that by January 1, 1992, some 264 of the 282 pieces of legislation proposed in the White Paper had been adopted by the Council. However, only 194 directives had been implemented into the national laws of the member states and just 79 had been implemented in all member states. Concern was also expressed about the knowledge of these new laws, especially among small and medium-sized enterprises (SMEs) and consumers. This led to fears that the new laws may not be respected because of this lack of understanding. If the laws are not effectively understood and implemented, it will be very difficult for mutual recognition of technical regulations to be widely accepted. Such a situation would undermine the expected change in trade flows and therefore the restructuring process would be limited because of the relatively small changes in intra-EU trade and the competitive environment.

The report also expressed the view that more legislation was required if the SEM was to operate effectively, particularly in the areas of consumer protection and public procurement. Consumers are unlikely to buy goods and services from companies in other member states when their rights (e.g., if products fail to meet acceptable standards) are not clearly specified. These concerns are likely to be most evident in the purchase of services and in manufactured goods with complex technical characteristics and/or where health and safety aspects are of importance. Concern was also expressed about how effective the laws on public procurement will be in the absence of effective monitoring and policing systems.

The Sutherland Report indicated that there were some short-comings in the legislative programme and in the effectiveness of the implementation of this programme. The report also considered that there were significant problems with regard to the understanding by companies and consumers about the content and importance of the SEM legislation. To ensure the smooth operation of the SEM, new EU laws were deemed to be required, especially in the areas of mutual recognition, consumer protection and public procurement.

The removal of fiscal barriers

The member states could not agree on the harmonisation of VAT and excise duties. However, a compromise agreement was reached to allow for the removal of frontier controls. This agreement required the acceptance of a minimum standard rate of VAT of 15% with a reduced rate of not less than 5%. Permission was also granted to allow for the continuance of exemptions and zero rates for some products. However, exemptions and zero rates could not be introduced or re-introduced if they had been changed by governments. Allowances for personal imports have been greatly expanded and have, in effect, become irrelevant in terms of any meaningful control by national governments. This has already led to a large increase in the personal importation of alcoholic beverages into Britain. Such taxation revenue loss caused by personal importation may limit the willingness of the British government to increase excise duties on alcoholic beverages. An incentive also exists for large increases in mail order shopping from low indirect taxation countries. In the absence of firm agreement on the harmonisation of indirect taxation, it is difficult to see how such a growth in direct mail ordering can be prevented. The problems of cross-border shopping are consequently likely to become more significant as economic agents react to the new opportunities that have been created by the failure to harmonise indirect taxation systems.

The restructuring of companies

That there have been significant changes in the strategies and organisational structures of many companies since the SEM programme began to be implemented is beyond question. Many companies have become more European-oriented in their production, marketing and distribution activities. However, there is no clear evidence at this stage as to the significance of these changes to the logistics chains of companies. The SEM programme has also stimulated foreign direct investment into the EU, particularly from Japan. This issue is examined in Chapter 12.

The *Financial Times* reported, on September 17, 1993, that cross-border merger and acquisition activities in the EU had increased from $23.1bn in 1991 to $42.0bn in 1992. However, in the first half of 1993, the volume of such cross-border merger and acquisition activities had reached only $12.3bn. The recession may have played an important part in the decline in merger and acquisition activities. It is not clear how important the creation of the SEM is as an incentive for merger and acquisition activities. The need to respond to changes in global competitiveness has also stimulated such activities. Reasons such as this seem to have been important in the merger and acquisition activities of European-based companies in the food processing industry, such as Nestlé, Unilever and BSN. They seem to have been influenced not only by the SEM, but also by the need to compete in global terms with large American companies, such as Mars, Philip Morris, Campbell and Kellogg in the branded food products market.

Attempts to rationalise in static or declining markets have been important in promoting strategic alliances such as the joint venture between ICI and Enchem – the European Vinyls Corporation. The fear that deregulation may lead to an increasingly competitive market has also induced some companies to enter into mergers or joint-ventures. This can be most clearly seen in the airline sector. For example, British Airways acquired the French carrier TAT, and KLM, SAS, Swissair and Austrian Airlines have sought to establish strategic alliances. The telecommunications services sector has also witnessed a growth in mergers and strategic alliances in response to the forthcoming privatisation of state-owned companies and moves by the Commission to deregulate this industry.

It is very difficult to ascertain whether the reorganisation of company structures that have taken place since the SEM programme began are due to this programme or to other factors. The report in the *Financial Times* indicated that a series of consolidations are taking place within Europe and that the SEM is an important factor in stimulating such merger and acquisition and strategic alliance activities. However, the privatisation programmes in Germany, France, Italy and Britain, the deregulation of the air travel and telecommunication services industries and the increasingly global competition in many markets may be at least as important in this consolidation process. These issues are explored in Harris and McDonald (1993).

Such consolidation also raises problems with regard to the future competitive environment in the EU. The dynamic benefits from the SEM depend upon creating and sustaining a more competitive environment than that which existed before the SEM programme started. However, it may be necessary to allow some companies to consolidate their positions in order to allow let to take advantage of the opportunities offered by the SEM. Nevertheless, such consolidations may also lead to the growth of market dominance which could lead to the potential for welfare loss resulting from companies abusing their market power. It would appear that the Commission will need to use wisely its powers with respect to the competition policy of the EU (see Chapter 13).

CONCLUSIONS

The SEM programme has moved the EU to a position where a common market among the member states is very nearly complete. However, some barriers and distortions to the effective working of the SEM still exist and these may impede the process of free movement. The Sutherland Report has raised doubts about the effectiveness of EU laws on free movement. Distortions caused by the failure to harmonise fiscal systems within the EU may also limit the effectiveness of the SEM. It is also not clear if the restructuring of the operational and organisational structures of companies was primarily due to the SEM programme or to other factors such as deregulation and the pressures of global competition.

The process of changing trading patterns and the restructuring of company operations in response to the SEM programme has not stopped because the 1992 deadline has been passed. The EU will have to take further steps to create an effective common market; including the removal of the remaining fiscal barriers; new laws on consumer protection; mutual recognition; and the monitoring and policing of the laws on free movement. Companies will continue to respond to the changes that have already been made and to those that will be made to improve the effectiveness of the SEM.

8

AFTER 1992

The Political Economy of the Single European Act

David Whynes

INTRODUCTION

By the mid-1980s, the European Union (EU) remained rather more than a customs union, but rather less than a common market (see also Chapter 7). The former status, entailing the elimination of tariffs and quotas between members and a common trade policy *vis-à-vis* the rest of the world, had been accomplished quite rapidly in the decade following the signing of the Treaty of Rome in 1957. Thereafter, the pace of progress had slowed considerably and the unified market, embodying a standardised legal framework for the conduct of economic affairs and a harmonised taxation and monetary system, seemed simply a pan-European's dream. Successive obstacles to its creation had regularly emerged, including Union enlargement, political disagreement over the long-term goals of the alliance and the severe economic difficulties experienced by all member states during the 1970s.

Beginning in the early 1980s, however, the drive towards the common market received a fresh impetus with a suite of policy proposals referred to simply by a date – '1992'. After their essentially individualistic responses to the economic crises of the 1970s, EU members were, quite simply, looking for something to be European about. In Copenhagen in 1982, a meeting of the European Council made economic unification a high priority, a pledge reiterated at the 1984 meeting (see Chapter 1). In consequence, as the theme of its programme for 1985, the Commission outlined a proposal for market unification within the EU:

> Unifying the market [of 320m] presupposes that member
> states will agree on the abolition of barriers of all kinds,

157

harmonisation of rules, approximation of legislation and tax structures, strengthening of monetary cooperation and the necessary flanking measures to encourage European firms to work together. It is a goal that is well within our reach provided we draw the lessons from the setbacks and delays of the past. The Commission will be asking the European Council to pledge itself to completion of a fully unified internal market by 1992.

(EC Commission, 1985)

The accompanying White Paper, entitled *Completing the Internal Market*, provided operational details of this, the 1992 proposal. The proposal was accepted and the twelve member states approved the 1986 Single European Act (SEA), formally committing themselves to market unification by the appointed date.

In view of the extremely slow progress which many proposals for greater European unity had achieved prior to this time, it is instructive to consider briefly why the 1992 package won such rapid and wholehearted respect. In the first place, much can be attributed to the strong personal advocacy of the then Commission president, Jacques Delors, who campaigned tirelessly for the project. Second, the ideological basis of the proposal was market liberalisation, a philosophy which greatly appealed to the liberal–conservative governments of Britain, Germany and, to some extent, France. Third, the proposal seemed to resolve satisfactorily a Europe-wide search for a new initiative to combat the high and rising levels of unemployment then existing in all member states (so-called 'Eurosclerosis'). Fourth, there was strong and vocal support in most countries on the part of leading industrialists, who viewed the creation of a single market as an expansion of the opportunities for profit. Fifth, the 1992 package gave the appearance of being narrowly and primarily economic; it thus seemed to steer well clear of the emotive political issues involving supra-nationalism and the surrender of national autonomy which had caused similar EU proposals to founder in the past.

A final reason for the rapid enactment of the proposal, and not one of least importance, was its administrative construction; the Commission had certainly 'drawn the lessons from the delays of the past'. The White Paper noted that the attainment of progress in Europe had often been hampered by attempts to develop pre-defined, all-embracing Union-wide targets and by the unanimity requirement in the Council of Ministers. It noted, first, that scope existed within the Treaty for the unanimity requirement to be relaxed to a majority requirement in certain policy areas and an extension of this facility was recommended. Second, it advanced a notion of 'sufficient harmonisation', implying that around a general target individual countries could be permitted a degree of policy idiosyncrasy. Finally, it extended the concept of harmonisation to 'mutual recognition and equivalence'. Thus with respect to a technical standard, for example, members would no longer have to agree on a common EU specification; rather, goods manufactured to the producing country's standards would have to be regarded as acceptable in all other member states (subject to conformity with general EU guidelines). Such easements, embodied in the 1986 SEA, naturally tended to facilitate an increase in enacted legislation.

THE SINGLE EUROPEAN ACT AND THE 1992 PROGRAMME

A unified market is one in which free trade and unimpeded factor mobility prevails and the potential benefits of such a market, including gains from comparative advantage and economies of scale, are easily demonstrated by economic theory (McKenzie and Venables, 1989). The 1986 SEA recognised that, whilst much had already been accomplished towards the creation of a common market within the EU (such as the elimination of internal tariff barriers), a number of obstacles remained. In effect, the SEA charged the Commission with the preparation of directives to member states to eliminate such obstacles. These directives (of which slightly less than 300 were involved in the 1992 package) were statements of required outcome, it being left to members individually to decide how the outcomes could best be achieved in their own contexts and to devise legislation to fulfil their requirements. Thus in Britain, for example, the 1985 Product Liability Directive became the 1987 Consumer Protection Act.

In that they were designed essentially to tidy up a very large number of loose ends, the directives covered an enormous range of subjects, ranging from the manifestly important to the frankly bizarre. However, some order can be imposed if we consider why a free flow of goods and services and factors of production in the EU was being impeded. In the first place there existed a series of technical impediments. Labour mobility, for example, was hampered by the lack of acceptance of the equivalence of training qualifications throughout the Union.

The flow of enterprise was constrained by the existence of twelve different sets of company law, making the formation of truly European companies a near impossibility. Goods made in one country might have been unacceptable to others owing to failure to meet technical specifications (e.g., wavebands for mobile telephones) or health and safety standards (e.g., permissible noise levels, exhaust emissions, food additives). On the principle of mutual recognition, subject to agreed EU standards, the SEA legislated away such technical impediments.

Second, there existed quite obvious fiscal barriers to trade, namely, differential rates of indirect taxation and excise duty which engendered price distortions. It was quite conceivable for low-cost producers in countries with high indirect tax rates to be out-competed by high-cost producers in countries with low tax rates and this was clearly economically perverse. One set of SEA directives involved the harmonisation of tax and duty rates and the establishment of a centralised payments mechanism. Third, and in spite of the removal of tariff barriers, all EU members tended to operate forms of restrictive practice which discriminated against producers in other member countries. Transport industries regularly operated under a quota system, giving preference to national suppliers, and government procurement was rarely put out to tender beyond the boundaries of the country in question. Under the SEA, these restrictive practices were to be eliminated.

The final set of barriers may be termed administrative, an example being the use of non-standardised documentation for import and export which contributed greatly to delays. To deal with this problem the SEA envisaged the use of standardised documentation to cover all intra-EU trade (the Single Administrative Document). Many administrative barriers were manifested at border crossings, although the SEA aimed to standardise customs procedures at these points. In any case, a number of administrative barriers were to be automatically removed by the elimination of the obstacles to trade mentioned above. Thus, products accepted as having been manufactured to a legitimate standard would not require a standards' inspection when crossing frontiers; also, a uniform structure and system of taxation would make this particular aspect of customs checking less significant.

Thus, the 1992 proposals were concerned to remove all these existing barriers, by creating consistent and mutually acceptable standards, by harmonising taxation, by eliminating national restrictive practices and by simplifying administrative procedures. According to a team of enquiry appointed by the Commission, the likely effects over the medium term were to be substantial. In their report (see Cecchini, 1988), the team classified expected future economic benefits under four main headings. In the first place, the easing of customs formalities and the streamlining of administrative procedures was expected to engender a price fall in traded goods owing to the elimination of excess costs (bureaucracy, border delays and complications arising). Price falls would precipitate demand and output rises and thus stimulate employment. The EU's overall balance of payments position was expected to improve, because demand for imports would fall with domestic price falls whilst demand for exports would rise.

Second, the liberalisation of public procurement would lead to falls in purchasing costs owing to enhanced competition between suppliers. Governments would then be able either to allocate the saved resources to other growth-inducing activities or to cut taxes, thereby stimulating consumer demand. Third, the harmonisation of regulations and procedures in the financial sector in particular would, via the creation of a truly European financial market and increased competition, lower the cost of credit. Public and private borrowing would become cheaper, leading to increased consumer demand and investment. Finally, a larger, more open and more competitive internal market could be expected to give rise to the aggregate supply-side effect of increased productive efficiency. Efficiency means lower costs and lower prices which, in turn, stimulate supply and demand. The harmonisation of standards was to be significant here, ensuring that the potential market was indeed 320 million people, thereby permitting economies of scale to be reaped in abundance. Overall, the '1992 effect' on EU prices was estimated to be a 6% fall, giving rise to output growth approaching 5% and an employment increase approaching 2 million across the EU.

THE ROCKY ROAD TO 1992

In common with all economic predictions, those given above were conjectural. As the expected price fall was the driving force behind the demand and supply growth, much would depend upon its precise extent and the speed of behavioural responses. Although these broad outcomes remained well in the future, some direct consequences of the 1992 programme soon emerged at the micro-level. By the late 1980s, a not insubstantial industry had set itself up in all member states to prepare entrepreneurs for 1992, entailing the imparting of language, legal and management skills. There was also a merger boom amongst small and medium-sized firms throughout Europe, merger being an effective method of obtaining increased capacity and trans-European market penetration in the brief period of time available before the unified market became established. It now seems clear that the anticipation of the single market contributed generally to an acceleration of European trade and investment during the late 1980s (but see Chapter 12).

All this having been said, 1992 was not quite so straightforward as some of its advocates apparently believed. To begin with, as the date approached, it became abundantly clear that, whenever 1992 was going to happen, it was not going to be in 1992. With the benefit of hindsight, it is now evident that the great majority (perhaps 95%) of the 300-odd directives had indeed been adopted by the Commission by the beginning of 1993. However, less than half of the 1992 programme had actually been translated into the legislations of the twelve national governments by that time (Barber, 1993). Even prior to the magic date, the simultaneous appearance in twelve statute books of laws embodying all the directives was logistically inconceivable. Put another way, that which happened by 1992 was not quite the same as that which was ostensibly intended. In fairness, however, this should not be too surprising because to have expected completion by the specified date would have been to misunderstand the nature of the exercise. The White Paper itself concluded as follows:

> Europe stands at the crossroads. We either go ahead – with resolution and determination – or we drop back into mediocrity. . . . What this White Paper proposes is that the Union should now take a further step along the road so clearly delineated in the Treaties. To do less would be to fall short of the ambitions of the founders of the Union . . . it would be to betray the trust invested in us. . . . That is the measure of the challenge facing us. Let it never be said that we were incapable of rising to it.
>
> (EC Commission, 1985)

This is rhetoric with a familiar ring and it has much in common with that accompanying indicative planning in the 1960s. The real purpose of the exercise was unambiguously to 'bounce' the members of the EU, to get things moving at an urgent pace by creating a sense of purpose with an imminent time horizon and a high public profile. Bouncing works by committing people and by sweeping them along with events. Without urgency, without deadlines, without positive involvement reinforced by the strength and momentum of a cause, no one feels the need to do anything. The year 1992 was clearly an attempt to reawaken a Europeanism which had lain dormant since the 1950s.

Turning to more specific matters, the harmonisation of taxation rates and excise duties along the lines suggested in the White Paper proved an immense stumbling block and a great many voices were raised in dissent. That this would inevitably have been the case can be seen immediately one considers the variation in VAT practices across member states by the end of the 1980s (see Table 7.2). All members, for example, had both a low-rate band (0–15%) and a standard band (12–25%); six, however, had an additional high-rate band (25–38%). Within these bands, specific rates differed between countries, some countries having multiple rates within a given band (Bos and Nelson, 1988). There was not, moreover, complete consistency across the membership of band classification for given commodities. Excise duties also varied enormously – beer, for example, was taxed at ECU 0.03 per litre in France and ECU 1.13 per litre in Ireland, whilst petrol duties per litre ranged from ECU 0.2 in Spain to ECU 0.53 in Italy (Smith, 1988). The 1992 proposals initially aimed at a harmonisation tending towards the Union average for tax rates and duties. Thus the suggested low rate for VAT became 4–9%, the standard band becoming 14–20% (the higher band was intended to be abandoned). Beer and petrol duties were to be harmonised at ECU 0.17 and ECU 0.34 per litre respectively, other duties following a similar averaging procedure.

Of the twelve member states only Germany operated with VAT rates in line with the original 1992 proposal (7% and 14%); all others would have been obliged to revise their rates and the scope for resistance was considerable. Countries required to move one or both of their rates upwards were concerned about the inflationary impact of such a movement. Countries whose low rates were too low or whose high rates were too high argued that harmonisation would precipitate adverse distribution consequences (lower rates generally being applied to necessities and higher rates to luxuries). Consequent increases in the cost of living on the part of the poorer groups in an economy would require compensation in the form of increased public spending, which would conflict with other national policy objectives. Governments required to lower their tax rates were concerned about the tax revenue and inflationary implications; those required to raise rates were concerned about domestic employment and, again, inflation.

Broadly equivalent remarks were made with respect to the harmonisation of duties. In the case of Britain, for example, alcohol and tobacco duties would have had to fall considerably to meet the 1992 targets (a requirement guaranteed to strike terror into the heart of any British Chancellor on Budget Day). In addition to the uncertain tax revenue implications, duty falls would have entailed price decreases and demand increases with consequences for public health. Increases in tobacco and alcohol consumption as a result of duty harmonisation were estimated at 4% and 39% respectively, which would have been likely to further increase the cost – several billion pounds annually – of treating the adverse health consequences of the consumption of such commodities (Appleby, 1988).

In order to prevent the VAT/excise controversy from destroying the momentum of the 1992 initiative, the Commission was soon obliged to signal the possibility of a greater degree of flexibility in this area. In 1989, Christiane Scrivener, the commissioner responsible for fiscal harmonisation, announced the abandonment of an upper ceiling on VAT rates and suggested that ways might be found of retaining the option of a zero VAT rate (as employed in Britain). The proposal for a common rate of excise duty was judged to have been misguided and revised policies on this matter were prepared (*The Economist*, 1989a). As events transpired, 1993 opened with a complex provisional VAT agreement, intended to ameliorate price distortions across borders. By that time, an agreement had been reached to set a minimum standard VAT rate at 15% and Germany, having been the model for the original VAT proposals, now emerged as the main deviant in this respect. A final agreement on VAT harmonisation has now been deferred until 1997, subject to a consensus being forthcoming.

Although flexibility might have been a necessary strategy to ensure compliance on the part of member states, it is not without its pitfalls with respect to the longer term. Assuming that the high degree of VAT flexibility will be retained in the future, the price distortions (which 1992 was trying to eliminate) will remain. Possibly internal competition might force rates into line (always assuming that such a competitive environment actually comes to prevail) although, if differential tax rates actually do represent major trade barriers (as they will if everything else is harmonised), then it will be the economically strong members of the EU which determine the final outcome. The combination of an open market with large disparities in duties would also tend, in the long run, to produce duty harmonisation. In the short term, however, we should anticipate substantial exportation from low-duty to high-duty countries. Individual states might well view this with disfavour on market protection (e.g., indigenous wine industry) and public health grounds. Many EU countries have persistently campaigned for the retention of a controlled market in dutiable commodities which, of course, hardly squares with the intentions of the 1992 proposals.

One aspect of the 1992 package frequently overlooked at the time was its 'social dimension', which embraced a series of policies specifically concerned with the implications for labour of the creation of a unified market (see Chapter 10). ECU 50bn were initially committed to cover the dislocation costs of structural adjustment (e.g., factory closures) but negotiations still continue on common health and safety standards at work, a European social charter (enshrining rights to social security, trade union membership, equal pay and rights to company information) and, most controversial of all, a European company statute incorporating worker participation in management. Some degree of long-term harmonisation on this issue is naturally vital to ensure the operation of fair competition within the EU, because firms operating with low safety standards and paying non-union or discriminatory wages would incur lower production costs and be in a position to undercut their more scrupulous rivals (a phenomenon known as 'social dumping'). Whilst member states agree on the objective of the social dimension, however, there remain wide differences about how such a suite of policies should be enforced. For example, the views of the former British prime minister, Mrs Thatcher, in 1988 – 'We emphatically do not need new regulations which raise the cost of employment and make Europe's labour market less flexible' (*The Economist*, 1989b) – do not appear to vary from those of her successor, Mr Major.

This social dimension is, in principle, an issue of enormous political weight. It is evident that, at the present stage of the proceedings, it has not been fully thought through and a great deal remains to be accomplished. Similar remarks can be made about monopoly policy (see also Chapter 13). EU monopoly policy remains rudimentary and relies heavily on individual monopoly and cartel control in member states. However, we have already noted that one of the most immediate effects of the 1992 programme was a merger boom, a trend which can only continue with the harmonisation of company law, the liberalisation of financial markets and increased factor mobility. Basic economic theory predicts that a likely outcome of a free competitive process is monopoly control and collusion, especially where the gains from economies of scale are substantial and the 1992 programme means that the environment for competitive battles to create monopolies will be improved. Other than its proposals to control very large mergers (*The Economist*, 1989a), the Commission has yet to develop an operational strategy to deal with Euro-monopolies. Were such monopolies to arise in the medium term they could well exert their powers in such a way as to nullify the economic gains to be brought about by price reductions.

THE LONG-TERM IMPLICATIONS OF 1992

Irrespective of the caveats noted above, it goes without saying that something recognisable as the creation of a unified market has happened and continues to happen. It is equally evident that, in its attempts to meet its own deadline, the EU was obliged to dilute some of the original proposals and to delay the implementation of others; many of the elements of the 1992 programme are unlikely to be effected until well into the next century. Accordingly, there has not been a sudden shift between 1992 and the years immediately following; the transition over time will be gradual. The most immediate impact over the next decade is likely to be felt in the financial and transport sectors. Finance capital is extremely mobile and is capable of responding almost instantly to regulatory changes – this proposition is evidenced by the profound changes in the London financial markets following deregulation in 1986. Variable capital in the transport industry (e.g., lorries, railway rolling stock) is likewise easily enhanced although fixed capital (e.g., roads, rail tracks) will prove more problematic. Furthermore, competitive pressure within the EU is certain to increase as a result of the 1992 package and this will lead, with equal certainty, to localised problems of structural adjustment. The most successful firms will be those which can merge or otherwise grow to a size sufficient to reap the economies of scale available in the extended market. The concentration of production is also likely to increase, for similar reasons.

Over the longer term, two implications of 1992 will be of particular interest. The first concerns the relationship of the EU to other trading economies. Ever since its formation, the Union has been viewed by outsiders in a dual light (see Chapter 1). On the one hand, the EU is an evolving giant economy, representing enhanced opportunities to foreign traders; trading with Europe offers better prospects than trading with any single European country. On the other hand, increasing economic integration threatens to strengthen 'Fortress Europe', a self-contained, insular and protected economic unit becoming increasingly impenetrable to foreign economies. The 1992 programme seemed set to enhance the depth of the dilemma – Europe was becoming more tempting as a market, but harder to penetrate owing to increased internal competition and external tariff protection.

The strategies of the Japanese economy with respect to the EU in recent years are instructive on this point (see also Chapter 12). Finding certain of their exports priced out of the market by penal duties, Japanese manufacturers began to move product assembly into Europe (Heitger and Stehn, 1990). In 1987, the EU responded by imposing rules of local content, requiring that, for duty to be waived, a proportion of the value of the final product had to be added using local resources. Since then there have been calls within the EU to increase this proportion, from the original 40% towards 70–80%, entailing a far more substantial employment of EU resources by Japanese companies. By 1990, the Commission had begun to consider even more stringent rules of origin requiring, in effect, not merely the transfer of capital from Japan to the EU, but the transfer of technology. In the case in point, semiconductors were considered to be only EU products (and thus exempt from duty and/or permitted entry) if the diffusion process (etching) took place locally (*The Economist*, 1989c).

In global terms, the EU is prosperous and, following 1992, gives every sign of becoming more so. It is not an economy, therefore, that the rest of the world can afford to ignore, as is evidenced by the fact that it can now seriously contemplate the extraction of substantial gains in the form of employment and investment from Japanese producers. Naturally, the Japanese do not regard the enhanced bargaining strength of the EU with a great deal of enthusiasm but, *in extremis*, they do not have a great deal of choice. Broadly similar remarks can be made with respect to the United States. Closer to home, non-EU economies elsewhere in Europe were already anticipating the effects of 1992 well before the implementation date. In 1989, EFTA proposed talks on closer EFTA/EU cooperation (which culminated in the creation of the European Economic Area in January 1994) and almost all the EFTA members subsequently announced their intention of applying for EU membership (*The Economist*, 1989d); see Chapter 9 for details. Such behaviour would seem to have indicated a global perception of 1992 as strengthening the walls of 'Fortress Europe', the appropriate strategy being to get within them.

The second implication of 1992 concerns the future style and scope of domestic policymaking. The 1992 programme can be seen as further evidence of a shift in economic and political power away from national governments and towards the central EU institutions. The SEA directives were no longer negotiable at a national level and the proposals implied the removal of certain conventional economic management tools from the hands of national governments. This was especially evident in the case of the tax/duty harmonisation proposals and, one suspects, forms one reason why that element of the package caused such widespread consternation. Further, the creation of a liberalised market in loanable funds severely constrains any independent monetary policy on the part of a national government (see Chapters 4–6).

It seems clear that the very momentum of the 1992 programme into the future must inevitably bring pressure to bear on economies who might attempt to continue an independent stance. For example, any country whose tax rates are consistently and significantly out of line with those of its partners will find itself at an economic disadvantage, being less able to compete. Britain's negative attitude to the monetary union appears to represent a particular obstacle in this respect. The full logic of 1992 requires a coherent monetary system (in the limit, monetary union) to prevent distortions and uncertainty in prices and to facilitate capital flows. Participating members will gain in these respects and non-participants will not. Such an asymmetry of benefits and costs will increase the pressure on deviant nations to conform to the norm.

CONCLUSIONS

Even from the time of the first visions of a united Europe, during World War II, the destination of the EU has been negotiable. One obvious tension has been between those who have seen the Union as an inter-governmental association of nation states and those who have viewed it as a step on the way towards the 'United States of Europe'. In terms of this polarity, the initial acceptance of the 1992 package was a clear victory for the pan-Europeans. More importantly, 1992 involved policy outcomes which, had they been fully realised, would have acted as a major force predisposing Europe towards continuing in that direction into the future. That this was appreciated within the Union could be seen by the opposition to the Delors faction on the part of those unhappy both with the implied consequence and with the Commission's overtly interventionist approach to liberalisation (see *The Economist*, 1989e). Clearly, in its ultimate manifestation, 1992 limited choices, both from the point of view of member states equivocal about their positions in Europe and of those outside the Union. In most respects, therefore, the precise details of the 1992 package, whether or not a specific piece of legislation was enacted by a certain date and the estimation of the economic benefits following fuller integration, are of far less significance than the overall tenor of the movement. The year 1992 was a crusade and crusades are never subject to a naïve economic calculus.

9

THE ECONOMIC IMPLICATIONS OF ENLARGING THE EUROPEAN UNION

Valerio Lintner

INTRODUCTION

Up to the early 1980s, it is probably fair to say that the issue of enlarging the European Union (EU) came to prominence only at times when the Union was actually busy absorbing new members, notably when the original six became 'the Nine' and when the Nine then incorporated the three Mediterranean states of Greece, Spain and Portugal to become the present EU of twelve. This 'widening' of the EU has always been, of course, of importance to its development in the sense that membership of the club was being increased, but during its early development most of the attention of the EU was probably concentrated on 'deepening' the Union; i.e., completing the customs union and the common market, developing common policies such as the Common Agricultural Policy (CAP) and regional policy and generally promoting economic convergence and monetary and political integration among the existing members.

More recently, however, enlargement has moved to the very centre of the EU's agenda. Recent events in Europe and elsewhere have called into question the whole direction in which the EU should develop and there is considerable debate as to whether the emphasis should be on widening, on deepening, or indeed on both in equal measure. The renewed interest in widening has resulted from a number of developments, principally:

1 the emergence of new independent states in eastern Europe following the collapse of the Soviet empire after 1989. These states are almost universally eager to cement their newly

acquired pluralist democratic systems and to embrace western capitalism as a means of securing greater material prosperity. They regard membership of the EU as the principal means of securing these objectives;

2 the increasing tendency for the deepening process to run out of steam. The middle and late 1980s were years of rapid development of the EU, with the 1992 programme and the moves towards monetary union contained in the Delors Report and the Maastricht Treaty. With the recession of the early 1990s and the economic problems caused by German unification, there has been a tendency for many European citizens and some European nation states to retrench and question the whole concept of further integration and the shape that this should take (see Chapter 1);

3 the increasing economic interdependence, or globalisation, that has resulted from expanding trade and vastly increased capital mobility. This has resulted in losses of real economic sovereignty (the ability of individual nation states to control their own economic affairs independently of events and policies in other nations), particularly among small and medium-sized European nation states. Many of these states have come to regard membership of the EU and the pooling of sovereignty that this involves as the only realistic means of maintaining control over their economic (and, indeed, political) destinies;

4 the temptation to use widening as a tactical weapon designed to slow down the deepening process. This has arguably been the British position over the last few years, culminating in its insistence on pushing forward the widening process at the Edinburgh Summit of December 1992;

5 the increasing tendency for the EU to be regarded as a vehicle for the provision of security in the context of the increasingly insecure world that has emerged from the upheavals of 1989; and

6 the trade gains and scale economies inherent in an expanded European market, particularly in the context of ever-increasing competition from newly industrialised countries (NICs) and of the increasing propensity for the world to operate in trading blocs, have proved attractive to countries, particularly those of the EFTA bloc. This process has of course been accelerated by the '1992' programme for the completion of the internal market

and can be seen as in many ways a defensive posture on the part of applicants to avoid being 'frozen out' of the EU trading bloc.

These factors have led to the emergence of a long list of applicants and potential applicants, the process of widening having been accelerated by the decision taken at the European Council held in Edinburgh in December 1992 to begin accession negotiations with the EFTA applicants at the beginning of 1993, thus removing the previous insistence that negotiations could not begin until the Maastricht Treaty had been ratified.

This, then, is the context within which this chapter is written. The second part of the chapter will outline the light that the economic theory of integration can shed on the likely effects of enlargement. The third part briefly surveys the nature and impact of previous enlargements, with particular reference to the entry of Britain. The following section will look at the situation with current and possible future applicants, while some conclusions will be presented in the final part. It should be noted from the outset that the motivation for and the impact of enlargement is not just, or often even primarily, to do with economics. To fully understand the issues here one has to additionally consider political and strategic factors.

THE ECONOMICS OF ENLARGEMENT: SOME THEORETICAL ASPECTS

Membership of the EU involves complete acceptance of the 'Acquis Communautaire'; i.e., the full diet of the Union's rules and legislation. The implications of membership are thus numerous and not all of them have an overtly economic dimension. From a strictly economic point of view and starting from the albeit unlikely assumption that there are no associations or other agreements prior to the enlargement, the main aspects of membership are:

1 membership of the customs union, which involves acceptance of internal free trade and adoption of the common trade policy *vis-à-vis* the rest of the world;

2 the common market aspect of the EU, which involves acceptance of the free movement of labour and capital within the EU. These first two aspects involve accepting all or most of the battery of standardisation and harmonisation measures which

form part of the '1992' programme to complete the internal market. These include the removal of frontiers, the adoption of common standards, accepting the principle of mutual recognition, new competitive rules on public procurement, the end of state monopolies, fiscal harmonisation, limits on industrial subsidies, etc. The costs here will include a surrender of economic and political sovereignty, to the extent that control over decisions such as whether to charge VAT on books or whether to operate state monopolies for tobacco and alcohol may be lost;

3 participation in the common policies of the EU, notably the CAP (Chapter 11), regional policy (Chapter 14), industrial and competition policy (Chapter 13) and social policy (Chapter 10). These policies are financed from the EU's budget, towards which new members have to make contributions in the form of customs revenues, a proportion of VAT receipts and a (at present small) payment related to gross domestic product (GDP); and

4 participation in moves towards full monetary union, although the prospects for this aspect of integration look dubious in the sense that the Maastricht Treaty is unlikely to be implemented in anything like its present form within the timetable envisaged. Nevertheless it is clear that the process has advanced to a significant extent over the last few years and will in all probability regain momentum at some time in the future.

These economic implications of EU membership have all to be taken into consideration when assessing the impact of an enlargement. An important dimension of assessing the impact of an enlargement concerns the question: effects on whom? For the distribution of any gains or losses will naturally be of considerable significance. In this context the approach adopted here is broadly to examine the economic effects of enlargement from three separate perspectives: the overall economic effects, the effects on applicant countries and the effects on existing members.

If we begin by examining the overall trade effects of an enlargement, then from a strictly neoclassical perspective what we are essentially concerned with is whether the enlargement is on balance a 'trade-creating' one or a 'trade-diverting' one (see Chapters 1 and 7). The factors that will determine the outcome are complex, but the following are likely to be of particular importance:

1 whether the structure of the traded goods and services sector of the entrant is competitive (overlapping) or complementary (dissimilar) *vis-à-vis* that of existing members. In general, competitive structures are more likely to result in welfare-enhancing trade creation; i.e., the displacement following enlargement of more expensive and less efficiently produced domestic goods and services by cheaper and more efficiently produced products from a customs union partner. Complementary structures, on the other hand, are more likely to result in trade diversion; i.e., the displacement of cheap and efficiently produced third country products by less efficiently produced partner products;

2 differences in costs of production between the entrant and existing members. In general, the greater the difference in costs, the more scope for trade creation and vice versa; and

3 the effect that enlargement has on tariffs and non-tariff-barriers (NTBs). If, on balance, it leads to an increase in tariff levels, then trade diversion is likely to be the result. On the other hand, if the enlargement results in an overall reduction in tariffs, then trade creation is more likely. NB, for a fuller treatment of the theory of customs unions and other aspects of the theory of integration, see, for example, Lintner and Mazey (1991).

Additionally, one has to consider the so-called 'dynamic' customs union effects of an enlargement. These consist principally of the possibility of exploiting economies of scale as a result of the growth of firm size that typically accompanies the change in the international division of labour following accession to a customs union. Clearly, these will depend on the scope for scale economies in the industries that are likely to grow in size after enlargement and the extent to which exclusion from the EU is, in fact, a barrier to their exploitation. Of some significance in this context is also the increased power that a larger EU is able to wield on the international trading scene and on its own terms of trade. Customs unions of increased size have more power to influence world market prices for the commodities they import and can thus better engineer increases in their own welfare by imposing (optimum) tariffs that cut imports and thus world prices (Johnson, 1965). This, it should be noted, can only be achieved at the expense of other countries and thus constitutes a classic 'beggar-thy-neighbour' policy.

In one way or another, what the above amounts to is the fact that enlargements are more likely to prove welfare-enhancing and thus desirable from a trade and welfare point of view when they involve the incorporation of countries whose economies are similar to those of existing members, which would explain why regional trade groupings tend to involve predominantly countries at similar stages of economic development. Conversely, one could argue that enlargement involving the accession and assimilation of dissimilar economies will tend to be more problematic. A further consideration here involves enlargements that encompass several states whose economies are similar to one another, but different from those of existing members. Here there may be scope for trade creation and welfare enhancement between the new members themselves and this may offset any losses that arise from relations with existing members.

If one then considers the trade effects from the specific point of view of the entrant(s) and/or existing members, then clearly the major considerations that will determine the distribution of the trade effects of enlargement and whether they will on balance be favourable to each party will be:

1 the extent to which accession results in the opening of domestic markets to competition from new partners and the extent to which domestic firms have enhanced access to partner markets. Put another way, the extent to which these markets were protected prior to accession;
2 (most crucially) the competitiveness of domestic firms in the traded goods and services sector *vis-à-vis* similar firms in partner countries;
3 the extent of trade diversion which results; i.e., the extent to which production from new partners competes with current imports from third countries; and
4 the dynamic response on the part of domestic firms to the competition from existing members.

The danger from the point of view of less economically developed entrants is that the welfare gains from entry may be skewed in favour of more advanced and competitive existing members. This is likely to happen if there are insufficient competitive industries in the acceding countries. What may ensue in this case is a transfer of economic activity from new entrants to existing members; i.e., an export of jobs and increased domestic unemployment. In this context, the length and nature of any transition period will be critical, as well as the dynamic response of domestic producers to competition; that is, the extent to which these respond to new challenges by becoming more efficient and developing new products that are in demand in existing member states.

From the point of view of existing members, enlargement may offer new markets for their industrial and other products, as well as cheap and secure sources of certain raw materials and primary products, but may also pose a threat to the extent that entrants are able to compete in existing domestic and EU markets in, for example, agricultural products. From a neoclassical perspective, the effect of the factor mobility aspect of EU membership can be shown to be welfare enhancing. Free movement will lead to labour and (particularly) capital moving to where it is most productive, thus improving the allocation of resources (but see Chapter 14). From the point of view of existing members this may result in gains from an increased supply of cheap migrant labour, although realistically the current importance of this is doubtful in the context of the high unemployment which the EU is now suffering.

The potential problem here again concerns distribution, needless to say to the possible detriment of any less advanced new entrants. Neoclassical theory would suggest that the free movement of factors tends to equalise factor earnings and thus lead to economic convergence between existing members and new entrants. However, the radical critique of this approach, pioneered in the 1950s by the Swedish economist Gunnar Myrdal, would suggest that the free movement of capital will tend to exacerbate national and regional differences in real income and welfare by causing a 'Polarisation Effect' by means of a process of 'Cumulative Causation' (Myrdal, 1957).

Broadly, the inflow of capital into areas where its marginal product is greatest may set in motion a dynamic process that reinforces the attractiveness of these areas at the expense of less prosperous ones. Thus, the more developed parts of existing member states grow in prosperity and attract more and more capital, while poorer entrants are gradually relatively pauperised. The free movement of labour may lead to similar effects, since it is the people with the greatest amount of human capital and enterprise who are typically the most mobile. There may be a flow of capital from the prosperous economic centre towards poorer new entrants, but this is unlikely to compensate for the polarisation effects. It is very difficult to test this hypothesis empirically, but it should at the very least serve as a salutary warning to the queue of potential EU applicants and potential applicants from eastern Europe and the Mediterranean area.

The impact of participation in the EU's common policies is, of course, likely to be dominated by the entrant's relationship with the CAP and, to a lesser extent, its claims on the EU's structural funds, particularly the European Regional Development Fund. The impact of the CAP on entrants will be determined by the size and competitiveness of their agricultural sectors, the agricultural support regime prior to entry and the extent to which, after entry, the price support mechanism covers the range of products they produce (see Chapter 11). The latter is likely to be largely determined by the political process in the EU and thus the degree of influence that the entrant wields at this level becomes crucial. A possibility is that prices to consumers will increase as a result of the CAP's system of subsidising agriculture via the price mechanism and of protecting the sector from foreign competition by means of tariffs (the Variable Levy). Claims on the structural funds will be determined by the objective needs of the entrant in terms of regional imbalances, but also by their influence in the EU's political process.

Entrants will have to contribute to the EU's budget. The budgetary implications of membership will depend on the extent to which contributions outweigh receipts from the budget or vice versa. This, in turn, will be largely a function of an entrant's success in obtaining funds from the CAP and the structural funds. The hope on the part of eastern European and the Mediterranean applicants is that the balance here will be favourable, but even if this proves to be the case, the overall impact is unlikely to be of excessive significance given the relatively modest size of the EU budget. In any case, entrants will have to compete with politically powerful existing members for the limited redistribution funds available to the EU. A more likely scenario is that the CAP and the EU's structural funds may be thrown into disarray by the absorption of relatively poor entrants with large agricultural sectors. A further problem may arise for existing members if the entrants can compete effectively in certain agricultural markets.

The impact of monetary integration concerns primarily the fact that integration in this area involves the most visible losses of economic sovereignty, since it involves surrender over key aspects of monetary and other macroeconomic tools and objectives, for example interest rates and the exchange rate. The importance of this will be determined by the extent to which such sovereignty exists in the first place in an increasingly interdependent world characterised by high levels of capital mobility (see Chapter 2). Also, monetary integration may involve accepting economic leadership from strong existing members. This may be advantageous or otherwise for new members, depending on the quality of the leadership available and the extent to which the economic philosophies and policies imposed by the leaders are appropriate to the needs of acceding countries. From the point of view of existing members, enlargement may exacerbate the problems involved in achieving the economic convergence required for monetary union or indeed other less ambitious forms of monetary cooperation.

Finally, it is worth noting that there may be economic benefits for new entrants from a variety of other sources, such as demonstration effects, spillover effects and an increased ability to attract Japanese, US and other direct investment (or indeed increased prospects of maintaining current levels of multinational activity in the domestic economy) – see Chapter 12. The likely extent of these is probably impossible to estimate.

ENLARGEMENT IN PRACTICE: FROM THE 'SIX' TO THE 'TWELVE'

Having outlined some theoretical aspects of the economics of EU enlargement, we can now apply these to examining the experience of the EU in practice. The original Union of six countries (West Germany, France, Italy, Belgium, the Netherlands and Luxembourg) remained in place from March 1957, when the Treaty of Rome was signed, until 1973 when the United Kingdom, Ireland and Denmark became members and thus completed the first enlargement of the EU. The second phase of enlargements, usually referred to as the 'southern enlargement', involved the absorption of Greece (in 1981) and the Iberian states of Spain and Portugal (in 1986).

In many ways, the first enlargement was eminently logical from an economic point of view. It mainly involved countries (Britain and Denmark) that were at roughly the same stage of economic development as the existing members and whose production and consumption patterns were broadly compatible with those of the original six. Ireland was somewhat different, being less wealthy and having a relatively large agricultural sector. But then Ireland is a small country whose needs could be accommodated with relative ease and which could hope to benefit from the CAP, redistributive EU expenditures and the increased foreign direct investment that membership might produce. In any case, the original EU six had hardly been a completely homogeneous grouping and agricultural areas such as the Italian Mezzogiorno had been accommodated with some success. The main economic effects of enlargement at this stage of European integration concerned trade and to a lesser extent the CAP and the EU budget. The overall economic effects were thus likely to be positive and what empirical work is available tends to confirm this.

If the global economic effects of Britain's entry were favourable, from a purely British perspective the economic impact of membership has been less clear cut – once again the issue of distribution rears its head. It is beyond the scope of this chapter to examine Britain's economic experience within the EU in detail – see El-Agraa (1983) or EC Commission (1983) for fuller accounts of this – but the economic impact of accession essentially consisted of:

1 the costs involved in joining the CAP. These included considerably higher food prices as a result of abandoning the 'deficiency payments' system of duty-free imports allied to subsidy of domestic agriculture directly from the exchequer. In addition, Britain had to abandon the highly favourable deals that had been struck with food suppliers from the Commonwealth. In fact, food prices in Britain increased by something like 300% in the decade between 1971 and 1981, partly no doubt reflecting increased world food prices during this period, while the Labour Party estimated that in the late 1980s every family was paying £13.50 each week to finance the CAP (Labour Party, 1989). The indirect impact of the CAP on employment has also been considerable. The best estimates suggest a job loss of around 860,000 in the largest four EU countries with Britain and Germany suffering most severely, as the result of a loss of potential gross output of between 1.1% and 2.5% (and between 4.4% and 6.2% of exports in manufacturing industries) in these countries (Demekas, 1988). The costs of the CAP have furthermore included the net budgetary contributions that resulted from Britain's small agricultural industry (employing approximately only 2.5% of the population) in the context of a CAP

that accounted for over 70% of EU expenditure and which resulted in the much publicised haggling over British rebates that took place during the early Thatcher administrations; and

2 the effects on British trade and production. These are again hard to estimate, since it is difficult to isolate the EU effect from other influences, such as long-term trends of falling competitiveness and inappropriate economic policies, on the British position. Nevertheless, the best estimates tend to suggest that membership of the EU reduced British output of manufactures and significantly worsened the trade balance in this area. Winters (1987) suggests that the loss of output that resulted from accession was at least £3bn (1.5% of gross domestic product), but that these losses might well have been outweighed by gains in welfare enjoyed by British consumers as a result of cheaper imports from EU partners.

These 'impact costs' were to an extent foreseen and were expected to be outweighed by longer-term 'dynamic' gains. For example, it may well be that membership has helped Britain to attract a greater amount of foreign direct investment from the United States, Japan and elsewhere. The overall impact of accession is impossible to quantify and is in any case largely immaterial, given that there is now no prospect of Britain withdrawing from the EU.

The southern enlargement was more problematic, involving as it did countries at a less advanced stage of economic development, with largely complementary productive structures and large agricultural sectors. On the other hand, there was the possibility of some welfare-enhancing trade creation between the new entrants themselves, given the competitive nature of their productive structures. This phase of the EU's development was, as ever, probably more motivated by political factors: the need to defend newly acquired pluralist democracies and the desire to integrate key parts of 'the soft underbelly of Europe' into the NATO block. For a full treatment of the southern enlargement, see Tsoukalis (1991).

Greece, in fact experienced severe difficulties in integrating its relatively weak industrial sector into the EU, despite a lengthy transition period. There was some internal pressure for withdrawal for a period, but on the whole the evidence seems to suggest that the impact of membership on the Greek economy has been positive and that it has been a net beneficiary from the CAP (Yannopoulos, 1986). In addition, Greece has benefited from the structural funds and in particular the Integrated Mediterranean Programmes. From the point of view of existing members, it is probably fair to say that the impact of Greek entry on the CAP has been contained, partly by excluding a proportion of Greek products from the price support mechanism (Nicholson and East, 1987). However, the Greek economy remains weak and its economic divergence from the rest of the EU has been a major problem in the context of recent moves towards monetary union (see Chapter 5).

Spain's entry was potentially extremely difficult, given that it had been a closed economy under the dictatorship of General Franco and that its productivity and quality standards had been well below those in the rest of the EU. In addition, Spain's agricultural sector threatened to exacerbate CAP surpluses, its olive oil output, for example, being greater than the rest of the EU put together. Nevertheless, the country has been integrated into the EU relatively painlessly and membership has proved to be a success. Spanish growth rates have been very rapid and its industrial sector in particular has grown impressively with the help of investment from the rest of the EU. Partly because of this, fears of large-scale labour migration into northern member states have proved to be unfounded. Portugal had more established links with the world trading system, having been a member of EFTA and having had traditional links with Britain. On the other hand, Portugal has the lowest per capita income in the EU (see Chapter 1) and low levels of productivity, particularly in agriculture. Portuguese membership has probably not been as great a success as that of Spain, but the worst fears of industrial decimation have yet to materialise.

In summary, we can conclude that, to date, enlargement has been broadly successful from an economic point of view and that the worst potential problems have been avoided. The distribution of any economic gains has been, however, less clear.

THE NEW APPLICANTS AND POTENTIAL APPLICANTS

As has been mentioned, the early 1990s has seen a veritable explosion in the number of states seeking or potentially seeking membership of the EU. Table 9.1 illustrates the enlargement position as it stands at the time of writing. The membership aspirants, actual or potential, can be conveniently divided into

181

Table 9.1 Applicants and potential applicants for EU membership

Actual/potential applicants	Existing arrangements	Path towards membership
I. EFTA Group: Austria Sweden Norway (withdrew) Finland Switzerland (withdrew)	Members of European Economic Area	Negotiations on accession from January 1993 Full membership in January 1995
II. Mediterranean States: Turkey	Association Agreement	Application blocked by Greece
Malta	Association Agreements	Have applied
Cyprus		Possible eventual membership
III. Ex-COMECON: Poland Hungary Czech Republic Slovak Republic Romania Bulgaria	Europe Agreements: Interim Agreements signed December 1991 Negotiations on Europe Agreement from May 1992	Principal of eventual membership established at Copenhagen Summit
Slovenia Baltic States Croatia Serbia Macedonia	Possible Europe Agreements None	Possible eventual membership Possibly an issue within next decade
IV. Former Soviet Union: Russian Federation Kazakstan Ukraine Belorussia	Negotiation of bilateral Partnership and Cooperation Agreements from 1993	Full membership less likely

four groups of states that, albeit diverse, have certain characteristics in common. The first of these are the applicants from EFTA: Austria, Sweden, Norway and Finland. These countries are currently part of the European Economic Area (EEA), an arrangement promoted by Jacques Delors since 1989. This comprises a common market between EU and EFTA countries, created by removing NTBs to the movement of goods (with some exceptions in the case of agricultural trade), services, labour and capital within the area by applying most of the EU internal market legislation throughout the EEA. Switzerland and (later) Norway rejected membership of the EU in popular referenda. Iceland has shown no interest in EU membership.

The EFTA enlargement is scheduled to take place on January 1, 1995, and is the least controversial and economically logical of the outstanding enlargements. It will probably be the last of the traditional or 'classical' enlargements, in that it involves the integration into the EU of economies that have broadly similar characteristics to the existing members. In fact, the EFTA countries are considerably richer: in the early 1990s Austrian per capita GDP was $16,592, Finland's $23,196 and Sweden's $22,443, compared with the EU average of $14,805. They are all small countries of between 4m and 8.5m inhabitants, with open economies in which trade accounts for 35–40% of GDP, most of it (55–60%) with the EU (Church, 1991).

There were a number of delicate problems in these negotiations with the EFTA applicants in which the EU insisted on full acceptance of the acquis communautaire: the issue of traffic transit, Sweden's state alcohol monopoly, Finland's Arctic and Sub-Arctic agriculture and its relationship to the CAP, the right to buy property in Austria and elsewhere. Nevertheless, all finally proved resolvable and ultimately accession depended on the ability of the EFTA countries' governments to sell membership to their populations at the referenda which were held to endorse membership. Popular approval was ultimately forthcoming in all EFTA states apart from Norway, where resentment against the EU is considerable.

The integration of the EFTA countries into the EU should prove to be relatively unproblematic and should, on the whole, lead to positive economic effects. Many of the trade effects of EU membership have already been experienced, given the close relations that already exist between the EU and EFTA, but there is likely to be substantial welfare enhancement as a result of the removal of NTBs. The Centre for Economic Policy Research (CEPR) has recently estimated that the EEA will increase EFTA's GDP by up to 5% (Centre for Economic Policy Research, 1992) and, interestingly enough, the distribution of welfare gains that arise from the removal of NTBs are likely to be skewed in favour of the EFTA countries (see Haaland, 1990).

The relationship between the EFTA enlargement and the CAP is unlikely to be too problematic, given that the issue of 'remote' agriculture has been resolved, since EFTA's agriculture is already even more heavily protected than its EU counterpart. In fact, EFTA subsidies amount to 68% of the value of farm output, compared to 49% in the EU and thus there may be gains for EFTA consumers from what would be a relative liberalisation of agricultural trade in EFTA. The EFTA countries are unlikely to call excessively on the structural funds and are likely to be net contributors to the EU's budget. The CEPR estimates that Sweden might be making net payments to the budget of around ECU 1.1bn, Finland of ECU 261m and Austria of ECU 661m, while in total an EFTA accession might increase the size of the EU budget by around 14% (Centre for Economic Policy Research, 1992). In addition, the EFTA countries satisfy most of the Maastricht convergence criteria for EMU and it is thus possible that their accession may actually *accelerate* moves towards integration in this sphere. Apart from the welfare gains that may result, the EFTA countries are keen on membership in order to attract foreign direct investment and to keep their own multinationals from locating elsewhere in the EU. However, their main reasons for seeking full membership are predominantly political (security), as are the main drawbacks (for example, the issue of neutrality).

From an EU perspective, the main problems are also political, for the prospect of an EU of fifteen containing three more small countries calls into question the efficacy of the whole institutional structure of the Union, while the whole issue of enlargement raises fundamental questions about the future direction and shape of the EU. For a fuller treatment of EU–EFTA relations, see *Journal of Common Market Studies*, Special Issue (1990).

The potential enlargements after the EFTA group are an altogether different proposition. The first group of these are the Mediterranean states of Turkey, Cyprus and Malta, which have been referred to somewhat unfortunately by Jacques Delors as the 'Mediterranean Orphans'. Turkey currently has an Association Agreement with the EU, providing some access to EU markets. It is of course much larger than the two small islands and has long sought membership. Its progress has been blocked by its dubious human rights record and by Greece, in protest over the partition of Cyprus. Turkish application would provide problems and opportunities analogous to those of the Greek case and its economic integration into the EU might prove difficult. Furthermore, for some people, Turkey's application calls into question the whole concept of 'Europe' and whether Turkey can legitimately be considered part of it. Malta and Cyprus have both applied for membership. The integration of the latter would probably be easier than that of Malta, given the structure and openness of the Cypriot economy. Their size poses potential problems, since it calls into question the EU's principle of treating applicants on the same basis as existing members of the same size.

The next group of potential applicants consists of the former non-Soviet Union members of the COMECON block, sovereign states that became independent following the collapse of the Soviet empire in the late 1980s. Arguably, the first ex-COMECON state has already been integrated into the EU with the unification of Germany. These states have new and fragile pluralist democracies and are almost universally attempting to establish market economies in a hurry. They are at present poor – average per capita GDP of the six potential eastern European members is around 13% of the EU average and (including the former Soviet Union) this group has a population which exceeds that of the EU (see Table 9.2).

The EU has, as yet, no concerted policy towards these countries, but it has negotiated a number of 'Europe Agreements' with them. So far Poland, Hungary, the Czech Republic, the Slovak Republic, Romania and Bulgaria have negotiated such interim agreements. These Europe Agreements have both an economic and a political dimension to them: they offer limited and selected access to EU

Table 9.2 Population of Eastern Europe, 1992

Albania	3.3m
Baltic States	7.3m
Bulgaria	8.5m
Commonwealth of Independent States (CIS)	272.7m
Czech Republic	10.4m
Hungary	10.3m
Poland	38.3m
Romania	23.2m
Slovakia	5.3m
Former Yugoslavia	23.8m
Total Eastern Europe	403.1m
European Union	343.0m
United States	250.0m

Source: Economist Intelligence Unit.

markets, together with some limited financial cooperation and they establish the principle of eventual membership, which was agreed at the Copenhagen Summit.

There is widespread unhappiness among these countries about the Europe Agreements, which are claimed to favour EU members in their trade provisions and provide insufficient help in dealing with the enormous problems that arise from the draconian structural change which is being attempted. They are also criticised for what in many quarters is regarded as the excessively neo-liberal economic agendas which they attempt to force on the new eastern European democracies. There is clearly a risk of social dislocation inherent in this approach, 'monetarism is the quickest route from socialism to socialism', as it has recently been put. Nevertheless, in the final analysis, the Europe Agreements are accepted as the best at present available.

Full membership is clearly out of the question for these states at the moment. The economic impact would be devastating for the nascent and fragile economies of the entrants and there would be potentially enormous problems for existing members, principally concerning claims on the structural funds and potential large-scale migration that might occur from East to West. The integration of the former German Democratic Republic into the united Germany provides a good case study of the problems that might be involved. The CEPR has estimated that annual budget transfers to the eastern European applicants might amount to ECU 13bn and that this may preclude membership for another twenty years, although this may be an unduly pessimistic view.

The potential economic and political benefits of accession are such that membership at some stage, perhaps in the early 2000s, is likely, assuming that the transition towards a market economy continues successfully in these states. Membership would provide significant economic stability and opportunities for the new countries of eastern Europe, while the existing members would be provided with new markets and investment opportunities. These are relatively large countries in population terms (see Table 9.2) that the EU is bound to regard as desirable future members. Even fears that freer trade with the eastern European states would threaten the economies of existing members may be unfounded. Rollo and Smith (1993) suggest that opening up trade in agriculture may lead to small losses in Greece, Ireland, Portugal and Spain, but that gains elsewhere would more than compensate for these, resulting in overall annual net gains of as much as 3bn, shared more or less equally between existing members and the eastern European six.

Next in the queue from this part of Europe are Slovenia and the Baltic States and conceivably even Croatia, Serbia and Macedonia if the war in the former Yugoslavia can be acceptably concluded. Membership for these countries is a more unlikely, but not inconceivable, prospect early in the twenty-first century. The same might also be said for the former Soviet Union itself, although at present the prospects of Russian or Ukrainian accession seem remote.

CONCLUSIONS

We are looking at the possibility of an EU with twenty or more members by around the year 2005. This, of course, assumes that everything runs smoothly, for example, that there are no further upheavals in eastern Europe, that the market transformation of the eastern European economies is a success and that existing members decide not to concentrate on deepening the EU. The extent to which this actually happens will probably be determined by factors such as the economic cycle, the quality of political leadership in the Union and the extent to which the EU can democratise its operations.

What is clear is that, at present, the EU has no concerted policy towards enlargement and needs to develop one. Also the process of enlargement calls into question the very nature of the Europe that is to be created. At the very least there are likely to have to be changes in EU institutions to accommodate enlargement and there may be a need to explore possibilities such as two-speed integration, partial integration and reversible integration, with the possibility of exclusion if relevant criteria cease to be met.

In 1989, something fundamental changed in economics, politics and international relations and there is a need to develop a post-1989 model for the EU. In particular, the EU needs to find some way of addressing the problems and challenges thrown up by the integration of small countries, given that most if not all of the likely new members fall into this category.

10

THE ECONOMICS OF SOCIAL RESPONSIBILITY IN THE EUROPEAN UNION

Peter Curwen

INTRODUCTION

The European Union (EU), remains a collection of nation states despite the expanding body of supranational rules and laws arising out of the Treaty of Rome, the Single European Act (SEA) and the Treaty on European Union (the Maastricht Treaty). The main thrust of supranationality is economic, but social responsibility has come increasingly to the fore in the debates about the future of the EU. The purpose of this chapter is to outline the economic effects of issues related to social responsibility and to examine the consequences of decisions reached at Maastricht in December 1991.

Social responsibility is approached via the social policy provisions of the EU. These arose initially in the provisions of the Treaty of Rome and were very limited in practice. Title III of Part Three (Articles 117 to 128) referred, under the heading of 'social policy', to the need for 'close co-operation between member states' in matters relating to employment, labour legislation, occupational training, accidents and diseases and social security.

It was clear at the time, however, and indeed subsequently, that no member state had the slightest intention of altering its social provisions in order to bring them into line with some European norm, nor indeed in the case of wealthier members to provide much by way of any subsidies to less-well-off members in order, for example, to equalise rates of unemployment.

The only specific provision of the Treaty applied to the introduction of national rules in relation to equal pay for equal work for males and females (Article 119). Some idea of the lethargic progress characteristic of the EU at that time can be gauged by the fact that this provision was supposed to have been implemented by the end of 1961, but could not be said to have been implemented in all member states (and even then in a less than clear-cut manner) until 1976. Given that this was the only specific matter referred to in the Treaty, it is hardly surprising that its more general aspirations mostly fell by the wayside.

THE SINGLE EUROPEAN ACT 1986

The passing of the Single European Act (SEA) which came into effect on July 1, 1987, provided a blueprint for the creation of the single European market (SEM). Whilst it was only peripherally concerned with social policy, it did contain two new social Articles, 118A and 118B, to be added to those contained in the Treaty of Rome and, perhaps more importantly, the SEA introduced a much improved system for implementing changes based upon these Articles.

The task set out in the SEA was necessarily more ambitious than that envisaged in the Treaty of Rome, if only because Greece, Portugal and Spain had joined the EU by the end of 1986 and their economic and social circumstances were quite different from those of established northern members. The need for unanimity agreed in the 1966 'Luxembourg Compromise' (see Chapter 1) could, therefore, have placed a block on progress as it had done in previous years, but this was prevented by a change in the decision-making procedures of the Council of Ministers.

In respect of social policy, the Treaty of Rome was amended by Article 118A of the SEA to provide for qualified majority voting on proposals to encourage improvements in the working environment, on proposals in respect of the health and safety of workers and in respect of harmonisation of conditions in these areas. This did not, however, remove all barriers to progress since the term 'working environment' was something of an ambiguous catch-all, the interpretation of which has remained an ongoing matter of dispute between member states, especially since unanimous voting was retained in the SEA for measures affecting 'the rights and interests of employed persons' (Article 100A) and the free movement of workers.

The passing of the SEA was seen as potentially threatening to social welfare. According to Rhodes (1992) the underlying rationale of the SEA was that:

market integration was the means by which pressure would be placed on the member states to sign up for political integration. This meant that social affairs were initially marginalised from the integration process and that market oriented forces dominated in defining the shape of the new Europe. For this reason the fight for a social dimension has been very much a rearguard action ... against the deregulatory threat of the 1992 programme and the market orientation of the SEA.

THE SOCIAL CHARTER

In the period subsequent to the SEA there were extensive discussions concerned with how to take account of the new pressures for social policy convergence. The outcome, in May 1990, was the European Union Charter of the Fundamental Social Rights of Workers, usually known as the Social Charter. The purpose of the Charter was to guarantee the basic rights of workers in the EU. It was formally adopted by eleven of the twelve member states on December 9, 1989, with Britain unilaterally objecting to a good half of its contents.

For a variety of reasons the Charter started out as a declaration without legal force. However, it contained a mandate allowing the Commission to set out detailed proposals on workers' rights in the twelve areas set out in Table 10.1. For the most part the twelve areas were outlined in very broad terms. Item (2), for example, stated that 'all employment shall be fairly remunerated' and that 'a decent wage shall be established' (EC Commission, 1990a). This approach recognised that national laws and negotiations between employers and unions within each country would already enshrine workers' rights such that it remained to be discovered to what extent it would be necessary to introduce detailed supranational laws in these areas.

The link between the SEA and the Social Charter was reiterated throughout the latter document. For example, 'completion of the single market cannot be regarded as an end in itself; it pursues a much wider objective, namely to ensure the maximum well being of all' (EC Commission, 1990a). Unfortunately, achievement of this objective raised a host of awkward issues, not least those pertaining to subsidiarity (see below) and 'social dumping'.

Table 10.1 Fundamental social rights: summary of the contents of the
Social Charter

The preamble refers to the importance of the social dimension 'particularly in view of the impending completion of the internal market' which 'must be accompanied, either at European Community level or at the level of the Member States or of their constituent parts, by a development of the social rights of citizens of the European Community, especially workers and self-employed persons'. Such 'rights must not, when implemented, provide grounds for any retrogression compared with the situation currently existing in each Member State' (CEC, 1990, pp. 92–3).

Title I   Fundamental social rights

Right of freedom of movement (paras. 1–8) covers rights to freedom of movement; freedom to pursue any occupation; equal treatment; recognition of qualifications; subcontracted labour; social protection and public works contracts.

Employment and remuneration (paras. 9–11) covers fair remuneration; freedom to pursue an occupation; and access to placement services free of charge.

Improvement of living and working conditions (paras. 12–13) covers working time, especially its maximum duration; contracts of fixed duration; seasonal work; part-time; temporary work; night work; procedures for collective redundancies and bankruptcies.

Right to social protection (paras. 14–15) covers access to social security and minimum income for the unemployed.

Right to freedom of association and collective bargaining (paras. 16–18) covers freedom of association; union recognition; right to strike; settlement of disputes. Para. 18 advocates development of a 'social dialogue'.

Right to vocational training (paras. 19–20) covers training and retraining opportunities, both national and cross-border.

Right of men and women to equal treatment (para. 21) covers intensification of existing arrangements.

Right to information, consultation and participation of workers (paras. 22–3) to be developed along 'appropriate lines', especially in multinationals in cases of technological change and restructuring and in respect of trans-frontier workers.

Right to health protection and safety at the workplace (para. 24) covers further harmonisation with particular regard to public works.

Protection of children and adolescents (paras. 25–7) covers minimum employment age (16), equitable remuneration, training and labour regulations.

The elderly (paras. 28–30) covers living standards, minimum income and social protection.

The disabled (para. 31) covers integration into working life.

Title II   Implementation

(paras. 32–5) Member states to do everything in their power to guarantee these rights either through 'legislative measures or by encouraging both sides of industry to conclude collective agreements'. The Commission to draw up an action programme and to report back regularly on implementation to relevant EC bodies.

SOCIAL DUMPING

Those who advocate that supranational rules are necessary in the realm of social policy have recourse to the social dumping argument. One variant of this argues that, in the absence of labour market regulation, poorer members of the EU will hold down wages and social benefits in order to control imports from richer members and to create better opportunities to export to them (in effect exporting unemployment). The other variant states that if investment is free to go wherever it wishes within the bounds of the SEM, it will end up for the most part in those countries where pay and working conditions are inferior. Hence, it is alleged, northern member states where standards of worker protection are relatively high will be obliged to lower them in order to maintain competitiveness. The purpose of the Social Charter is thus to protect the living standards and working conditions of employees threatened by the move towards the SEM.

There can be no doubt that there are at present large differences between gross wage costs in different member states. Taking salaries/wages together with various social benefits, the labour cost per worker in western Germany is five times as high as in Portugal and four times as high as in Greece (see EC Commission, 1990a). Nevertheless, it does not follow as a matter of simple logic that wage differences in a single market will lead to the distortion of competition once adjustments are made for differences in productivity, since in practice wage differences tend to be very closely related to productivity differences.

Furthermore, locational decisions are not driven purely by differences in wage costs. The existence of a pool of trained labour, high quality component suppliers or excellent transport links may have much to do with a preference to locate in a high-wage economy. Under such circumstances, relatively underdeveloped countries must rely upon cheap labour in order to compete effectively and this should not be opposed on 'social dumping' grounds (Kotios and Schafers, 1990). It may be counter-argued that deliberate social dumping is analogous to economic dumping (that is, export prices held below domestic prices). However, there is little evidence to support the idea that this happens in practice, especially since countries engaged in deliberate dumping of any kind should be exhibiting (much larger) trade surpluses (than they are).

But if social dumping is a naturally occurring phenomenon, upward harmonisation of labour regulations may serve only to worsen the position of less-developed member states. As Rhodes (1992) has noted:

> Unless the southern countries are able to upgrade their product quality . . . market integration could well mean further specialisation in labour-intensive, low demand growth sectors such as clothing and footwear where fierce competition from the NICs is already occurring. Rather than convergence, this could produce cumulative divergence. For contrary to the fears expressed in the 'social dumping' argument (which ignores the dependence of capital productivity on labour quality) a vicious circle could develop in which investment in well-regulated, high wage/high productivity economies offers consistently better returns than the loosely-regulated, low wage/low productivity areas, permitting neither convergence nor social harmonisation.

THE SOCIAL ACTION PROGRAMME

It is hardly surprising that organised labour has been anxious to formalise the Social Charter and the governments of the countries allegedly threatened by social dumping are understandably sympathetic. It is curious, on the face of it, that there is so much support from Spain, Portugal and Greece which seem unlikely to benefit from explicit regulations governing the labour market. A 'Eurosceptic' would argue that their support stems from the knowledge that they will anyway be unable to enforce such regulations and that it represents a trade-off for improved financing via the Cohesion Fund (see Chapter 14). Nevertheless, it has to be recognised that the Social Charter provided a rallying call for socialists throughout the EU in the face of the increasingly dominant economic doctrine of deregulation in the SEA.

Mrs Vasso Papandreou, the then EU Commissioner for Social Affairs, latched upon the apparent widespread enthusiasm (other than in Britain) for the Social Charter to push through a series of draft directives as part of what is known as the Social Action Programme. It was quickly appreciated that most of these directives, which when approved by the Council of Ministers must be converted into national law in each member state, needed to be subject to qualified majority voting rather than unanimity, given Britain's entrenched position, if they were to have a realistic chance of success.

The Social Action Programme presently consists of 47 individual measures, of which 27 are in the form of directives or other binding measures (see Addison and Siebert, 1993). The Programme is to all intents and purposes fully issued, but it is not yet fully enacted. The sections below analyse some of the most contentious directives and provide specific illustrations of the opposing views taken of social legislation.

WORKING TIME

The draft directive for the Adaptation of Working Time was issued on July 25, 1990 (EC Commission, 1992c). This was proposed as a health and safety directive because such directives can be approved by qualified majority vote and it was clear from the outset that both the British government and UNICE, the European employers' federation, would be utterly opposed to the directive. At the time, all member states except Britain and Denmark had laws governing the maximum daily working period, although many exceptions were permitted. The limit to the working week ranged from 39 hours in France to 48 hours in half a dozen states, although in practice only Portugal actually had a working week in excess of 41 hours with all other states falling between 39 and 41 hours. It followed, therefore, that the main impact of the directive was inevitably going to be felt in Britain in respect of aggregate hours worked (although it is interesting to note that workers in relatively poor member states have become much less willing than in the mid-1980s to forgo a nominal rise in income for shorter working hours) – see EC Commission (1991a).

However, the directive was more controversial insofar as it addressed shift and night work. On average, 20% of EU employees were doing shift work, with the highest rates in Britain and Spain (roughly 30%) and the lowest in Germany, Portugal and Denmark (below 15%). According to the Commission there was an established link between long hours of night work and ill health. On the other hand, several surveys had shown that, given the choice, many workers preferred to work longer shifts over shorter periods and it was observed that British workers habitually took fewer days off work on average than their counterparts in Germany and the Netherlands.

The prevalence of extended shift work and overtime in Britain meant that it would bear the main brunt of the draft directive, with adjustment costs estimated initially at roughly £2bn a year. The British government accordingly fought hard to hold back the directive, but finding itself continually isolated it eventually abstained on June 1, 1993, with the other eleven member states voting in favour. The main provisions of the directive are:

1 a minimum daily rest period of eleven consecutive hours;
2 at least one day off a week;
3 mandatory daily rest breaks after six hours;
4 four weeks' annual paid holiday; and
5 no more than eight hours per shift for night work averaged over a period to be determined by each member state.

The directive was formally adopted in 1994. All countries bar Britain will be required to implement its contents within three years, whereas Britain will need only guarantee three weeks' holiday for a further six years and has ten years overall for full implementation (a 'derogation' which may be extended subject to 'review'). There are also exemptions for transport, agriculture, fisheries, all work at sea and doctors in training. British employees who wish to work more than 48 hours a week will be able to do so; those who do not will have the protection of the law.

PART-TIME AND TEMPORARY WORK

There are currently three directives under consideration concerned with part-time and temporary work. Because there are so many different contractual forms which fall under this heading, the Commission has been driven to refer to contracts and employment relationships 'other than full-time open-ended contracts' (EC Commission, 1990a; 1992a). The Commission (1990a) justifies the need to legislate in this area on the grounds that:

> Unless safeguards are introduced, there is a danger of seeing the development of terms of employment such as to cause problems of social dumping or even the distortion of competition at Community level.

The intention of the draft directives is to provide the same treatment for part-time and temporary workers as that accorded to 'typical' full-time employees (hence the common use of the term

'atypical workers' to refer to the former). Given that the discrimination against part-timers comes in many forms, the directive seeks
to encompass working conditions, access to training and social
security and other measures of social protection.

The first draft directive is essentially concerned with the
harmonisation of working conditions. The second concentrates
on harmonising the laws on employment relationships and a key
clause requires member states to 'ensure that part-time workers are
afforded the same entitlements to annual holidays, dismissal
allowances and seniority allowances as full-time employees, in
proportion to the total hours worked' in the pursuit of the level
playing field. The third draft directive extends health and safety
protection for temporary workers. A key issue here is the threshold
of weekly working hours below which protection will not apply. In
Britain this was until recently sixteen. It was argued that such a
high threshold invites employers to offer slightly lower hours than
this figure in order to avoid even the impact of existing British
legislation. The draft directives set the threshold at eight hours,
thereby encompassing the great majority of part-time workers and
proposed that permanent status must be provided once workers
have been 'temporary' for three years.

Britain, like the United States, has a particularly large proportion
of its workforce employed in a part-time capacity and was expected
to be significantly affected by new legislation in this area (Jackman
and Rubin, 1991). For example, the qualifying period for those
working sixteen hours or more per week in respect to statutory
redundancy payments was two years, whereas for those working
fewer hours it was five years. Not surprisingly, therefore, the
Confederation of British Industry (CBI) went on record that 'the
added costs would force employers to reduce the number of part-
time and temporary contracts'. However, the House of Lords ruled
in 1994 in a case brought by the Equal Opportunities Commission
that the government was obliged under national legislation against
sex discrimination to give statutory rights to part-timers in line
with the directive, and the government agreed to this on 21
December 1994.

Temporary working is not all that common and hence is not a
major issue in Britain, whereas it has become extremely prevalent
in countries such as Spain precisely because it is extremely costly
there to hire and fire permanent employees.

The opposition to the draft directives has caused them to be held back from consideration by the Council of Ministers since November 1990.

The UK government once again vetoed the part-time work directive only days before conceding the House of Lords' ruling. Further opposition would accordingly appear to be pointless, although the government remains convinced that part-timers will have little to celebrate as the playing-field will tilt back in favour of full-time employment. In addition, meeting the provisions of the three directives can be expected to impose a substantial additional cost on British industry and discourage the offering of new jobs in small businesses.

PROTECTION IN PREGNANCY

A particularly contentious attempt to improve the position of women workers relates to the provision of maternity leave. It is interesting to note that the United States is the only advanced economy which provides no statutory maternity benefits nor permits a job-protection leave of absence. An attempt to introduce this in a draft Family and Medical Leave Act was vetoed by President Bush in 1990. Whilst a number of US states grant unpaid leave of varying duration, the effect is said to be a dramatic reduction in the pay of full-time female workers with children relative to their male counterparts because of the 'lost years' while caring for babies.

The current situation in Britain is somewhat better, but is the worst among the EU member states. Currently, women qualify for maternity leave only if they have two years' continuous service in full-time employment or five years in part-time employment and have no rights if working fewer than eight hours a week. As a result, almost one-half of working women in Britain do not qualify for maternity benefits, which amount to six weeks' leave at 90% of regular pay followed by a flat-rate £47.95 for a further twelve weeks (which can be compared to the minimum sick pay of £52.50). Any additional period of leave is unpaid.

It may be noted that even relatively poor member states such as Portugal and Greece provide much longer periods of leave than Britain – and at full pay. The draft directive concerning measures to encourage improvements in the safety and health of pregnant workers, women workers who have recently given birth and those who are breastfeeding, originally proposed that all women be granted fourteen weeks' leave at full salary together with a guaranteed return to the job being done prior to going on leave. In addition, women were to be granted two weeks' compulsory rest before birth, whether working full-time or part-time and pre-natal visits to the doctor were to be counted as paid work time. Employers were also expected to improve workplace facilities for pregnant and breastfeeding women.

At a meeting in October 1990, the draft directive was laid before the Council of Ministers concerned with social affairs (EC Commission, 1992c). It was proposed that maternity benefits (for women who had paid social security contributions for one year) should be set at the same level as sick pay, thereby much reducing the payments made to pregnant women and new mothers in most of the EU. Mrs Papandreou responded by threatening to withdraw the directive on the grounds that pregnant women were not sick, but normally very healthy. In the event, although there was general support for the draft directive in the Council, there were also substantive disagreements about whether jobs should be protected since there could be legitimate reasons for dismissing workers who happened also to be pregnant and, more significantly, as to whether the draft directive was a health and safety directive and hence subject only to majority vote or concerned with social security provisions requiring unanimity.

The directive was eventually accepted on October 19, 1992, in a watered-down version, on a majority vote, with a deadline of October 1994 for introduction in member states as national law. Its key provisions were contained in the Trade Union Reform and Employment Rights Act 1993, operative from the end of August 1993, which gave British employees the right, when pregnant, to a minimum entitlement of fourteen uninterrupted weeks' maternity leave and enhanced protection against dismissal on maternity-related grounds, but omitted any details beyond maxima and minima. Proposals published during August reaffirmed that maternity benefit would be raised to equivalence with sick pay, but left open whether this would be for fourteen or eighteen weeks and also whether women would qualify after either six or nine months with their employer for the six-week period on 90% of pay.

These measures will accordingly be more costly than those currently ruling and also because women eligible for current higher rates of maternity pay can continue to claim under existing regulations. All told, additional costs are expected to amount to between £55m and £75m, which the British government has decided to pass on to employers.

WORKER REPRESENTATION

Currently under discussion are draft directives concerned with worker representation which, whilst they are in many ways the descendants of more ambitious attempts to impose worker representation such as the 'Vredling Directive', are different in certain significant respects. One key difference, for example, relates to the fact that previous directives have been exclusively concerned with national bodies whereas the current directives are essentially transnational in nature.

A draft directive on informing and consulting employees was issued in December 1990 which, if implemented, will require worker representation on boards of directors of companies with more than 1,000 employees where at least 100 workers are employed in each of two member states. Also, a draft directive concerned with the establishment of a 'European works council' will, if implemented, require any company with more than 1,000 employees and at least 100 employed in each of two member states to set up a European works council, effectively a consultative council at group level where strategic decisions will be discussed which touch on plant closures, employment contracts, new working practices and the introduction of new technology. Each council will be obliged to meet at least once a year.

British companies would be most affected by the plans for mandatory works councils since Britain has 332 qualifying companies representing more than one-third of the 900 total. Germany has 257, France 117 and the Netherlands 83. Furthermore, Britain is also the base for nearly half of all companies passing the threshold (130 out of 280) which have their headquarters outside the EU. By contrast, Germany has only 50.

It is possible to argue that Britain's continual use of the veto for a directive which requires unanimity (two other member states also have reservations) is unnecessary, given that little more than annual briefings appear to be required. It is equally possible to argue that the entire exercise is anyway pointless, because forward-looking companies have already learned from the evidence of Japanese team-working methods that it pays to keep employees informed.

The majority of British employers nevertheless argue strongly that the councils will merely serve to interfere with existing channels of information. They are also very concerned that the enthusiasm shown by the unions reflects the latters' view that councils will promote the introduction of EU-wide collective bargaining systems.

Some twenty European multinationals have already created EU-wide councils, including most recently Ford, and a further 30 are being planned, but they are mostly operated in a fashion which is insufficiently well-defined to meet the requirements of the directive. Nevertheless, it is anticipated that works councils will be a priority item under the Social Protocol (discussed below) from which Britain has opted out and which could be operational in 1995. If so, British companies will not remain untouched since more than a hundred will qualify for councils even if their British operations are excluded.

BRITAIN VERSUS THE REST?

Both the Commission and many member states have exerted continuous pressure to subject as much as possible of the Social Action Programme to majority voting, while Britain has grimly held to the view that majority voting should apply only to health and safety legislation narrowly defined. On many occasions, Britain has stood ready to exercise its veto if need be and, as a consequence, it has created the image that Britain is wholly antithetical to EU-wide social legislation.

Such a conclusion would nevertheless be quite erroneous. Many of the Social Action Programme measures outlined rights to, for example, a safe working environment, training and trade union representation which already existed under British law. Such laws also covered equal opportunities and the protection of young, disabled and elderly workers (see EC Commission, 1992c). Furthermore, measures designed to enhance the transferability of benefits or pensions and the mutual recognition of vocational and educational qualifications, are very much in line with the British government's free-market philosophy. Indeed, it is slightly ironic that Britain was the first member state to implement at national level all of the eighteen directives on social policy which the European Council had adopted by the end of 1990.

It is of particular interest, given the scale of unemployment throughout the EU, to note the underlying philosophy of the Social Charter:

> In addition, and this is possibly more fundamental than the question of social dumping, the creation of jobs must not be achieved at too high a price (in particular in terms of health and safety and social protection.
>
> (EC Commission, 1990a)

By way of contrast, the then British employment secretary stated in June 1991 that 'the most important social dimension of the single market is the creation of jobs'. This is a view with which the unemployed might well concur, even if their governments are obsessed with the level playing field, the avoidance of social dumping and the view that relative inequality is socially damaging and a cause of labour unrest.

In the latter respect, however, the British government has arguably been resisting the inevitable because the Social Action Programme can be seen as an attempt to persuade employees that the SEM is not simply a charter for capitalists. As the Social Charter stated:

> This is why [the Commission] will continue to take and propose whatever measures are needed to strengthen cohesion between social groups. The Union is concerned to show solidarity.
>
> (EC Commission, 1990a)

Nevertheless, the Commission has embarked upon a path which clearly runs the risk of, first, making labour markets much more rigid at precisely the time that they need to be made more flexible in order to tackle the problem of unemployment and, second, raising labour costs relative to those in Japan and the United States and thereby creating for the EU a competitive disadvantage in world trade at a time of recession. This does not appear to worry the Commission overmuch. Indeed, it argues that:

> Flexibility of employment may be a factor which is detrimental to competitiveness as it acts as a disincentive for workers. For firms too, flexibility may have negative effects in the medium

and long term, as it may reduce the motivation to invest in 'human capital', which has become one of the factors essential to growth.

(EC Commission, 1990a)

Similar sentiments were expressed by the Commissioner for Social Affairs and Employment in September 1993. On the other hand, it worries the British government very deeply that more than a decade spent fostering the deregulation of the labour market (see Paterson and Simpson, 1992) has produced results which are incompatible with the Commission's vision of a supranational labour market. Politicians in other member states beset by unemployment have become increasingly sympathetic with the views expressed by the British government and it must be remembered that whereas they are often constrained from stating this in public for fear of offending coalition partners, they have found it helpful to treat Britain as a scapegoat when it has delayed measures about which they themselves are unenthusiastic.

As the full programme of directives comes into force, smaller member states will face the realisation that they are no longer able to exploit their comparative advantage in trade. This will probably oblige them either to seek additional EU funds by way of compensation, or alternatively protection against 'technological dumping' by northern members (Kotios and Schafers, 1990). Much the same effect will be felt in individual regions even within northern states. Harmonising social conditions must inevitably assist core regions at the expense of those on the periphery and this must be viewed as undesirable at a time when relocation decisions are increasingly necessitated by the advent of the SEM (see Chapter 14).

Harmonisation of social standards will anyway come about in the natural course of events as living standards rise in poorer member states. It can therefore be argued that it is unnecessary to enforce it and indeed that it is inadvisable at this stage. It is also worth observing that once the directives come into force, it will be much more difficult to widen the EU's membership by the addition of less-developed states such as those from eastern Europe.

Eurosceptics in Britain are somewhat cynical about the enthusiasm of certain other member states for the Social Action Programme. They note, first, that those among them who (unlike Britain) trade comparatively little outside the EU feel little concern about any loss of competitive advantage relative to the United States and the Far East; second, that industry in countries such as Germany is already so heavily regulated that the directives will make them more competitive relative to other member states; and third, that some governments, notably Italy and Greece, have a patchy record of implementing and enforcing directives and those they do not really support are rendered *de facto* inoperative.

THE TREATY ON EUROPEAN UNION

When the Inter-Governmental Conference (IGC) on Economic and Political Union convened at Maastricht in December 1991, it was hoped that social policy would form a Social Chapter within the draft Treaty on European Union. However, a Treaty amendment requires unanimity and, predictably, the British government rejected outright any such amendment to the Treaty of Rome.

The original five pages in the draft Treaty were reduced to 'Present EEC Treaty Provision Unchanged (cf. Annex III)'. The annex contains a Protocol on Social Policy (frequently referred to in practice as the Social Chapter) which as part of the Treaty has been ratified by the British government. However, annexed to this Protocol is an Agreement signed by all member states bar Britain (which 'opted-out'). The Protocol contains the agreement of the twelve signatories to authorise the eleven parties to the Agreement to give effect to its contents.

The Protocol is undoubtedly a Treaty amendment. The Agreement may or may not be (see Whiteford, 1993). Article 1 of the Protocol commits its eleven signatories to:

> the promotion of employment, improved living and working conditions, proper social protection, dialogue between management and labour, the development of human resources with a view to lasting high employment and the combating of exclusion.

In the Council of Ministers, from which Britain will absent itself, there will be qualified majority voting (52 out of 78 votes required) in five areas covered by the Protocol, namely improvement of the working environment to protect workers' health and safety; working conditions; information for and consultation of workers; gender equality; and the integration of persons excluded from the labour market. However, unanimity will be required in respect of: (i) employee representation and co-determination; (ii) social security; and (iii) protection against dismissal. In addition, the Protocol excludes consideration of pay, the right of association, the right to strike and the right to impose lock-outs.

It is unclear how all of this will operate in practice. For example, matters stemming from the Treaty of Rome and the Social Charter prior to the enactment of the new Treaty are unaffected and hence require the participation of the British government even if they also form part of the Agreement. Second, certain draft directives, such as that on works councils, are now likely to go before the eleven, acting as the European Social Union in order to circumvent a British veto, whereupon, as noted previously, many British companies may either compulsorily or voluntarily become subject to their prescriptions. A third complication is that if at some future date the British government should decide to accept the Agreement, it will have to honour any decisions previously agreed in its absence. Finally, it is possible that where practices in Britain are perceived to provide an 'uneven playing field', they will be taken before the European Court of Justice and struck down.

SUBSIDIARITY

It is possible to argue that the extension of the competence of the Commission in the field of social responsibility represents a development which is incompatible with the principle of subsidiarity, itself a recurrent theme in the Social Charter. The Treaty on European Union defined subsidiarity as follows:

> in areas which do not fall within its exclusive competence, the Union shall take action, in accordance with the principle of subsidiarity, only and insofar as the objectives of the proposed action cannot be sufficiently achieved by the member states and can therefore, by reason of the scale or effects of the proposed action, be better achieved by the Union.

In practice, this can be interpreted in various ways, the British government's preference being for the view that the EU should only do things which Britain cannot do at all. Clearly, this principle would exclude virtually any attempt by the Commission to introduce new social policy legislation and the Commission understandably prefers to interpret the concept in a less restrictive manner.

Nevertheless, the initial rejection of the Treaty in Denmark and the manifest lack of enthusiasm for further supranational control over their lives among the general public in, for example, France as much as in Britain, has induced the Commission to tone down considerably its ambitions for a new improved Social Europe. The Green Paper on social policy is less detailed and introduces 'framework directives' which will set binding objectives, but leave governments and companies to decide how they should be met. One area where this could be applied is that of works councils.

CONCLUSIONS

In the end, Britain may feel obliged to join in Social Europe, although it will take a change of government for this to be a truly voluntary act. If so, Mrs Thatcher's nightmare vision of 'socialism by the back Delors' may yet come to pass. In the meantime, the Social Action Programme will largely come to fruition in Britain, although there may be some dragging of feet in other member states ostensibly more enthusiastic about its content.

It is worth reiterating that, irrespective of the merits of legislation to enforce social responsibility, it cannot be divorced from the economic circumstances of the time and these have undoubtedly deteriorated badly over the past few years. It is the low-skilled, poorly paid sections of the workforce who are supposed to be protected by existing and proposed legislation, yet they tend to bear the brunt of a levelling of the playing field, as do small companies which have provided a disproportionate number of new jobs over the past decade (see Addison and Siebert, 1993; Johnson, 1992).

In refusing to be party to the Agreement Britain may indeed gain at the expense of other member states, but it also suffers many ongoing disadvantages in respect, for example, of its education and training systems, so it is not unreasonable that it should utilise such comparative advantage as is available, especially as the Cohesion Fund does not exist for its benefit. It is easy to level accusations of social irresponsibility at the British government, but under present circumstances they are largely wide of the mark.

11

THE COMMON AGRICULTURAL POLICY

Its Operation and Reform

Robert Ackrill

INTRODUCTION

For a variety of reasons, the European Union (EU) has in recent years become an important focus for economic analysis. The most important development has been the movement towards closer economic integration between the member states of the EU, known as the 1992 programme (see Chapters 7 and 8), and subsequently the debate over even closer links in the future under the Maastricht Treaty (see Chapters 4–6). There has, however, been one policy operated by the EU for a number of years that has continually put the EU in the public eye – that is, the operation and effects of the Common Agricultural Policy (CAP). This is the means by which the EU provides financial support for its farmers. It has been popularly associated with massive budgetary expenditures and the infamous mountains and lakes of surplus products as diverse as cereals, skimmed milk powder, beef and alcohol.

These problems have, of themselves, caused great consternation and have brought forth a number of attempts to correct imbalances in agricultural production and the resulting rising expenditures. However, these problems have had wider implications. For the success of the 1992 programme, a larger EU budget was necessary to fund larger and new policies (for example, greater regional spending and the expansion of the EU's activities into areas like research and development and new high-technology industries – see, for example, Chapter 14). This had to be accompanied by an effective reform of the CAP in order to ensure the larger budget was not simply swallowed up by ever-expanding support costs for agriculture.

In this chapter, simple microeconomic theory is used to consider the principles underlying the operation of the CAP, the reasons why the levels of surpluses and budgetary expenditures have risen over time as a result and how the reforms implemented to try and control the growth of agricultural output and expenditures have actually operated. The system of support operating up to 1993 will receive particular attention, in order to understand how the problems of the CAP came about and why the reforms implemented prior to the MacSharry reforms agreed in 1992 proved ineffective. Although reference will be made to a number of the different products supported under the CAP, the main reference will be to cereals, because of its importance to farmers across the EU, both as a final product and as an input into other production processes, notably as a feed input into livestock production.

WHY SUPPORT AGRICULTURE?

Most developed economies' governments intervene in agriculture to some degree, with a variety of aims in mind. The two principal motives conventionally stated are: (i) to counter unstable market prices; and (ii) to support farmers' incomes. Taking the question of price stability first, the nature of the agricultural production process means that for most products, arable and livestock, one production cycle lasts several months. Thus, *ceteris paribus*, supply is relatively price-inelastic in the short run.

Moreover, there is a relatively low income elasticity of demand for food, so that in the high-income western economies, a relatively low proportion of income spent goes on food. Thus food takes a smaller and smaller proportion of total consumer expenditure over time. This, coupled with the fact that unprocessed farm products face relatively price-inelastic demand (even when a processed form of the food may face relatively elastic demand), as well as the more obvious point that 'food' in total has no close substitutes, results in farmers facing a relatively price inelastic demand schedule. It therefore follows that, given inelastic demand and supply, changes in either demand or supply will result in proportionately greater changes in the equilibrium price. Moreover, whilst demand tends to be relatively stable over time, supply can fluctuate quite significantly, given its reliance on such external factors as the climate (witness, for example, the high potato prices in Britain in 1976 when the drought of that year cut harvests significantly).

The second point, that of supporting farmers' incomes, stems (at least in part) from the argument stated above, namely that in developed economies demand for food rises more slowly than general demand in the economy as a whole. In addition to this, whilst consumers' expenditure on food is rising over time, this in no way guarantees a rising return to farmers, with the food bought by consumers increasingly being processed (e.g., convenience foods, 'TV dinners', etc.). Thus a larger and larger fraction of total expenditure on food goes on the marketing margin – processing, etc. Moreover, technological progress acts to increase supply over time, by developing higher-yielding varieties of seeds and improved inputs. Coupled to relatively static demand for farmers' products, if not for food in total, the price *faced by farmers* will be driven down over time.

SUPPORT UNDER THE CAP PRIOR TO 1993

During the period under consideration, the EU has used a number of different methods of support, all aimed at fulfilling the aims of the CAP as laid down in Article 39 of the Treaty of Rome. These were and remain (author's emphases):

1 to increase agricultural productivity;
2 to promote the optimum utilisation of factors especially labour;
3 to ensure *thereby* a fair standard of living for the agricultural community;
4 to stabilise markets; to ensure certain supplies; and
5 to ensure supplies to consumers at *reasonable* prices.

The principal method of support involved maintaining a market price for each commodity within the EU which was normally higher than the price in the rest of the world and, moreover, above the equilibrium price. Simple microeconomics suggests that, without further intervention, this policy would result in the price charged being driven down to the equilibrium level. In the particular case of the CAP, there were two ways in which this high price could be undermined and thus there were two distinct, but closely related, policies operated by the EU to protect this higher price.

First, the EU had to protect against cheap imports from the rest of the world entering the EU and undermining the high EU price (see Chapters 1 and 7 for a discussion of the welfare effects of trade protection). It achieved this by applying variable import levies (VILs) to all imports coming into the EU. These were set by reference to the 'target price'. This was defined as the market price at Duisburg in the Ruhr, assumed to be the place of greatest cereals deficit in the EU and therefore the place with the highest market price. From this were deducted transport costs from Rotterdam (the main point of import into the EU) to Duisburg. This then gave the 'threshold price'; that is to say, the minimum price at which imports were allowed into the EU. Thus the VIL was calculated as the difference between the price of the cereals landing at Rotterdam and the threshold price.

Second, to prevent domestic over-supply from putting excessive downward pressure on the EU price, a system of intervention buying was available for most products. This acted to put a floor in the market, so that when the market price fell below this level, the member states, on behalf of the EU, were obliged to buy in what farmers decide to offer to them for sale, subject to certain requirements such as minimum quality and current stock levels. When the products were sold out of intervention, they normally went for export to third countries. Resale onto the EU market would have undermined the reason for the intervention buying in the first place, namely that of domestic over-supply, by simply adding to that over-supply. This, like all exports to third countries, required a payment to cover the difference between the EU price and the world price – the export restitution payment (though more commonly called the export refund or subsidy, funding the process popularly known as 'dumping'). Note that, for a number of reasons, the unit export refund was generally lower than the unit VIL. This system of protection operated by the EU can be seen in Figure 11.1.

The target price, P_t, is above the threshold price, P_{th}, by the transport costs from Rotterdam to Duisburg. P_{in} is the 'intervention' or buying-in price and P_W is the world price. S_{EU} and D_{EU} are the EU's supply and demand curves for this particular commodity. What these show is that at the institutional prices set by the EU, the EU is a net exporter; i.e., supply is greater than demand at those prices. At the world price, however, the EU is assumed to be a net importer. Because the intervention price theoretically put a

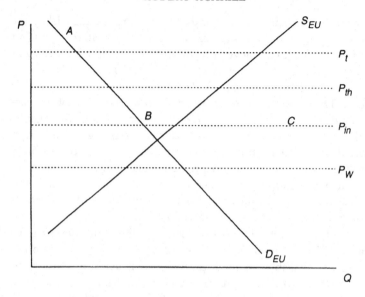

Figure 11.1 The price regime of the CAP

floor in the market, the effective demand curve facing producers is given by *ABC*.

Over time, the EU moved from being a net importer to being a net exporter. Demand for many agricultural products remained fairly stable over time, but technological advances, encouraged by high support prices, continually increased supply. Given a higher unit VIL than export refund, being a net importer meant that this system of supporting agriculture was originally a net income generator for the EU. More recently however, as the EU moved from being a net importer for most products to being a net exporter (the situation shown in Figure 11.1), the cost of supporting agriculture rose. Although the unit VIL was still greater than the unit export refund, a far greater quantity of many products was exported than imported.

This last point also demonstrates that whilst small cereals farmers are often cited as an example of perfectly competitive producers (even ignoring the impact of government intervention on this point), this example is highly questionable. The output of small cereals farmers can be highly differentiated. Thus the EU imports large quantities of 'hard' wheats suitable for milling, whilst simultaneously exporting larger quantities of 'soft' non-milling

210

wheats – all basically wheats, but very different in consumption and trading at very different price levels on international markets.

As production rose, not only were greater quantities of the surplus products exported, requiring greater expenditure on export refunds, but for most products, greater quantities were also sold into intervention. Thus expenditures rose here as well, to cover the operations involved in moving the products into and out of store, as well as the costs of keeping them there. Therefore, as surplus production rose over time for the reasons set out above, so too did the level of stocks (the 'mountains' and 'lakes' the media have always been so ready to highlight) with the costs of the CAP threatening, *inter alia*, the progress of the EU towards the completion of the internal market in 1992 – a danger highlighted by the Commission president when the Single European Act (SEA) was first agreed upon. We have now established the principles that underpinned EU support to agriculture until 1993 and showed how this led to the emergence of surpluses. By considering the financial implications of dealing with these surpluses, we have also seen how the EU's expenditure on agricultural support has risen over time.

THE ATTEMPTS AT REFORM

Because of the market developments outlined above and the consequent rise in expenditure, by 1984 the EU was, in a technical sense, bankrupt, though the member states provided sufficient short-term injections to ensure the continued functioning of both the EU and the CAP. The fact that these additional payments were made reflected the value placed by the member states on the EU. Rather than let this imbalance in agriculture risk the future of the entire EU, as some commentators suggested a budgetary crisis would, the EU was able to continue functioning. It was apparent, however, that this situation could not continue indefinitely and that, moreover, simply providing more money would not solve the problem, since if the CAP were left unchanged, the extra money provided would simply go straight into agricultural support.

Thus in 1984 an attempt was made to secure both extra funds for the EU budget as a whole, while at the same time trying to control the amount spent on agricultural support via rules on 'budgetary discipline'. The formula agreed was one which set an informal limit equating the growth of agricultural expenditure to total EU expenditure. The agricultural price decisions (i.e., the setting of the target price, the threshold price and the intervention price) were to be taken so as to respect this lower growth in agricultural expenditure, but there was no legally binding mechanism to guarantee that the expenditure guidelines were respected. In practice, the measures simply failed, as the price decisions taken left no chance of total expenditures falling below total revenues. The lower real prices paid to farmers were intended to slow or halt the growth in agricultural production, but the decisions taken were insufficient to outweigh the effects of steadily improving technologies and so extra payments were needed from the member states in 1984 to 1987 as production, and hence costs, kept rising.

THE 1988 REFORMS

In February 1988, the European Council took the decisions that tightened the budgetary discipline guidelines referred to earlier and made them legally binding. It was, however, a time when certain external (and internal) factors were also coming to the aid of the EU. Principally, there was a drought in the United States during the summer of 1988. International cereals prices tend to be determined by US domestic policy, since it is the dominant supplier to the world market. Thus the large fall in US output caused by the drought led to a sharp rise in world cereal prices and so savings by the EU on unit export refunds. Also, the seemingly inexorable rise in nominal EU support prices began to slow. Support prices had been increased very dramatically during 1980–81. Indeed, for the first (and only) time, the prices increased in real as well as nominal terms. Since then, however, the real price had fallen. Indeed, the automatic increase in the nominal price every year had become a thing of the past, with the target price and the intervention price being frozen in nominal terms during the mid- and late-1980s.

Increases in production have been driven by yields, rather than area planted, for some time now. Thus the effect of measures such as 'set-aside', whereby farmers receive a financial inducement to take land out of the production of certain surplus crops, was always going to be debatable (especially as only around 1% of the total arable area was set aside each year). For example, with cereals the area planted has been in secular decline for many years, but rising yields have outweighed this effect, resulting in steadily rising production.

In addition, reform measures known as 'stabilisers' were passed at this Brussels summit. The principal weapon was an automatic cut in the intervention price whenever production exceeded a particular level, known as the Maximum Guaranteed Quantity (MGQ). This, *ceteris paribus*, also cut the per-unit export refund. This price cut to farmers, it was also hoped, would slow down the rate of growth of agricultural production – i.e., slow down the rate at which the supply schedule shifted to the right over time. Coupled to this agreement was an increase in the EU's 'own-resources' (i.e., total revenues), which was felt necessary to fund the policies needed to achieve a single market by December 31, 1992, and extend the number of common policies operated by the EU.

AN ASSESSMENT OF THE REFORMS OF THE 1980s

The foregoing discussion of policy reforms suggests that, although the EU introduced a number of ways of trying to control agricultural production and resultant expenditure, perhaps the most significant feature to note is that the underlying principle of high prices (i.e., prices maintained well above their world levels) remained unaltered. Reform simply consisted of a gradual lowering of this price, in the hope that farmers would respond by producing less, therefore yielding savings to the EU budget. If one considers the experience of the EU's cereals sector, however, it can be seen that this path would prove to be ineffective. Calculations by this author suggest that between the early 1970s and 1989, the real price paid to cereals farmers in the EU roughly halved. During this same period, the total area planted to cereals in the EU fell by around 4–5%. Yet despite these two effects, total cereals production in the twelve member states rose by approximately 33%.

These figures show that the EU's reform policy of gradually cutting support prices paid to farmers in order to correct market and financial imbalances would not work. The reason can be seen quite clearly in Figure 11.1. Whilst the levels of the different support prices were changed over time, those changes were too small to have any significant effect on production and expenditure levels. The intervention price *was* cut, but it was always chasing a moving target, as the steady increase in excess supply pushed down the world equilibrium price.

This point is further evidenced by the market events of late 1990 and early 1991. Following the reforms of 1988, CAP expenditures did fall, but this was against the background of the drought in the United States. Most commentators felt that the cause of the expenditure cut was the drought, rather than the stabiliser reforms. Their prediction was, therefore, that once world production rose (with production in the United States returning to 'normal' levels and production elsewhere responding to the higher world prices realised in 1988), CAP expenditures would once again rise. This process started in earnest in 1990, with rising surpluses in a number of sectors and increasing quantities of products going into store and for export. Official stock figures (taken at the end of the accounting year) indicate that the previous highest level of cereals intervention stocks in the EU occurred at the end of 1985, when the figure was 18.5m tonnes. The data indicate that, by mid-1993, cereals stocks had risen to about 29m tonnes – i.e., *considerably* above the level of the mid-1980s.

In addition to the cereals sector, a number of other sectors faced major difficulties. Among those was the beef sector. Here, however, the causes of the problems were somewhat different. First, there were large quantities of cheaper beef 'entering' the EU from the former East Germany, resulting in more producers in the rest of the EU trying to sell their beef into intervention. Second, in Britain in particular, demand was affected by the BSE 'mad-cow disease' scare, causing producers to increase their 'demand' for intervention, as 'market' demand fell.

From all of this, it can be seen that attempts at reform failed *de facto*, because they in no serious way altered that fundamental underlying method of support under the CAP. Those 'adjustments' that were made can be seen to have failed to address the imbalances in both the product markets and also in the budgetary expenditures incurred.

A RADICAL REFORM OF THE CAP

The discussion so far therefore begs the question of what sort of reforms could be implemented that would succeed in containing the growth in production and support expenditure. What is set out now is a consideration of the MacSharry Reforms agreed upon in May 1992. The MacSharry Reforms represent the most radical changes in the CAP ever undertaken. The reason for this is that, for the first time, the basis for support has been changed fundamentally. Over a three-year transition period, the selling price of farmers' output will fall, with farmers being compensated for this with direct government payments. Additionally, all who produce more than 92 tonnes of cereals (calculated at average historical regional yields rather than actual yields, *ex post*) must set aside 15% of their arable land (defined as the area of land on which they grow cereals, oilseeds and protein crops – peas, beans and lupins – and also land that was set aside under the schemes agreed upon in 1988).

The larger farmers are not compelled to set aside their land, but if they do not, they will not be eligible for the compensatory payments which offset the lowering of the selling price of their output. This is the first time 'cross-compliance' (i.e., having to satisfy a pre-condition before being eligible to receive support) has played a major role in the operation of the CAP. By setting aside land, these larger farmers then also become entitled to claim compensation for that obligation as well. In all cases, the per-unit level of compensation is initially stated as a sum per tonne of production. The *actual* payment, however, is now based on area, so the per-unit or per-tonne compensatory payment must be multiplied by the average regional yield figure, in order to establish the sum paid. It must also be noted that this 'base' yield figure is not the actual current yield, but the average of the yields over the period 1986–90, excluding the highest and lowest figures. Thus support is now based on area planted rather than the level of production, unlike the old system of support. The principle is best illustrated by a simple example.

The new versus the old regime

To illustrate the difference between the two regimes, suppose a farmer has 100 hectares planted to different cereals, oilseeds and protein crops. He must now set aside 15% of this area (i.e., fifteen hectares) and farm only 85 hectares. Suppose also his average base yield is five tonnes per hectare. With a per-unit compensatory payment of ECU 45 per tonne, he is eligible for a per-hectare payment of (ECU 45 × 5 =) ECU 225. This is payable on the 85 hectares that he is allowed to plant and thus he receives, for this area of his farm, a total compensatory payment of (ECU 225 × 85 =) ECU 19,125. In addition, he can claim compensation for having to set aside 15 hectares of his land. This is compensated at a rate of ECU 57 per tonne. Thus, he also receives a per-hectare set-aside compensatory payment of (ECU 57 × 5 =) ECU 285, giving total set-aside compensation of (ECU 285 × 15 =) ECU 4,275. The farmer thus receives total compensatory and set-aside payments of ECU 23,400. In addition, he will also receive the revenue from selling his crop at the (lower) market price. Assuming the producer price continues to follow the level of the intervention or buying-in price, this will be ECU 100 per tonne. He is producing on 85 hectares at five tonnes per hectare, which gives him a total revenue of ECU 42,500. Thus, he has a total income of (ECU 42,500 + ECU 23,400 =) ECU 65,900.

Under the old system, in contrast, the price received by farmers also tended towards the level of the intervention or buying-in price. This was approximately ECU 155 per tonne. He would, however, be producing on all his 100 hectares. Thus, the same farmer under the old regime would sell his crop for (ECU 155 × 5 × 100 =) ECU 77,500. The hypothetical farmer is therefore worse off under the new system by ECU 11,600. This calculation, however, only looks at income and thus excludes costs incurred in production. One way in which a farmer could make savings is via the lower use of variable inputs such as fertilisers and pesticides. Under the new system, the yield figure (here taken as five tonnes per hectare) is based on past yields, *not* current levels. Thus, whilst a lower use of such inputs may cut current yields, this would not affect the calculation set out above. Hence, savings on purchased inputs may be made.

In terms of the effect on production, economists predict that the growth in output will be affected. The large fall in crop selling prices will be most influential in this. Over the space of the three-year transition period, the drop in nominal selling price will be about ten times the average annual price cut under the stabiliser mechanism. Moreover, there will be a much larger area of land taken out as set-aside. Under the schemes agreed in 1988, the area came to approximately 1% of all arable land. Under MacSharry, however, allowing for small farmers who are exempt from set-aside requirements, about 9% of all arable land will be removed from production. One forecast (see Ackrill *et al.*, 1993) suggests that by 1999 production may be at least 15–16m tonnes per annum lower under MacSharry than had the old stabiliser system continued.

Regarding the control of production, therefore, it appears that the new policy could be relatively successful. The main grey area surrounding this forecast remains 'slippage'. This occurs when the cut in area planted is not fully represented in the cut in production. Whilst it has been suggested that farmers could cut the use of inputs and therefore cut production more than proportionately, it is also conceivable (based on years of experience in the United States) that farmers could farm their remaining 85% of land more intensively. This would push up average yields and reduce the effects of set-aside on cuts in production. Thus a net 9% cut in area may only result in perhaps a 6–7% cut in production.

For consumers, there is generally modest and qualified good news. As noted earlier, there is an increasing element of processing going into food nowadays and it is unlikely that the price cuts under MacSharry will make any serious difference to the marketing margin. Thus whilst food processors will be paying less for their raw material inputs, their other costs are unlikely to change and so the net effect on the price of food in the shops is likely to be modest at best.

The third main group in the analysis – i.e., the taxpayers who pay for the EU budget via their domestic tax contributions – are also likely to suffer. The costs incurred in paying for export refunds and intervention storage are expected to fall significantly under Mac-Sharry. Estimates put the savings at about ECU 2.4bn by 1999 (see Ackrill *et al.*, 1993). The problem, however, is that the budget must now pay for the difference between the price paid by consumers of the farmers' production and the final sum received by producers; i.e., the total compensatory payments. Ackrill *et al.* (1993) estimate that this figure could exceed ECU 7bn by 1999. Other estimates have put the figure even higher.

There are, however, two possible gains for the EU with the expenditure under the new system, even though total expenditure is likely to rise. First, the bulk of the expenditures (the two forms of compensation payments) will be much more stable and predictable than the expenditures on export refunds and intervention storage. This gives an advantage to the EU in trying to predict the level of own resources needed in any year to cover total expenditure plans. Second, the total expenditure arising from CAP support will now be much more directly under the control of the EU. It was shown earlier how cutting support prices had no significant effect on production and budget costs. Now, however, by cutting the per-tonne level of the compensation payment and/

or set-aside payment, the EU can realise immediate and significant savings. Estimates suggest that, for 1997, a one-off cut on the levels of the two compensatory payments of ECU 5 per tonne would result in budget savings of between ECU 750m and ECU 800m (Ackrill *et al.*, 1993).

THE CAP AND GATT

It is also worth referring in this discussion to the international pressures that have helped, albeit only indirectly, in shaping the new CAP. The EU and its member states are all members of the General Agreement on Tariffs and Trade (GATT). Within the recently concluded 'Uruguay Round' of trade negotiations sponsored by GATT (1986–93), there was great pressure on the EU from the United States and the 'Cairns Group' of agricultural free-traders, which all want the EU to reduce its support for agriculture because of the trade-distorting effects such intervention has – notably the use of export refunds, which depress the world price and permit the EU to compete, unfairly as these other countries perceive it, in export markets.

Considering the MacSharry Reforms detailed above, it can be seen that these will reduce the trade distortion resulting from the CAP since they will cut the market prices of agricultural products within the EU to levels much closer to world prices, thereby requiring much lower export refunds on trade. Indeed, if world prices were to rise by about 15–20% for whatever reason, then such a strong market would mean that the EU would be able to export without subsidy. It is, however, worth examining the commitments that might be asked of the EU in more detail. If the CAP reforms outlined above do not achieve these require-ments, further changes to agricultural support in the EU will be necessary. Ingersent *et al.* (1993) sets out in detail both the pro-posals contained in the 'Dunkel Draft' paper of 1991 and also the amendments contained in the bilateral Blair House Accord, agreed between the EU and the United States late in 1992. In brief, the key issues as outlined in the Dunkel Paper are:

1 to improve market access by tariff reductions. These were to be reinforced by specific minimum import figures for each year;
2 to reduce domestic support by 20%, this to be applied to all supported commodities. In this process, credit is given where

reductions in support for a commodity have occurred since 1986. In addition, support policies that create little or no trade distortion (so-called 'green-box' policies) are to be exempt; and
3 export volumes are to be cut by 24%, with budgetary expenditure on exports being cut by 36%. Both requirements relate to each commodity individually.

The CAP reforms of 1992 unquestionably made the possibility of a multilateral GATT agreement more likely and the purpose of the subsequent bilateral talks was to try to iron out specific concerns between the EU and the United States. Included in this was an attempt to finally resolve the long-standing disagreements between the EU and United States over the EU's support policy for oilseeds (now incorporated into a broader 'arable' regime under the MacSharry Reforms). The Blair House Accord amended the issues outlined above in a number of ways:

1 on market access, the EU was permitted to retain 10% Community Preference. Community Preference has always been a key pillar of the CAP and in practice this now means that the EU would be able to retain a tariff on imports of 10%;
2 on domestic support, the EU got the United States to recognise the new area and headage payments as 'green-box' support instruments, even though they are not fully 'decoupled' (i.e., not fully independent of the level of production);
3 on exports, the 24% volume reduction figure was lowered to 21%. This applies to *all* exporters; and
4 on oilseeds, the EU agreed to a minimum figure of the 15% set-aside requirement that should come from areas planted to oilseeds. The purpose of this is to contain oilseed production within the EU to 10m tonnes.

In the end, an agreement was reached between the EU and the United States in early December that permitted a full GATT agreement to be completed on December 15, 1993, the deadline date for the Uruguay Round. To a great extent, the final deal accepts the proposals from the Blair House Accord, although with a few noteworthy amendments. In accordance with the earlier proposals, domestic support is to be cut by 20%, with the agreed exemptions for 'green-box' policies. In addition, subsidised exports are to be cut by 36% in value and 21% in volume.

There is, however, an important change to the base against

219

which this cut is judged. As agreed between the EU and the United States immediately prior to the conclusion of the Uruguay Round, the base period is to be changed from the average of the period 1986–90, to the average of 1991–92. In practical terms this means that over a six-year period, the EU will be able to export an additional 8m tonnes beyond the limit had the earlier base period applied. Finally, it was agreed that all import barriers are to be converted to tariffs or tariff equivalents and reduced by 36%. This relates to the simple mathematical average of all tariffs – each individual tariff must be reduced by a minimum of 15% over the six-year period. It is estimated that world prices will rise by up to 10%, resulting in gains to the EU in terms of lower unit export refunds (important in terms of the required 36% reduction in export refund expenditures).

One feature of this reform package is that it asks countries to reduce domestic support and address trade issues (notably, market access and export competition). Both the EU and the United States have now made significant changes to their domestic policies and further major cuts would be politically very difficult. It needs to be considered, however, if further changes to the CAP will be needed in order to meet the requirements of the GATT agreement. Considering first the 20% reduction in domestic support required, this has already been met, aided by the classification of new EU support measures as 'green box'.

With regard to the trade measures, things are rather less clear-cut. A number of studies have been carried out to see if the MacSharry Reforms of the CAP would actually result in the EU being able to meet the requirements of the GATT agreement without further changes. The results are dependent on the assumptions made about the affects of price cuts on, *inter alia*, production and consumption and hence on the exportable surplus. Some studies feel that for cereals, the new EU regime will lead to the GATT commitment being met, whilst others feel further change would be necessary. For beef, however, there appears to be more general agreement that further changes would be needed. Work by Rayner *et al.* (1993) perhaps summarises the work best by showing that, for cereals, the result is very much on a knife-edge. It is suggested that for the period 1998 to 2000, the EU may well breach the subsidised export volume limit. If, however, the world price were to rise, it may be feasible to export some cereals without refund, thus meeting the requirement concerning *subsidised* exports.

A few straightforward ways in which the EU could, if necessary, match the GATT obligations are:

1 to increase the set-aside requirement, by either or both of increasing the set-aside percentage for farmers already setting aside land and reducing the exemptions for small farmers (either by reducing the ceiling for a farmer to be exempt, or requiring all 'small' farmers to set aside a low percentage of land); and/or

2 to cut intervention price, thus lowering the internal price. This would reduce the per-unit export refund and could ultimately lead to the abandonment of subsidised exports; and/or

3 to subsidise exports up to the ceiling permitted and export the rest without subsidy (such as occurs in the EU's sugar sector currently); and/or

4 to store the extra quantities if, for 1998–2000, the EU is unable to meet its GATT obligations by the above means. Given the budgetary reforms implemented since 1988, however, this could only ever be a short-term palliative.

One point here is that an implicit assumption is made about the conditions in the rest of the world remaining unchanged. As was seen in 1988 with a drought in the US mid-West, changed circumstances elsewhere in the world could affect the EU's position quite dramatically, for the good in the case of such a drought with budget savings and greater export opportunities. It could be negative, however, if, for example, a major grain importer were to purchase less grain and the supplies they would have bought then needed to find a new market elsewhere. This has often meant larger subsidies being used, driving down the world price and increasing the EU's unit export refund.

Overall, therefore, it can be seen that the various reforms implemented unilaterally by the EU and multilaterally by GATT are to a large extent compatible. For the key cereals sector, some of the support reductions asked for by GATT have already been met by the EU. Other reductions meeting the GATT obligations will, to a large extent, depend on variables outside the control of the EU. Even if these work against the EU, it is suggested that it would be straightforward to amend the CAP as it now stands ('reform' is perhaps too strong a word) so that it will become compatible with GATT.

CONCLUSIONS

Since its inception, the CAP has been a cornerstone of the operations of the EU. The policy has, however, generated much political
and economic discussion over the way in which it operates. It has
been shown that the method of support used under the CAP since
its inception was instrumental in generating the much publicised
surpluses of agricultural products and also creating financial crises
for the EU. Both outcomes are shown to be entirely consistent
with simple microeconomic theory.

Although it was 'reformed' throughout the 1980s, the policy was,
in essence, the same as when it was instituted over 30 years ago. It
has also been shown that the 'radical' reform of the CAP agreed
upon in 1992 will help to contain production and therefore intervention storage and export refund expenditures. The EU budget
will, however, have to face the significant added burden of the
compensatory payments agreed in 1992. These are effectively
comparable to the 'hidden' transfers from consumers that
occurred under the old support system, but now, coming from
taxpayers, they are quite 'visible'. Consumers may be a little better
off, although only marginally, and it is suggested that producers
may be better or worse off, depending on specific circumstances,
although it is also indicated that larger farmers, like many in Britain,
may well be worse off. Taxpayers, it is suggested, will also be worse
off, because of the extra cost incurred with the compensation
payments.

Future further changes to the policy will depend to a great
extent on whether or not the reformed CAP is able to meet the
EU's international obligations determined during the Uruguay
Round of the GATT. It has been suggested here that even if the
new CAP cannot meet these without further change, for some
sectors at least, notably cereals, the additional changes needed will
not be significant and could be met by simple adjustments to the
policy variables under the reformed CAP.

12

JAPANESE FOREIGN DIRECT INVESTMENT

The Impact on the European Union

George Norman

INTRODUCTION

The past decade has seen a remarkable transformation in trade and direct investment flows, particularly between the developed economies, but also between the developed economies and the newly industrialising nations. This transformation has been characterised by a particularly rapid growth in foreign direct investment (FDI). Over the period 1983–89, the outflows of FDI grew at an annual rate of approximately 29%, more than twice as fast as the previous decade and three times faster than the growth of world exports and the growth of world output (see Table 12.1). There is an intensified effort on the part of most countries to attract this investment. Transnational companies are emerging from the developing countries as well as the developed economies and they are increasingly adopting an explicitly global strategy in many of their business activities.

This implies: (i) that FDI is likely to become the dominant method for international economic integration; and (ii) that multinational firms will produce an increasing share of world output. It

Table 12.1 Growth of foreign direct investment, exports and gross domestic product, 1973–89

	1973–83 compound annual growth rate (%)	*1983–89 compound annual growth rate (%)*
World FDI	13	29
World exports	12	9
World GDP	8	8

Source: Dunning (1988), United Nations (1991), OECD.

223

might be felt that this is of little consequence since, in a Heckscher–Ohlin–Samuelson world, trade in factors of production can be treated as a substitute for trade in goods (Mundell, 1957), but the generality of this proposition can be questioned. In an imperfectly competitive or, in particular, an oligopolistic international economic environment, the relationship between trade in goods and trade in factors is at best ambiguous. It is possible, and indeed likely as Norman and Dunning (1984) and Markusen (1987) have suggested, that international factor flows are complementary to trade in goods.

The implications for trade, technology flows and the competitiveness of individual nations are significant. Rather than being neutral as suggested by Mundell's analysis, FDI is likely to have a direct and important influence on a host economy in a number of ways that the same volume of trade flows need not have, notably:

1 the effect on the local economies in which the investment is located;
2 the potential for effective technology transfer;
3 export/import-substitution potential; and
4 employment and growth in the host economies and the receiving regions.

It is impossible to cover all of these issues within the confines of a single chapter. This chapter will, therefore, present an overview of Japanese FDI in the manufacturing sector in the EU. The motives for this investment are then considered, since these will shed light on the consequences of the investment for the EU. The impact on the local economies is likely to be determined both by *why* Japanese companies choose to establish operations in Europe and by *how* those operations have developed. There is more likely to be a long-term, beneficial impact if the investment is closely integrated with the local economies, exercises effective local decision-making and is associated with research activities.

THE EMERGENCE OF THE TRIAD

The United States remains the dominant source of FDI in terms of the stock of investment but the rapid growth of FDI flows in the past decade has been accompanied by the emergence of a new leading source of this investment (see Figure 12.1). Japan has overtaken both Britain and the United States to become the major

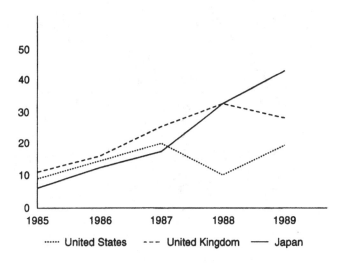

Figure 12.1 Outflows of foreign direct investment, 1985–89 (US$bn)
Source: International Monetary Fund.

source of new FDI outflows. This has had the effect of changing the global pattern of FDI stocks and flows. In the early 1980s this pattern could be described as being roughly bi-polar, dominated by the United States and the EU. By the beginning of the 1990s a tri-polar pattern is emerging based upon the United States, the EU and Japan (see Figure 12.2).

This Triad accounts for approximately 80% of total outward FDI stocks and flows but only about 50% of world trade. In addition, an increasing share of the investment flows are being concentrated in the Triad. Nevertheless, there remains a considerable asymmetry in the flows. Recent years have seen the growth, not only in intra-industry trade but also in intra-industry FDI, but the latter has occurred primarily between the United States and the EU: see Cantwell (1989), Norman and Dunning (1984). By contrast, there have been relatively low FDI inflows to Japan, a phenomenon that has emerged as an important source of friction between Japan and her trading partners.

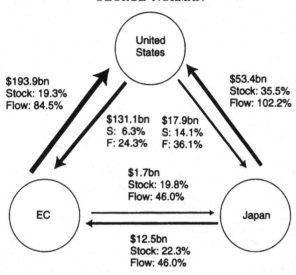

Figure 12.2 Intra-Triad foreign direct investment, 1988
Source: UNCTC.

THE GROWTH OF INTERNATIONAL REGIONALISM

Over the same period there have been considerable changes in FDI flows within the EU that are likely to have significant impacts on the investment decisions of non-EU members. The 1992 programme (see Chapters 7 and 8) and the general process of regional integration in the EU have been reflected in a rapid growth in intra-EU FDI: from 25% of the total inward stock in 1980 to 40% by 1988. In a number of industries, in particular the technology-intensive industries, EU corporations are becoming increasingly regionalised within the Union. The home markets of such firms are seen as the EU rather than the country of origin of the firms within the EU.

Similar comments can be applied to those firms from the United States that have been long-established within the EU. Many of these companies have developed a pan-European view (e.g., Ford, General Motors), with high levels of local sourcing and highly devolved local management structures to such an extent that it is difficult to think of them as being other than EU

companies. While few of the Japanese companies currently established in the EU can yet be described as 'Euro-giants', this can
primarily be explained by their relative youth – as will become clear
when their motives and objectives in establishing their European
bases are established.

There has been a change in strategy by Japanese firms. The
1970s and early 1980s could be characterised as a period of market
dominance through exports, with FDI intended mainly to support
exports. In more recent years, by contrast, 'there is evidence that
Japanese transnational corporations are building regionally integrated, independently sustainable networks of overseas investments centred on a Triad member ("regional core networks")'
(United Nations, 1991). These networks are intended to secure
access to the relevant Triad markets and to protect the Japanese
companies from the real or imagined threat of trade sanctions by
the United States and the EU – see also Gittelman and Dunning
(1991).

Until recently, the majority of Japanese investment has been
targeted at North America but there is evidence of a change in
emphasis with an increased focus on the EU and the rapidly
growing markets in the Far East. The industrial structure of
Japanese investment varies across the three members of the Triad
(see Figure 12.3). More than 50% of the investment in the EU is
in the service sector, whereas in North America and Asia the
emphasis is much more on manufacturing and (in Asia) mining

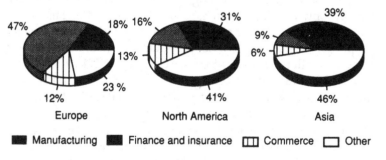

Figure 12.3 Japanese foreign direct investment by industry (stock as of
March 1990)
Source: Ministry of Finance, Japan.

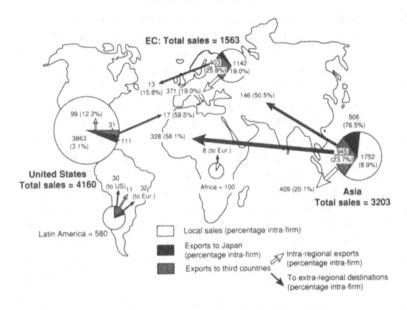

Figure 12.4 Sales of Japanese affiliates in manufacturing, 1987 (billion yen)
Source: United Nations.

or resource extraction. These differences are reflected in the very different proportions of outputs exported (see Figure 12.4).

These data are only partly consistent with the suggestion that FDI by Japanese corporations replaces intra-Triad exports. Such substitution appears to be strongest in the United States where the vast majority of sales are intended for the US market. This is less true of investment in the member states of the EU, where a higher proportion of sales is exported. It should be noted, however, that there is a high proportion of intra-EU exports (92% of total sales exported in 1987). If the EU is treated as an integrated market in much the same way as the United States, then the EU strategy has much in common with that adopted in the United States.

The strategy underlying investment in Asia is rather different, reflecting only in part the longer history of this investment. It is no longer possible to explain such investment solely by the desire to gain access to sources of relatively cheap labour and raw materials. That such an explanation still has some force can be seen by the high proportion of affiliate sales that are exported intra-firm.

Nevertheless, we can perceive a clear shift in focus with the Japanese corporations positioning themselves to take advantage of the spectacular growth in consumer demand in the rapidly growing economies of the Asia–Pacific region.

If attention is confined to the United States and the EU, these data further support the idea that the Japanese transnationals are adopting a regional core network strategy – in the United States because it is already an integrated market and in the EU because it is becoming one with the completion of the single-market programme. The establishment of extensive networks of local suppliers to serve the overseas affiliates discussed below is consistent with this hypothesis, as is the fact that the Japanese transnationals are attempting to form close, long-term relationships with these suppliers and are now developing regional research potential through the creation of research and development facilities in the EU.

What we are seeing is the emergence in the EU of Japanese transnational corporations whose market orientation is towards the whole EU region rather than any one country within the region. This is likely to lead, as these companies mature within the EU, to characteristics that are already common in EU and US transnationals in the EU – increased cross-border trade between affiliates to take advantage of economies of scale and the benefits of specialisation.

One feature that remains unclear is the extent to which these companies will be oriented to exports to countries outside the EU regional bloc. If the 'regional core network' hypothesis is correct, then such exports are unlikely to be extensive. Rather, there will be an emphasis on deepening the intra-regional network of trading relationships. This should, however, be interpreted as a benign rather than malign characteristic of the investment. The size of the EU and the North American regional markets are each sufficient to allow an operation sited in either one of these regions to achieve most of the available economies of scale without exporting to any of the other regional markets in the Triad.

JAPANESE INVESTMENT IN THE EU

There has been a rapid growth of Japanese FDI in the EU (see Figure 12.5) with Britain as the major recipient, although we are

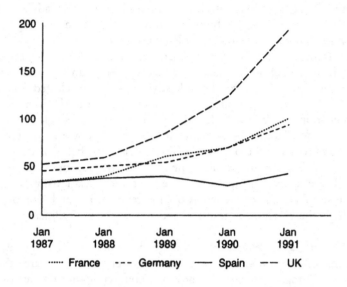

Figure 12.5 Japanese manufacturing enterprises in Europe
Source: JETRO (1991).

Table 12.2 Investment plans for the EU (number of projects)

Britain	52
France	31
Germany	51
Italy	17
Spain	21
The Netherlands	21
Belgium	14
Portugal	3
Greece	0
Denmark	1
Ireland	7
Luxembourg	1
Total	219

Source: Export–Import Bank of Japan.

now beginning to see the re-emergence of Germany as a host country. A recent survey by the Export–Import Bank of Japan (1991) indicated that nearly as many companies have investment plans involving location in Germany as in Britain (see Table 12.2). The majority of this investment is in high-technology, engineering-based industries, notably consumer electronics, chemicals, general machinery and transport.

THE MOTIVATION FOR JAPANESE INVESTMENT IN THE EU

Simply stated, a world view lies at the heart of the overall FDI strategy of the majority of the larger Japanese transnationals and investment in the EU forms part of this world view. The Japanese transnationals have switched increasingly from exporting to over-seas production and in doing so have chosen to establish opera-tions in the EU as well as elsewhere in the Triad. There have been several surveys aimed at identifying the reasons for this change: see, for example, Dunning (1986), Export–Import Bank of Japan (1991, 1992) and JETRO (1984–91). A major problem in compar-ing these surveys and in trying to draw conclusions from them is that they do not share a common methodology. Each survey offers different possible responses to those being surveyed. Even the JETRO surveys that have been conducted on a regular basis since 1984 use questions that have been changed over the years, making inter-temporal comparison difficult.

Given this caveat a number of conclusions can be drawn from both the JETRO surveys and others such as those of the Export–Import Bank of Japan. One prediction of theory suggests that much of the Japanese investment in the EU has been motivated by negative influences such as, for example, the apparent increased use of anti-dumping actions by the EU (Tharakan, 1991) and the possibility that the regional integration that is part of 1992 will lead inevitably to the emergence of closed regional blocs – 'Fortress Europe' as it has occasionally been labelled. If this is indeed the main motivation for the investment, then it is probable that the investment has merely been brought forward in time rather than increased in volume compared to what would have happened without the change in policy – see Thomsen and Nicolaides (1991).

The evidence does not, however, appear to support this negative view. In addition, theory can be used to give a richer and more positive set of predictions. There is no question that Japanese companies feel that increased regional integration within the EU will make market access more difficult. In addition, they have been influenced by factors that come under the general heading of trade friction as a consequence of which, *ceteris paribus*, FDI from Japan is likely to continue at least at its present level. But even here it is possible to discern a positive rather than purely defensive response in the reasons for continuation of overseas investment.

By far the greatest motives for investment in the EU relate to the positive factors already discussed. Regional integration increases accessibility to the host-country market. Rather than talking of the 'British', or the 'French' or the 'German' markets as a series of separated markets, we should talk of the European or EU market. Improved market accessibility resulting from the Single European Act (SEA) is increasingly encouraging companies, no matter what their original nationalities, to adopt a pan-European view. Since the change in market accessibility is additional to any increase in market size it will lead to more investment in the EU than would have occurred as a consequence solely of market growth. As one Japanese businessman recently stated, 'even if "Fortress Europe" is a reality, it is better to be in one single, unified and large fortress than in a number of small, separated fortresses'.

This is reflected in the JETRO and Export–Import Bank of Japan surveys of Japanese manufacturers' motives for establishing EU operations (see, for example, Figure 12.6). The evidence of the investment being a negative or defensive response to increased protectionism within the EU is weak. Much greater importance is placed upon market access and, more recently, upon the establishment of a global corporate strategy. This is consistent with the suggestion that the investment is intended to establish regional core networks and in turn is consistent with the view that economic integration, by improving intra-EU market access, will encourage investment by companies from countries that are not members of the EU.

Such surveys must, of course, be treated with caution. It has been suggested by at least one Japanese businessman, for example, that the importance of 'Fortress Europe' is not fully reflected in the survey responses to JETRO. Nevertheless, the largely positive message coming from these survey results suggests that the

232

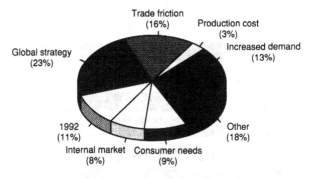

Figure 12.6 Motivation for production in Europe
Source: JETRO (1991).

volume of investment will be greater than would have been the case without regional integration.

THE IMPACT OF JAPANESE INVESTMENT

While there have been some studies of the local regional impact of Japanese investment in the EU – see, for example, Munday (1990) – I shall concentrate upon a number of broader issues. Apart from the immediate impact of new FDI, significant long-term benefits are dependent upon the quality of that investment measured along at least three important dimensions:

1 the extent of local sourcing;
2 the degree to which managerial autonomy is granted to the EU affiliate; and
3 research and development (R&D) activity in the EU.

Local sourcing

The higher the degree to which inputs are sourced locally, the greater the likelihood that there will be multiplier effects from the incoming investment and that there will be effective technology and knowledge transfer. Progress in this area has been significant. A recent JETRO survey (1991) indicates (see Figure 12.7) that the average local content has increased from 55.1% at the start of operations to 68.9% in 1990. Local content is highest among enterprises bought out by the Japanese and lowest among

233

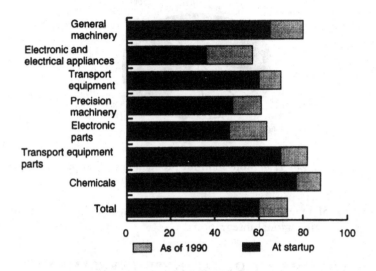

Figure 12.7 Local content of parts and material (per cent) (per cent sourced within the EC and EFTA)
Source: JETRO (1991).

those which have 100% Japanese ownership, but the rate of increase in local content is greatest in the latter group of companies. The initial level of local content is particularly high among companies that have entered the EU after 1989 – over 67%. While this has undoubtedly been influenced by pressure from within the member states of the EU, it is also consistent with the establishment of corporations in the EU that are European in outlook.

There is, however, a significant negative side that must be recognised, as illustrated in Figure 12.8. The degree of satisfaction expressed with respect to local suppliers remains depressingly low. The 1991 JETRO survey indicates that nearly 70% of respondents have expressed some degree of dissatisfaction with their local suppliers, roughly evenly split between quality, price and delivery.

It is clear from these results that local suppliers still have much to learn if they, and the local economies in which they operate, are to benefit fully from the incoming investment. This evidence also points to at least two potential future developments. First, if the EU supply base is inadequate there is at least the possibility that

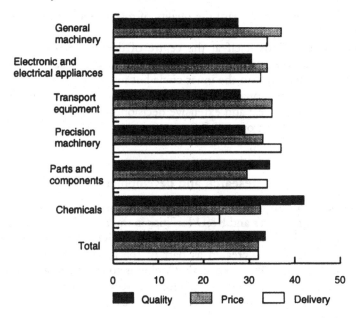

Figure 12.8 Reasons for dissatisfaction with local suppliers (per cent)
Source: JETRO (1991).

new investment will be diverted from the EU to other regions in the Triad, in particular to the rapidly growing economies in the Asia–Pacific region. Second, a natural response to dissatisfaction with local suppliers in the EU is to encourage a secondary flow of investment by Japanese specialist suppliers who are well versed in the requirements of their Japanese clients. This secondary flow of investment may supplant local (EU) suppliers and so limit the technology, knowledge and managerial skills transfer that could otherwise be achieved.

Managerial autonomy

Here the message is much more positive. A significant minority (about 30%) of Japanese companies in the EU now have locally recruited chief executive officers (CEOs), and determined moves have been made to localise management. It does appear that the Japanese transnationals are aiming to become regional 'insiders' rather than foreign companies operating in the EU. It also appears that they are satisfied with the quality of managerial staff available. What remains to be seen, of course, is the extent to which local management finds itself at the centre of decision-making within the corporation. It has been suggested that local management will never find its way into the inner circle but much the same was said about US transnationals when they first came to the EU. Only time will tell whether real and extensive decision-making independence is ceded to the European affiliates.

Research and development

The same positive message appears. There has been a rapid build-up of design centres and R&D facilities in the EU, with the number nearly doubling between 1990 and 1991. A significant proportion of these have been created as part of the global strategy of the parent company. Their prime motivation is to design products for the regional (in this case the EU) market. It is felt increasingly that this is most effectively achieved by being close to the market and to the competition.

CONCLUSIONS

Conclusions are inevitably mixed. The rapid growth of Japanese FDI in the EU is a response only in part to increased protectionism. It is to a much larger extent a response to the increased market accessibility that has followed from the completion of the single market in 1992. While both negative and positive factors are important, surveys of the motivations of those companies that have established operations in the EU indicate that their actions have been much more influenced by the positive rather than the negative implications of 1992. This implies that more Japanese FDI has and will come to the EU than would have occurred without the policy changes.

Japanese investment in the EU is part of a wider strategy. What is emerging with the continued flow of FDI from Japan is a set of global corporations whose aim is to develop as regional insiders in the three big regional blocs of the Triad. These corporations are taking an integrated view of the EU and other Triad markets. To compete with them both within the EU and in other parts of the Triad, it is clear that EU and US corporations will have to rationalise their activities along roughly similar lines. This will lead in the future to an increasing proportion of trade flows taking place *within* the relevant Triad region rather than *between* regions of the Triad. It also implies that countries that are not currently part of the Triad will have increasing difficulties in penetrating the Triad markets. This might mean, of course, that we shall see yet further regional blocs emerging in the future.

The quality of the investment coming to the EU is high, particularly with respect to progress in devolving managerial autonomy and establishing EU-based research and development activities, but problems remain. In particular there are important concerns with the supply base that is such a crucial part of making the Japanese investment in the EU work to the real long-term benefit of the host countries and regions. It is to be hoped that the EU can make significant progress to be made in this respect in the future.

13

COMPETITION POLICY IN THE EUROPEAN UNION

Eleanor J. Morgan

INTRODUCTION

The progressive reduction of trade barriers to create a single European market (SEM) has exposed many firms in the European Union (EU) to increased competitive pressures (see Chapters 7 and 8). There are two possible responses to this change in the competitive environment. Firms may take advantage of the opportunities offered by the larger internal market to become more competitive, so benefiting consumers. Alternatively, they may react defensively to protect themselves from increased competition by acting anti-competitively through restrictive agreements and monopolistic practices, for example. National governments may also try to protect their domestic firms from the increased competition by granting subsidies and other forms of assistance.

Competition policy has an important role in the context of the SEM to ensure that anti-competitive behaviour, both by firms and national governments, is controlled so that the potential benefits of integration are realised and consumers gain, not simply the producers and shareholders. Its importance was recognised in the Treaty of Rome, and Articles 85–94 of this Treaty provide a system to ensure that 'competition in the common market is not distorted'. As the pace of integration gathered momentum from 1985, the existing framework of competition policy has been more actively applied and new powers have been introduced so that this is now one of the most prominent parts of EU policy.

Decisions on competition are taken largely by the European Commission although appeals can be made against its decisions to the European Court of Justice. Cartels and restrictive practices and the 'abuse of a dominant position' (i.e., misuse of monopoly power) can be prohibited under Articles 85 and 86 respectively of the Treaty of Rome. Powers have been extended beyond the original Treaty provisions with the introduction of a Merger Regulation in 1990. Article 90 of the Treaty of Rome provides control over nationalised undertakings and Articles 92 and 93 allow the Commission to restrict 'state aids' (i.e., government assistance or subsidy). These aspects of policy will now be discussed with particular emphasis on the recent developments associated with the move towards the SEM.

RESTRICTIVE PRACTICES

Under Article 85 of the Treaty of Rome, any agreements between enterprises which affect trade between member states and prevent, restrict or distort competition within the EU are generally prohibited. The main targets of this prohibition have been market sharing, price fixing and quota arrangements between competitors, supply restrictions and certain types of discriminatory distribution arrangements.

Such arrangements are seen as not only leading to costly inefficiencies but also as conflicting with the aims of the EU in establishing a single market. For example, market sharing agreements have the same effects as quotas on trade. The European sugar cartel is a good example of such an arrangement. This cartel, which was banned in the early 1970s, was based on the 'home market rule' under which the members agreed to operate only in their own territories rather than competing across the larger internal market.

Most cartels are treated as illegal but more generally, an agreement which limits competition may be exempted under Article 85 where its harmful effects on competition are counter-balanced by a number of possible beneficial effects. The conditions for exemption, laid down in Article 85, are that the agreement contributes to 'improving the production or distribution of goods or to promoting technical or economic progress, while allowing consumers a fair share of the resulting benefit'. Further conditions for exemption are that the agreement is the only way of achieving the benefit and that competition is not eliminated from a substantial part of the industry.

If the agreement eliminates competition in a substantial part of the industry, it must be condemned, no matter how beneficial its other effects. This still gives the Commission considerable discretion to trade-off competition against efficiency or international competitiveness. For example, an agreement in 1990 between the French company Alcatel Espace and ANT Nachrichten Technik of Germany on research and development, production and marketing of electronic components for satellites was allowed largely to help them compete with their larger non-European competitors (especially those in the United States) which have a wider spread of space technology activities.

As well as case-by-case investigations under Article 85, block exemptions have been granted for some types of collaborative arrangements where it is expected that cooperative behaviour, while restricting competition, may still lead to efficiency and other socially desirable benefits. These include arrangements relating to joint research and development, patent licensing, specialisation in the manufacture of products involving small and medium-sized enterprises (SMEs) and the development and application of common standards. This system of exempting classes of agreement from the requirement to notify allows industrial policy objectives to be recognised and avoids the necessity for detailed scrutiny by the Commission, reducing its workload as well as the degree of discretion in Commission policy.

Article 85 has been vigorously applied towards price fixing and market-sharing arrangements in recent years but its powers were little used until 1962. This was mainly due to disagreements among the member states, especially concerning possible grounds for exempting agreements from the competition rules. The problem was dealt with in 1962 when the Council of Ministers adopted Regulation 17/62 which clarified policy and gave the Commission wide powers of enforcement.

If the Commission finds against an agreement, the companies concerned usually agree to end the agreement voluntarily or to modify it so that it is acceptable after an informal recommendation from the Commission. Otherwise the agreement can be ended by issuing a formal decision. Table 13.1 reveals a gradual increase in the number of formal decisions. Most of the decisions relate to manufactured products and, over the period 1960 to 1990, services accounted for only 12% of all decisions. From 1980 to 1990, however, 20% of decisions were concerned with services (see Sapir *et al.*, 1993). This was due to the Commission's efforts to complete the internal market in previously protected areas such as

Table 13.1 Individual formal Commission decisions under Articles 85 and 86 published in the Official Journal, by sector

	Manufacturing			Services		
	1964–69	*1970–79*	*1980–90*	*1964–69*	*1970–79*	*1980–90*
Article 85	25	108	120	2	1	28
Article 86	86	0	6	0	0	5

Source: Sapir *et al.* (1993).

futures markets, insurance, banking, transport, construction and the media. Emphasis on the service sector has increased since and fourteen of the 40 formal Article 85 decisions related to the service sector in 1991 and 1992.

The number of unnotified agreements which are actually in operation is unknown but the Commission has wide powers to obtain evidence and, if it finds that Article 85 is being infringed, the agreement is automatically banned. Heavy fines of up to 10% of the turnover of each company concerned can be levied. There has been a marked increase in the level of fines actually imposed in cartel cases in recent years. This indicates a substantial toughening of policy towards cartels in contrast to the relatively relaxed treatment of other types of collaboration which have become more common in recent years.

MONOPOLIES

EU competition policy towards monopoly is contained in Article 86 which provides that 'any abuse by one or more undertakings of a dominant position within the common market or in a substantial part of it shall be prohibited as incompatible with the common market insofar as it may affect trade between member states'. There are three important elements in this policy:

1 there has to be a dominant position;
2 it is abuse of the dominant position which is controlled rather than dominance itself; and
3 there must be the possibility of an effect on trade between member states (as is the case with Article 85).

Before being able to assess the degree of market dominance, the Commission has to decide the boundaries of the relevant market both in terms of the products involved and its geographic extent. Defining a market has been problematical and in Continental Can, the first case considered under Article 86, the company won an appeal against the Commission on the grounds that the Commission had defined the product market too narrowly and had therefore underestimated competition from substitute products.

Article 86 does not define what a 'dominant position' is. However, past decisions suggest that a firm with less than 40% of the market will not be regarded as dominant and usually much higher shares are involved. A high market share does not automatically give monopoly power so other factors are taken into account to see whether the firm has the ability to act independently of competitive pressures. These include the structure of the firm, including the degree of vertical integration and control over distribution channels, as well as the structure of the market, for example the number and strength of actual competitors and the degree of potential competition. The judgements have also referred to behavioural and performance aspects such as a firm's success in defending market share even when prices are higher than those charged by competitors.

The dominant position itself is not illegal, only the abuse of dominance. Certain types of abuse have been singled out for particular attention, namely unfair buying or selling prices, limitations on production, applying dissimilar conditions to equivalent transactions and 'tying agreements' whereby a manufacturer, for example, will sell product 'A' to customers only if they agree to accept product 'B' as well.

The recent Tetra Pak decision provides a good example of the abuse of dominance which Article 86 is designed to control. Tetra Pak, a Swiss-based company, is the largest supplier of cartons for liquid food (mainly milk and fruit juices). In some of its markets, such as packaging machinery and cartons for long-life products, Tetra Pak has a virtual monopoly with about 95% of the market. In 1992, it was fined ECU 75m and required to end the various abuses of its dominant position.

The Commission found against on Tetra Pak on four main grounds involving almost all aspects of its commercial policy. First, it had a marketing policy aimed at separating national markets within the EU. Second, its consumer contracts policy was designed to exclude potential competition by imposing exclusivity clauses on customers, for example by requiring that on Tetra

Pak machines, only Tetra Pak cartons could be used. Third, its pricing policy discriminated between member states with differences of some 50–100% for cartons and 300–400% for machines. Fourth, it operated various predatory pricing and other practices aimed at eliminating competitors. For example, in Italy, Tetra Pak's sale of certain types of cartons at a loss forced Elopak, its main competitor, to close a new production plant and almost forced it out of the market.

The Commission first applied Article 86 in 1971 and, as Table 13.1 shows, there have been comparatively few formal Article 86 decisions. In total, 25 were published by the end of 1992. This compares with the 340 formal decisions published in relation to Article 85 over the same period. As with Article 85, attention given to services has increased with the services sector accounting for about half of all recent cases.

MERGERS

The Treaty of Rome contained no specific powers to control mergers, and although both Article 85 (e.g., Philip Morris) and Article 86 (e.g., Continental Can) had been used to try to control mergers, the Commission was hampered by the lack of a merger regulation. It first proposed such a regulation in 1973 but could not gain acceptance from the member states, some of which (notably Britain and West Germany) already had well-developed merger policies of their own.

In the late 1980s, there was a substantial increase in mergers, acquisitions and joint ventures between firms as they restructured their operations in readiness for the SEM. The increase in cross-border activity was particularly marked and led to the agreement to adopt a European Merger Regulation in December 1989. One aim was to reduce the transactions costs large firms could face in getting approval for cross-border mergers by introducing a 'one-stop shop' and eliminating the need to get approval nationally, often in more than one country, as well as in Brussels. Another was to ensure that the gains from market integration were not eroded by defensive mergers whereby firms attempted to build up market share and protect themselves from the increased competitive pressures.

The new regulation, which came into operation in September 1990, gives the Commission prime responsibility for controlling mergers involving the very largest firms. The scope of the regulation is defined by the size of turnover and its geographical distribution within the Union. It covers mergers and merger-like transactions where total turnover of all the parties concerned exceeds ECU 5bn and the total Union-wide turnover of each of the parties is more than ECU 250m. The ECU 250m figure is designed to exclude relatively insignificant transactions where large firms acquire very small ones. If two-thirds or more of total Union-wide turnover is within the same member state, the merger is excluded from the regulation, as it is considered better dealt with nationally. The legislation and regulatory structures of member states remain in place and mergers which do not meet the criteria for EU intervention are dealt with by the relevant national authorities.

Mergers which satisfy the regulation thresholds have to be notified to the Commission and are examined solely by the Commission (subject to limited exceptions which have so far rarely been requested). Each case is examined individually in terms of its likely effects on competition. Investigations are conducted for the Commission by a Mergers Task Force, which was set up for this purpose. Decisions have to be reached within tight time-scales; after notification, the Commission has a month to decide whether to open a full enquiry and if so, a further four months to reach a decision. As with Articles 85 and 86, the Commission has wide remedial powers and can, for example, require divestiture, impose conditions on the merger and levy fines for breaches of the regulation.

Before the regulation came into force, it was estimated that the Commission would have to examine between 50 and 60 mergers a year. This estimate has been fairly accurate; in the first three years of operation, 178 transactions were notified to the Commission (see Table 13.2). In view of the strength with which the case for an effective merger control at Union level had been advocated, it is perhaps surprising how few of the small number of mergers falling within the scope of the regulation were fully investigated. The approach to date appears fairly lenient, and the Commission has been prepared to accept undertakings from firms to remove the anti-competitive features of their transactions as a condition for clearance, rather than banning them outright. Of the 178 cases, fourteen went to full proceedings and only one of these has been banned (ATR/De Havilland). Three of the mergers which were

Table 13.2 Decisions on cases notified under EC merger regulation,
September 20, 1990 to September 19, 1993

Notification withdrawn	3
Outside scope of regulation	18
Article 9 referral	2
Stage 1 clearance	141
Full proceedings opened	14
of which	
cleared unconditionally	3
cleared conditionally	8
banned	1
abandoned	1
decision awaited	1
Total number of cases	178

Source: Commission decisions.

fully investigated were cleared unconditionally and eight have been cleared subject to conditions designed to eliminate aspects of the merger causing concern about the likely effects on competition.

The regulation is based on a competition test and the framework within which the likely effects are assessed is very similar to that of Article 86 (Morgan, 1993). A merger can be prohibited if it creates or strengthens a dominant position which will impair competition in the EU or a substantial part of it. In the Nestlé/Perrier decision of July 1992, the interpretation of dominance under the regulation was extended to include structures where no single firm dominates, but a group of firms together have a dominant position and the oligopoly seems likely to act in a coordinated way.

Unlike Article 85(3), the appraisal criteria allows no trade-off between competition and other aspects of performance; the development of technical and economic progress can be taken into account only 'if it is to the consumer's advantage and does not form an obstacle to competition'. It was difficult to reach agreement on this aspect of the regulation as the way in which mergers are assessed in different member states varies, reflecting differences of philosophy towards the respective roles of competition and industrial policy considerations. French competition policy allows mergers to be cleared if the anti-competitive effects are counterbalanced by beneficial effects in terms of the cost savings and effects on technical innovation, for example, but the German and British governments, in particular, were concerned that the

Commission might be tempted to use an efficiency defence as a means of introducing industrial strategy into decisions – e.g., attempting to create 'European champions' to compete with large Japanese and American companies – and that competitiveness might actually suffer rather than improve as a result.

The November 1991 decision to ban the proposed acquisition of De Havilland, the Canadian subsidiary of Boeing by ATR, a joint venture between two state-owned companies, Aerospatiale FNI (France) and Alenia Spa (Italy) was particularly contentious and tested the Commission's resolve to apply a strict competition yardstick in the assessment of mergers. The acquisition was prohibited because it would create a dominant position in the turbo-prop aircraft market, with adverse effects on competition in the EU. The Italian and French governments, in particular, demanded a re-examination of the case, claiming that the analysis was flawed and the Commission had taken insufficient account of the need to build up the European aerospace industry. The Commission refused, stating that any appeal should be made to the European Court of Justice. The membership of the Commission was split on the decision and it is reported that the prohibition of the merger was based on a majority of only one vote and that the decision owed much to the strong line taken by Sir Leon Brittan. Following the ban on ATR/De Havilland, it remains to be seen whether the Commission will resist calls for a more broadly based analysis of mergers, taking into account considerations other than those solely concerned with competition effects.

Beside the standard of assessment to be applied, another stumbling-block in the original negotiations was over the size of mergers to be included within the scope of the regulation. The Commission only accepted the high thresholds to gain approval and provision was made in the regulation for the thresholds to be reviewed by December 1993. The Commission proposed that when the thresholds were reviewed, the scope of the regulation should be extended by reducing the aggregate turnover thresholds from ECU 5bn to ECU 2bn and the Union-wide turnover threshold from ECU 250m to ECU 100m.

Thresholds based on size are bound to be arbitrary and, wherever they are set, some mergers with effects going beyond a single country will be excluded and mergers with effects in only one member state will be included. There are a number of instances of recent mergers which appear to raise possible competition concerns at EU level, but which were not subject to Union control because of their failure to satisfy the thresholds for investigation. For example, Reed (Britain) and Elsevier (the Netherlands) merged their activities in the publishing industry in 1992 to form the largest publishing group in the Union and the second largest in the world, yet escaped scrutiny under the regulation because their combined world turnover was less than ECU 5bn. The merger of Hoesch and Krupp to create one of the largest steel producers in the world was outside EU control because both of the parties had more than two-thirds of their turnover in Germany. Instead, the national competition authorities had to be consulted in Germany, France, Ireland and Belgium.

Any lowering of the size thresholds and, particularly, any lowering or abolition of the two-thirds rule would be bound to increase the number of purely national mergers falling within the merger regulation. One way of dealing with this would be to have a more liberal policy of referral back to the member states and this has already been proposed. Many member states are now better equipped to deal with mergers nationally, having recently introduced merger controls of their own. However, more liberal referral would be at the cost of detracting further from the 'one-stop shop' principle on which the regulation was intended to be based.

Recent unease about the centralisation of power in Brussels, as well as the substance of some of the merger decisions (e.g., ATR/De Havilland) meant that the Commission's attempt to widen the scope of the regulation in 1993 was strongly resisted, especially by the French, German and British competition authorities. Some industry representatives were also concerned that any significant increase in the workload of the Commission in this area would reduce the speed of decision-making and possibly divert resources from other parts of EU competition policy where there is already a substantial backlog of cases.

REGULATED INDUSTRIES

In recent years, major new initiatives in the application of existing competition law have been taken in policy towards 'regulated' enterprises. There are a number of important fields of activity where member states have traditionally granted special or exclusive rights, essentially giving monopoly positions to enterprises providing basic or essential services. Energy, post and telecommunications are the major examples, although similar rights often exist in railways and other transport facilities, broadcasting and financial services. Along with the special rights, the ownership of these sectors has often been partially or wholly nationalised.

A number of countries, most notably Britain, have recently taken steps to privatise the ownership of some of these industries and at the same time to liberalise their provision. The Treaty of Rome does not regulate the system of ownership, but Article 90 is designed to ensure that public enterprises and state monopolies operate in accordance with EU competition rules. Article 90(1) of the Treaty of Rome states that competition law is to apply to public undertakings and to undertakings to which member states grant special or exclusive rights. According to Article 90(2), the same goes for enterprises which provide services of general economic interest as long as the application of these rules does not hinder them from carrying out the particular tasks assigned to them. Even then, 'the development of trade must not be affected to such an extent as would be contrary to the interests of the Union'. Article 90(3) allows the Commission to lay down general rules ('directives') setting out the obligations of member states with regard to such undertakings and to require compliance by member states if a particular national measure is found incompatible with the competition rules.

Article 90 was not used by the Commission until 1985. Its previous interpretation of Article 90 was in favour of granting monopoly rights on the basis that this was the best way of providing goods and services to all consumers on an equal basis, especially in utilities which tend to be 'natural monopolies'. It did not require member states to prove that their exemption from competition rules was necessary for them to perform their tasks.

Commission policy has become much more active in this area largely as a result of efforts to move towards a single market in previously regulated service sectors. The need for member states to grant exclusive rights is being closely scrutinised. It is now argued that by dividing the market on national lines, such rights not only limit the scope for domestic competition and facilitate the abuse of the dominant positions, but are also in conflict with the right of freedom of establishment and the right to provide services across all member states which are among the fundamental principles underlying the EU.

As well as trying to ensure that any monopoly or exclusive right is defined as narrowly as possible (compatible with providing the necessary services), more radical alternatives to state-funded monopolies are currently being considered at EU level as well as in some member states. First, the implications of changes in technology are being examined to see if the original reason for granting a monopoly still holds or whether supply conditions have changed as a result of technical change or the removal of trade barriers so that the industry no longer has the features of a natural monopoly. Second, if monopoly provision is regarded as necessary because of the characteristics of the service, alternatives to permanently granting a monopoly position which might be less detrimental to competition are being investigated. For example, one possibility is that firms can compete for the right to offer the service, perhaps with a direct subsidy as part of the contract to ensure services are provided on reasonable terms to all customers.

Markets are being liberalised through the removal of exclusive rights in a number of ways. Some countries are taking the initiative in altering their own national policies, but Article 90 is the main policy instrument at EU level. Article 90 is most frequently used to deal with individual cases in individual countries, in particular in postal services (e.g., the Netherlands) and air transport (e.g., in Germany). However, perhaps the best known application of Article 90 is in the telecommunications sector across the EU.

The market for terminals equipment (e.g., telephones and fax machines) was opened up by an Article 90 directive in 1990 so that purchasers would not be dependent on the monopoly telephone suppliers for these ancillary services. In 1991, another directive introduced competition in telecommunications providing for the abolition of exclusive rights for all telecommunications services other than satellite and mobile communications (the latter was already liberalised in most EU countries) and voice telephony. Telephone calls, which account for the majority of services, were not included in the original liberalisation measures because it was argued that a national monopoly was regarded as important to generate sufficient revenue to allow a universal service to be maintained. This is now being reassessed as technical change means that several competing networks can now coexist and the large price differences between member countries imply that the introduction of competition might reduce prices to the benefit of consumers.

Liberalisation of the voice telephony market is likely to be strongly resisted. The Commission's power to adopt the two Article 90(3) telecommunications directives was highly controversial and challenged by several member states. They argued that Article 90 only gives the Commission powers to oversee existing rules under the Treaty of Rome, not to take a proactive stance in breaking up monopolies. The decision of the European Court of Justice in November 1992 confirmed the Commission's powers, but although the decision could be seen as giving the Commission the 'green light' to continue using Article 90 in this way, the level of resistance from the individual member states makes it likely that the speed of liberalisation itself will be slowed down for political reasons.

STATE AIDS

Until recently, the Commission's reluctance to conflict openly with the governments of member states has also constrained its use of Article 92 of the Treaty of Rome. This deals with the various types of assistance national governments may give to their domestic firms which affect trade between member states.

Subsidies ('state aids') which distort competition by favouring certain enterprises and giving them an artificial advantage are considered incompatible with the common market, and the Commission can require such aid to be abolished or modified. If the government responsible does not comply, the matter can be taken to the Court of Justice. Difficulties in enforcing controls on state aid have not been uncommon. Investigation of aids is also difficult as the Commission does not have the same sweeping investigatory powers as under Articles 85 and 86 and has to rely on cooperation from member states.

Article 92 condemns all state aids which distort competition. There are, however, large areas which are either exempted or may be considered in the common interest despite the harmful effect on competition because of their contribution to economic growth, to structural adjustment and to encouraging development in poorer regions. Examples of aids allowed on these grounds include regional aids, support for research and development and for staff training, development aid for SMEs and aid to help export to third countries.

There is a considerable temptation for individual states to use subsidies as a means of protecting domestic industry, especially in recessions. This pressure has increased as the tariff and other non-tariff barriers (NTBs) to intra-Union trade have been progressively dismantled and competition from the newly-industrialising countries has intensified. Member states have been ingenious in exploiting the available exemptions and introducing new types of aid schemes.

Initially the controls over state aids were not rigorously applied. In the 1970s, recession and the addition of new Union members resulted in a proliferation of aids. The first survey of state aids across the member states which was published in 1989 revealed the extent of state support to industry. According to the report:

> in 1986, the volume of state aids . . . amounted to ECU 93bn or 3% of gross domestic product (GDP) and represents an average of 9% of public expenditure. In the manufacturing sector, state aids represent over 6% of value added and amount to ECU 49bn. . . . In most member states, expenditure on aids exceeds the corporate taxes paid by companies.
>
> (EC Commission, 1989a)

Evidence about the high level of industrial subsidies, especially in the relatively prosperous regions of the Union, and the drive to complete the SEM encouraged the Commission to apply the existing Article 92 provisions more comprehensively and strictly and to require more information about their aid schemes from member states. Recognising that the mix of public and private companies differs in each member state, the application of the rules has been extended to public enterprises to control the subsidies they receive and ensure that they compete on more equal terms with private operators. In addition, since 1990, aid schemes already in existence are being reviewed as well as new notifications.

In 1983, the Commission warned that the repayment of illegal aid could be required. The implementation of this policy has recently led to a number of well-publicised confrontations with national governments, especially in the case of aid to the motor industry. The challenge to a debt write-off granted to Renault in France (1990) led to eventual agreement that Renault should repay or start paying interest on FFr6bn, half the sum originally demanded by the Commission, after Renault agreed to certain conditions. In the case of Rover in Britain, £44.4m had been paid to British Aerospace by the British government in addition to the approved sum as a 'sweetener' after it acquired Rover in May 1988. After lengthy proceedings, it was finally agreed in March 1993 that this sum should be fully repaid, including the repayment of interest of some £13m.

Partly as a result of these various initiatives to apply state aid policy more strictly, the level of aid notifications rose markedly to 326 in 1987, 429 in 1990 and 459 in 1992. According to the Commission, this reflects the increased efficiency of Union policy in controlling aids. However, as a higher percentage of the cases considered under Article 92 are being allowed than previously, the number of cases regarded as incompatible with the common market has not risen so significantly.

The third survey of state aids (EC Commission, 1992a) provides data for 1989 and 1990 and shows that although spending has decreased slightly, the overall level is still high. It averaged ECU 89bn in the period 1988–90, excluding aid given to eastern Germany. Control of aid to the former GDR and extending the application of the competition rules is, of course, one of the major tasks now facing the Commission. Of the ECU 89bn of total aid, 40% went to manufacturing, transport received 29%, coal 18% and agriculture and fisheries received 13%. Steel and shipbuilding are the main recipients in the manufacturing sector.

The negotiations for the reduction of subsidies in the steel industry concluded towards the end of 1993 provide a good illustration of the problems the Commission faces in controlling state aid to specific sectors in recession. A 'crisis' cartel was allowed in the steel industry under Article 85 as a means of achieving a planned reduction in capacity. The Commission can require production quotas and capacity cutbacks, but rationalisation plans have often been thwarted by national government subsidies. The logic of competition policy is that 'lame duck' enterprises which are otherwise uncompetitive should not be allowed to receive subsidy on a continuing basis. However, pressure from individual member states to continue state aids in steel as elsewhere has been hard to resist.

CONCLUSIONS

The framework of existing EU competition policy was laid down in the Treaty of Rome and the aims have remained much the same as they were when the Union was first founded in 1958. Since the mid-1980s, the existing rules have been applied more vigorously, especially in the control of aid, to help create and protect fair competition in the emerging SEM. The application of the Commission's powers has been extended to areas such as telecommunications, energy, transport and financial services, which were previously little affected by EU competition policy, as part of the drive to complete the internal market in services. In addition, the introduction of a merger regulation in late 1990 has given important new powers to regulate the build-up of uncompetitive market structures.

As the application of EU competition policy has intensified and its scope increased, it has also become more controversial. Two aspects of the debate which surrounds its operation have become particularly prominent recently. The first concerns the objectives of policy, particularly the part that the promotion of competition can play in ensuring international competitiveness (see, for example, Hughes, 1992). The second concerns the division of responsibility for competition policy between member states, the EU and more widely in the post-Maastricht era, an issue which is usefully explored in Gatsios and Seabright (1993).

It is generally agreed that EU competition policy is necessary to secure the benefits of European integration but there is an ongoing controversy about whether encouraging competition in the EU is the best means of ensuring that Europe is competitive in international markets. This is a source of continuing tension in the application of policy. A concern for the competitiveness of industry is built into the possibilities for exemption in Article 85, for example, but each of the annual competition reports published by the Commission stresses the paramount importance of competition. In the run up to the SEM, Sir Leon Brittan (the Commissioner responsible for competition policy between 1989 and 1992), strongly championed the cause of competition, as illustrated in ATR/De Havilland. However, others, both inside and outside the Commission, would prefer a more sympathetic approach to anti-competitive strategies and such pressures have become stronger with the general slowing of economic growth in the Union. The Competition Commissioner has considerable discretion in the application of the competition rules, so much will depend on the approach of the current Commissioner, Mr Van Miert, and whether he will continue to adopt the tough stance of his predecessor. Early indications suggest that this is unlikely (Hill, 1993).

As EU competition policy has become increasingly assertive, relationships with member states have become more confrontational. The recent vigorous policy towards public undertakings and state aid has been strongly resisted nationally. There has been much debate about the appropriate division of jurisdiction over competition policy within the EU as well as how the powers are applied. This is particularly acute in the case of the merger regulation which gives the Commission exclusive powers (subject to referral back to member states at its discretion) over mergers within the thresholds for investigation. This is in contrast to restrictive agreements and monopolies, for example, where the Commission has jurisdiction if there is an appreciable effect on trade between member states but the national authorities can also investigate and act in such cases. The backlog of cases at the Commission, which have resulted in lengthy delays, and the formal adoption of the principle of 'subsidiarity' at Maastricht, have encouraged the Commission to work more closely with the national courts in the application of Articles 85 and 86. However, self-policing of state aids and privileges enjoyed in public undertakings by the national authorities is unlikely to be successful, so any devolution of responsibility is unlikely here.

This chapter has focused on the development of EU competition policy in the context of the SEM. It must not be forgotten that many types of agreement and anti-competitive behaviour still only have effects in one country or even a regional sub-market. In parallel with the development of European policy, a number of member states (e.g., Belgium, Ireland, Italy and Portugal) have introduced new competition laws to fill previous gaps. This means that there is now a more adequate machinery to cope with purely domestic cases nationally than there was before.

At the other end of the spectrum, as business globalises and markets extend beyond EU borders, behaviour by firms and governments outside the Union which affects the prospects of EU businesses is increasingly a matter of concern (see Healey, 1991c). For the future, it seems likely that policymakers will put greater emphasis on trying to secure a more 'level playing field' for business at international level, whether by bilateral agreements (as recently concluded with the United States), regional agreements (as with the EFTA countries in the 1992 European Economic Area Agreement) or multinationally (through GATT, for example).

14

THE REGIONAL POLICY OF THE EUROPEAN UNION

Harvey Armstrong

INTRODUCTION

The final ratification of the Treaty on European Union, or Maastricht Treaty (Council of Ministers 1992), in 1993 represented an important step towards full integration. The economic and monetary union (EMU) provisions of the Maastricht Treaty will have far-reaching effects on regional disparities within the EU, particularly as they will be superimposed upon the effects of the single European market (SEM), most of which have yet to be fully experienced (see Chapters 7 and 8).

With these considerations in mind, the EU has introduced a new package of regional policy reforms and has agreed a series of changes to the financing of EU regional policy for the period 1994–99 (EC Commission, 1993). These reforms have been deliberately designed to coincide with the implementation of the Maastricht Treaty. They represent an attempt to build upon an earlier major reform package introduced in 1989, which was designed to accompany the SEM process (EC Commission, 1989b).

This chapter examines the 1994–99 EU regional policy. The following section begins with an examination of the growth processes which lie at the heart of Europe's distinctive pattern of regional disparities. This is followed by a discussion of the importance of regional policy for the attainment of economic and social cohesion in the EU. The particular regional effects of the SEM and EMU are considered. The 1994–99 EU regional policy is then set out and appraised in the final section.

THE REGIONAL GROWTH PROCESS IN THE EU: CONVERGENCE OR DIVERGENCE?

One of the most important, and as yet unresolved, controversies is whether growth and economic integration in the EU leads to a narrowing of regional disparities ('convergence') or a widening (cumulative growth or 'divergence'). Those favouring a convergence view of regional disparities have drawn their arguments from neoclassical economic theory. Neoclassical models have a long history in economics (Borts, 1960; Borts and Stein, 1964) and have evolved into the more sophisticated 'catch-up' models in use at the present time (Barro and Sala-i-Martin, 1991, 1992). In neoclassical convergence theories of regional growth, the main equilibrating mechanisms are:

1 labour migration and capital mobility – regions with lower per capita income levels will automatically shed labour through out-migration and attract capital inflows seeking to exploit the higher returns available in regions with lower labour costs. These factor flows will continue until returns to both labour and capital are equalised;

2 technology diffusion – regions with a technological head-start find that the knowledge spreads rapidly to the lagging regions;

3 capital accumulation – regions with higher productivity and per capita income levels find further growth more difficult as capital accumulation inevitably runs into diminishing returns. Regions starting from a lower base do not face this disadvantage and, as a result, will grow faster. This is the key equilibrating process in neoclassical growth models; and

4 free trade – which allows regions to concentrate on those goods and services in which they have a comparative advantage. If, for example, a region has surplus labour, then it will concentrate on goods which intensively use the labour available. The resulting surge in exports will reduce unemployment and increase incomes.

Views of the growth process as a cumulative one in western Europe also have a long pedigree. A series of alternative cumulative growth theories have, however, evolved over time, the main ones being:

1 cumulative growth models of Myrdal (1957) and Hirschman (1958). These models distinguish between a series of forces,

256

some of which cause divergence (i.e., 'backwash effects') and some of which cause convergence (i.e., 'spread' or 'trickle-down' effects). If the former predominate, cumulative growth will result and regional disparities will widen. In an EU context, this can occur if the central regions having initial advantages in the form of lower assembly and distribution costs and proximity to the richest markets, build on their head-start by exploiting plant economies of scale, external and agglomeration economies (e.g., skilled labour pools, transport and business facilities, etc.). These backwash effects are then reinforced by inward migration of the youngest and most skilled members of the workforces of the peripheral regions. Any spread effects (e.g., higher congestion costs, land and labour costs in the central regions tending to encourage firms to leave) may be overwhelmed by the backwash effects;

2 growth pole theory of Perroux (1950). This stresses the role of key (i.e., propulsive) manufacturing industries. These draw other activities towards themselves through a combination of input–output links to 'upstream' activities (e.g., steel fabricators using the output of iron and steel works) and also 'downstream' activities (e.g., components and equipment suppliers). Local demand multiplier effects reinforce this process; and

3 modern cumulative growth theories. These include those of Kaldor (1970) and Dixon and Thirlwall (1975) which stress the role of Verdoorn's Law, in which regions with a head-start reap additional productivity gains through scale economies and specialisation of production. More recently, new growth economics has pointed to technological change and skills acquisition as a key cause of cumulative growth (see Crafts, 1992, for a survey).

With supporters of convergence and divergence theories at logger-heads, it is not surprising that attention has switched to the analysis of actual regional disparities within the EU. As Figure 14.1 shows, the EU exhibits a pronounced core–periphery pattern in regional GDP per capita disparities. The more prosperous regions lie close to the centre of the EU. Patterns of regional unemployment rate disparities and other indicators such as net migration rates also bear out the broad core–periphery nature of EU regional disparities (see EC Commission, 1991a, 1991c, 1992b).

Further support for those favouring a cumulative view of EU

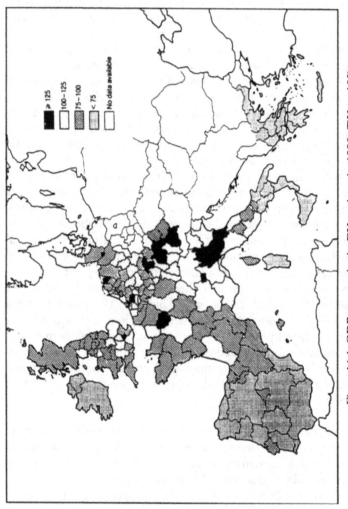

Figure 14.1 GDP per capita in EU regions in 1990 (EU = 100)
Source: Eurostat (1993) *Rapid Reports: Regions 1993(1),* Luxembourg.

regional disparities is provided by international comparisons of regional disparities. EU disparities are very wide by international standards. Regional disparities in per capita gross domestic product (GDP), for example, are over twice as large in the EU as in the United States (EC Commission, 1991c; OECD, 1989). Comparisons with other countries produces even starker contrasts (OECD, 1989).

While the existing pattern of regional disparities within the EU suggests that forces in the past may have systematically favoured the more central regions, this does not necessarily mean that current growth is cumulative. If the poorer peripheral regions are catching up with the more prosperous core of the EU, but the process is a slow one, then the neoclassical explanation may be compatible with the evidence of Figure 14.1. Analysis of per capita GDP data for the period 1950–90 suggests that a process of very slow convergence over time in regional disparities seems to be occurring. The best evidence currently available suggests that the regional inequality gap appears to be closing within the EU at approximately 2% per annum (Barro and Sala-i-Martin, 1991). Some idea of just how slow the convergence process is can be seen from Barro and Sala-i-Martin's estimate that at this rate it would take eastern Germany 35 years to halve its per capita income gap with western Germany in the absence of government intervention.

In summary, the debate on whether EU regional growth is convergent or divergent remains a finely balanced one. The best available evidence suggests that an extremely slow process of convergence is under way, but with wide disparities remaining. Whether the convergence process will continue in the future depends in part on the regional impact of EU integration, particularly the SEM and EMU. It is to these that attention is now turned.

ECONOMIC AND SOCIAL COHESION AND EU REGIONAL POLICY

The fact that convergence appears to be taking place within the EU leaves no room for complacency. As we have seen, the process is an extremely sluggish one. This in itself constitutes a strong case for intervention in the form of an EU regional policy as a means of 'speeding' matters along.

In addition, the EU is in the middle of two programmes designed to greatly improve economic integration – the SEM and EMU. The SEM, in the form of legislation phased in between 1989 and 1993, is designed to create a genuine single market for goods, services, labour and capital in Europe. Its principal targets are the many non-tariff barriers (NTBs) which still exist within the EU (Emerson, 1988). Prime candidates picked out by the SEM legislation are technical and safety standards in different countries which are frequently used as an excuse to block imports, the deliberate bias of member state governments in placing government contracts with local firms ('public procurement'), internal frontier formalities and a whole raft of barriers to trade in services (e.g., banking and insurance). While the legislative programme of the SEM has gone well and is largely now in place, the full economic effects will take many years to work their way through the European economy, even with the active steps being undertaken by the EU in the wake of a special committee (the Sutherland Committee) designed to push matters along (see Chapter 7).

Alongside the profound economic changes being introduced as the SEM takes effect is another major step forward in economic integration, namely EMU. While the initial Maastricht Treaty timetable for attaining monetary union now seems optimistic, the ratification of the Treaty does mean that in the years to come a slow process of further integration in the EU will be set in motion with a single currency as a final outcome (see Chapters 4–6).

Each successive strengthening of economic integration in Europe brings with it far-reaching structural changes to EU industry. In order to reap the benefits of additional trade in the form of lower prices for consumers, more jobs and more competitive European industries, it is necessary that a process of large-scale reorganisation takes place. Indeed, the faster the process of restructuring of European industry, the quicker will the benefits of integration be realised. As trade becomes freer, industries in some regions will decline, while other industries will expand. Industrial concentration is likely and considerable movement of labour and capital between industries and regions is necessary if the gains from freer trade are to be realised. EU regional policy can be seen as a vital adjunct to the SEM and EMU programmes. It can be used to help to speed up the structural changes which accompany them and it can be used to ameliorate the problems of industrial decline and unemployment which inevitably surface as restructuring occurs.

The case for an EU regional policy to accompany SEM and EMU is reinforced by the fact that no two 'rounds' in the process of EU integration ever have the same regional impact. Take the SEM process, for example. Some industries are more affected by NTBs such as technical and safety standards than others (e.g., food processing, telecommunications). Removing the barriers will therefore affect these industries (and hence the regions where they are concentrated) more than others. Some 40 manufacturing industries and a number of key service sectors are thought likely to be the ones eventually most affected by SEM (see EC Commission, 1990c; Booz Allen and Hamilton, 1989; PA Cambridge Economic Consultants, 1989). EMU too will have its own distinctive regional impact across the EU (Emerson, 1992).

In view of the likely regional restructuring effects accompanying SEM and EMU, it is not surprising that the EU has stepped up its regional policy effort since the SEM programme began in 1989, and has chosen to step it up again in the aftermath of the Maastricht Treaty (see below). The EU has placed great emphasis on developing a stronger regional policy in order to attain economic and social cohesion. Article 130A of the Maastricht Treaty sets out this goal as follows:

> In order to promote its overall harmonious development, the Community shall develop and pursue its action leading to the strengthening of its economic and social cohesion. In particular the Community shall aim at reducing the disparities between the various regions and the backwardness of the least favoured regions, including the rural areas.
>
> (Council of Ministers, 1992)

While it is possible to argue that the precise meaning of 'cohesion' has not been spelled out adequately and is therefore open to interpretation (European Parliament, 1991), its importance for the future of the EU is not in doubt.

EU REGIONAL POLICY: THE STRUCTURAL FUNDS

The structural funds lie at the heart of EU regional policy. They comprise the European Regional Development Fund (ERDF), the European Social Fund (ESF) and the Guidance Section of the European Agricultural Guidance and Guarantee Fund (EAGGF). The 1993 reforms to the structural funds were triggered by the need to increase the financial resources available for regional policy in the aftermath of the Maastricht Treaty, and by a desire to fine-tune the regional policy which had been set in place in 1989 at the time of the SEM legislation (EC Commission, 1989b). The 1989 legislation formed by far the most important piece of regional policy legislation ever introduced by the EU and laid the foundations of the regional policy which we see today.

The three structural funds have, since 1989, been required to act in a closely coordinated manner even though each plays are rather different role. The ERDF is designed to provide help principally for industrial and infrastructure projects in the disadvantaged regions. As with the other two structural funds, assistance is in the form of grants. Help is by no means confined to manufacturing industries. Many service sectors (e.g., tourism) are also assisted. Since the 1980s there has been a much greater emphasis on helping small and medium-sized enterprises and innovating sectors. The ESF concentrates on what in Britain would be called employment policy. Help is targeted on schemes for training and retraining, helping unemployed persons back into work, and on reducing labour market discrimination (e.g., against women and disabled workforce members). Although not strictly a 'regional' fund, the ESF by virtue of the type of help it gives inevitably operates with a bias towards the more disadvantaged regions of the EU. Indeed, under the 1989 and 1993 regulations the ESF is required to operate with a deliberate regional bias. The EAGGF Guidance Section is designed to be an instrument for restructuring the farming sector (e.g., new investment in farming and agri-businesses, land consolidation, etc.), and is also used to try to stimulate new firms in the non-farm sectors of the rural economy. As the traditionally dominant Guarantee Section (used to pay for the EU's price support policy) is reined in, the Guidance Section is gradually becoming more important.

Table 14.1 sets out the five common objectives of the structural funds for the period 1994–99. Table 14.1 also shows the various structural funds responsible for tackling each objective. As can be seen from the table, only three of the objectives are explicitly regional policy objectives in the sense that they involve the ERDF. These are Objective 1 ('lagging regions'), Objective 2

Table 14.1 The five priority objectives of the EU's structural funds, 1994–99

	Structural funds responsible
Objective 1 Development and structural adjustment of the regions whose development is lagging behind	ERDF, ESF, EAGGF (Gu)
Objective 2 Converting the regions or parts of regions seriously affected by industrial decline	ERDF, ESF
Objective 3 Combining long-term unemployment (more than 12 months) and facilitating the integration into working life of young people (under 25 years of age) and of persons exposed to exclusion from the labour market	ESF
Objective 4 Facilitating the adaptation of workers of either sex to industrial changes and to changes in production systems	ESF
Objective 5 Promoting rural development by: (a) speeding up the adjustment of agricultural structures in the framework of the reform of the Common Agriculture Policy (b) facilitating the development and structural adjustment of rural areas	EAGGF (Gu), FIFG ERDF, ESF, EAGGF (Gu)

Notes:
1. ERDF = European Regional Development Fund; ESF = European Social Fund; EAGGF (Gu) = European Agricultural Guidance and Guarantee Fund, Guidance Section; FIFG = Financial Instrument for Fisheries Guidance.
2. The Financial Instrument for Fisheries Guidance (FIFG) is a new instrument created in 1993 to group the funds available to tackle the serious problems being faced by communities dependent on fishing and aquaculture. The 1993 regulations chose to follow this route rather than creating a separate priority objective solely concerned with the fisheries and aquaculture sector (for which there had been intense lobbying prior to the 1993 reforms).

Source: EC Commission (1993).

('regions affected by industrial decline') and Objective 5b ('rural areas'). It is the three 'regional' objectives on which this section will focus. It should be noted, however, that although the other objectives are non-regional in the sense that all parts of the EU are eligible for help under them, the nature of the objectives (e.g., help for the long-term unemployed) means that they inevitably result in a regional bias in operations designed to tackle them.

In orchestrating its attempts to meet the priority objectives which it has set itself, the EU has devised a regional policy which embodies four key principles:

1 concentration of help where it is most needed;
2 partnership between the EU and other participants (e.g., member states, regional and local authorities);
3 the careful programming of help (effectively a system of regional planning);

Figure 14.2 Regions eligible under Objective 1 of the EU's structural funds, 1994–99

Note: The Objective 1 regions are those whose development is lagging behind that of the rest of the EU.

Source: EC Commission (1993).

4 stress on the principle of 'additionality' (i.e., the use of EU funds as a complement to member state money and not as a substitute).

Concentration of policy assistance

The need to target help where it is most needed is an obvious one. EU regional policy has several mechanisms for concentrating financial help on the most disadvantaged regions. The first mechanism involves limiting the areas eligible for help. Figure 14.2 sets out the regions of the EU eligible for help under Objective 1 (the lagging regions). These are supposed to be limited to regions with GDP per capita levels under 75% of the EU average. In practice, special reasons are also used to justify an extension to other areas (e.g., Northern Ireland, Merseyside). A worrying feature of Figure 14.2 is the way in which the Objective 1 regions have expanded from the 21.7% of the EU's population covered by the areas between 1989 and 1993, to the 26.6% designated for the period 1994–99. Any laxity in the targeting of Objective 1 money is particularly worrying given that some 70% of all structural fund expenditure is earmarked for Objective 1 (a figure rising to 80% of the total when the ERDF alone is considered).

Figure 14.3 shows the map of Objective 2 ('industrial decline') and Objective 5b ('rural areas') regions, as well as Objective 1. The Objective 2 regions are initially for a three-year period (1994–96), after which further revisions are possible. Objective 5b regions are for the full budget period 1994–99, as are the Objective 1 regions shown in Figure 14.2. The Objective 2 and 5b regions are based on very different criteria to those of Objective 1 regions. The Objective 2 regions are designated using data on unemployment rates and employment in declining sectors. Special considerations have been brought in to handle West Berlin and the fisheries areas – communities for which there is currently a heightened concern. The Objective 2 regions encompass 16.8% of the EU population. Objective 5b regions (encompassing 8.2% of the EU population) are designated using a combination of criteria, including the level of economic development, the level of employment in agriculture, agricultural incomes and measures of depopulation. Again, as with the Objective 2 regions, special provision is made to identify areas where the decline of fishing is having an effect.

Simply controlling the designation of maps of assisted areas is

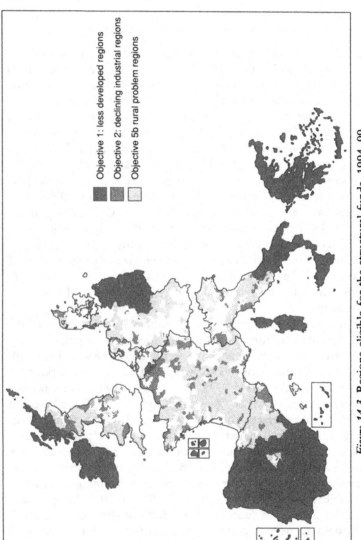

Objective 1: less developed regions
Objective 2: declining industrial regions
Objective 5b rural problem regions

Figure 14.3 Regions eligible for the structural funds, 1994–99
Source: Commission of the European Communities.

not, in itself sufficient to ensure that the bulk of the money goes to the worst affected regions of the EU. Three other mechanisms are used to concentrate structural funds' spending:

1 the deliberate earmarking of the bulk of EU structural fund money for the Objective 1 regions. Table 14.2 sets out the situation which has prevailed between 1989 and 1993, together with the EU's plans for the 1994–99 budget period. As can be seen, there has been a huge increase in the overall size of the resources devoted to the structural funds. This reflects the EU's concern for the regional implications of the SEM and EMU. The process of concentration of money is encouraged by deliberately earmarking money for the very poor Objective 1 regions (e.g., 80% of ERDF allocations between 1989 and 1993, and no less than 70% of all structural funds spending between 1994 and 1999);

2 the Commission makes indicative allocations for each objective and for each member state. These are best interpreted as targets for the country-by-country breakdown of spending under each objective. These indicative allocations are deliberately 'indicative' and are not rigid country quotas. That is, their attainment depends in part on the quality of the applications for help coming to the EU from the member states. Careful manipulation of these indicative allocations does, however, allow the EU some control on where the money is eventually spent and is therefore part of the targeting process; and

3 the targeting of money on the most disadvantaged regions can also be controlled to a limited extent by detailed day-to-day decisions by the Commission on which schemes put forward by the member states to give approval to. The EU also has a sum of money set aside for initiatives of its own (called Community Initiatives) and for which very flexible targeting rules apply.

Partnership and programming

The EU is not content to simply pay over the money from its structural funds to the member states. In involving itself in the implementation of its regional policy, however, the EU has a serious problem in that it does not have an established civil service at member state, regional and local level. The EU therefore has no choice but to work closely in partnership with the member state

Table 14.2 EU commitments for structural fund operations, 1989–99

(a) Under the Commision (1989) reforms

Year	ECU million (at 1988 prices)
1989	9,000
1990	10,300
1991	11,600
1992	12,900

(b) Under the Commission (1993) reforms

	ECU million (at 1992 prices)		
	Structural funds		
Year	Total	Objective 1	Cohesion Fund
1993	19,777	12,328	1,500
1994	20,135	13,220	1,750
1995	21,480	14,300	2,000
1996	22,740	15,330	2,250
1997	24,026	16,396	2,500
1998	25,690	17,820	2,550
1999	27,400	19,280	2,600

Note: The Cohesion Fund is not strictly one of the structural funds, but has been introduced as part of the broader financial package accompanying the 1993 reforms.

governments and to use the bureaucracy of the member states as the 'delivery system' for regional assistance. There are two other reasons for the EU's emphasis on a partnership approach to regional policy. First, the EU is committed to 'subsidiarity'; that is, wherever possible, powers are decentralised within the EU. If the EU wishes to be involved in regional policy, therefore, it must tolerate an active role by the member states, regional governments and local authorities. Second, the EU can play an important role as a coordinator, bringing together all of the organisations and governments trying to regenerate industry in the depressed regions.

In encouraging a partnership approach to its regional policy the EU has not been content to deal only with the member state

governments. It has tried to involve regional and local organisations, too, at all stages. This has not always been popular with
member state governments, particularly in countries such as Britain
where the central government is all-powerful. Most notably of all,
the EU has encouraged partnership by developing a distinctive
system of regional planning (or 'programming') which is designed
to involve regional and local participants as well as the member
state governments. As well as ensuring a good mix of partners,
the programming system is the key instrument for trying to get
the various participants to coordinate activities. Money from the
structural funds is used as an inducement to closer coordination.
For 1994–99, the programming system is essentially a four-stage
one:

1 stage one – member states, together with regional and local
  partners, draw up detailed regional development plans. The
  best designed of these plans will contain an analysis of the
  problem, clear quantified goals, an indicative financial table
  showing how each partner (including the EU) will contribute,
  and the main thrust of the regional strategy. These plans are
  supposed to dove-tail with the EU's own analysis of the regional
  situation (see EC Commission, 1991c, for an example) and the
  EU's stated regional policy guidelines;
2 stage two – after considering the regional development plans,
  the EU responds, in consultation with the member state, with a
  Community Support Framework (CSF) or Single Programming
  Document (SPD). This sets out the EU's priorities and the
  amount and manner of its structural fund help for the 1994–
  99 period. Care is taken to tie in the EU's help closely with that
  offered by the member state and the other participants;
3 stage three – the implementation of the jointly agreed programmes of help is normally left in the hands of the member
  state governments and the other regional and local organisations
  involved. EU money can be used in a huge variety of flexible
  ways. These range from direct grants to firms for investment to
  advisory services and infrastructure provision. The vast bulk of
  the aid is channelled through Operational Programmes (OPs).
  These are detailed regional and sub-regional schemes. Each is
  designed to run for several years (usually on a renewable basis),
  with clear local goals, drawing in a range of public and private

partners and using coordinated packages of different types of help; and

4 stage four – the programmes of assistance are subject to a process of continuing monitoring and evaluation. The planning process is therefore a continuing, iterative one. At each new round, the results of the monitoring and evaluation are used to design improvements to the programmes.

Although the bulk of the EU's structural funds' help for depressed regions is channelled through OPs, there are a number of other mechanisms for providing help. Direct help to individual large (mostly infrastructure) projects on a one-off basis can be given. The EU can also simply part-finance member state aid schemes if it wishes. There is also a limited use of global grants. These involve the EU paying money to some intermediary agent which acts on its behalf. Global grants are particularly useful in channelling help to small firms where 'hands-on' work would simply swamp the EU or member state government. Finally, mention must be made of Community Initiatives (CIs). These are programmes of aid initiated by the EU from the 9% of the money set aside for this purpose. Unlike the OPs, which are confined to a single member state (or part of a single member state), the CIs are designed to tackle regional problems which are common to many member states. Table 14.3 sets out the CIs introduced between 1989 and 1993. As can be seen, some of the CIs attack problems caused by an EU-wide decline of a single industry (e.g., RECHAR and the coal industry), or are designed to meet a common goal (e.g., REGEN and energy supply networks to disadvantaged regions).

Additionality

The principle of additionality is one of the most important for the success of EU regional policy and at the same time one of the most difficult to achieve. Additionality refers to the situation in which the EU structural funds inject money into the depressed regions in a manner which prevents member states from exploiting the opportunity to cut back their own domestic regional spending. There are three main reasons for the importance of the concept of additionality:

1 EU regional policy is designed in part to meet new regional problems arising from processes such as the SEM and EMU.

270

Table 14.3 The Community Initiatives (CIs) adopted by the EU, 1989–93

Name	Nature of programme	Allocation (ECUm)
ENVIRAG	Environmental protection	500
INTERREG	Cross-border cooperation	800
RECHAR	Coal-mining areas	300
REGIS	Remotest regions	200
STRIDE	Research and technology	400
REGEN	Energy networks	300
TELEMATIQUE	Telecommunications	200
PRISMA	Business services	100
EUROFORM	Skills acquistion	300
NOW	Equal opportunities (women)	120
HORIZON	Equal opportunities (handicapped persons and others)	180
LEADER	Rural development	400

Source: EC Commission (1993).

New problems call for a net injection of new money, something which is frustrated if additionality is avoided by member states;

2 the EU's structural funds budget, large though it now is, cannot possibly solve Europe's regional problems on its own. The money must therefore act as a catalyst, triggering matching injections from the member states, regional and local organisations and from the private sector. Additionality is crucial if this is to occur; and

3 the period 1994–99 will see member states desperately attempting to fulfil the convergence criteria of the Maastricht Treaty (see especially Chapter 5). Cutting budget deficits is a key element in this struggle for economic convergence. The temptation for member states to use EU money as a substitute for their own regional spending will be strong.

The EU attempts to ensure additionality by two methods. The first is its use of a matching-grant process in awarding structural funds' help. The EU will not be the sole provider of assistance to projects and programmes. Member state aid must also be given and ceilings on the EU contribution are set. Second, the EU operates a 'maximum disclosure of information' policy designed to put pressure on member states to stick to their additionality promises. Under the 1993 regulations, for example, member states are required to 'maintain, in the whole of the territory concerned, its public structural or comparable expenditure at least at the same level as in the previous [i.e., 1989–93] programming period' (EC Commission, 1993). Information checks are also included in the regional development plans and at the monitoring and evaluation stage. It must be admitted, however, that member states in the past have often proved masters at disguising cut-backs in regional policy spending and there is little to guarantee that the 1993 regulations will be any more successful than their predecessors.

THE REGIONAL POLICY ACTIVITIES OF OTHER EU FINANCIAL INSTRUMENTS

In addition to the EU's structural funds, a number of other financial instruments also operate with a pro-regional policy bias, including:

1 the Cohesion Fund – an entirely new fund created in 1993 as part of the Maastricht Treaty process. It is designed to help certain member states to become more fully integrated into the EU economy as part of the EMU process. Member states with GDP per capita under 90% of the EU average are eligible, currently Spain, Portugal, Greece and Ireland. Eligibility will be reviewed in 1996. The money is earmarked for transport infrastructure and environmental improvement projects. The Cohesion Fund will increase from ECU 1.5bn in 1993 to ECU 2.6bn in 1999 (at 1992 prices). Spain is to get between 52% and 58% of the fund's spending, Greece 16–20%, Portugal 16–20% and Ireland 7–10%;

2 the Financial Instrument for Fisheries Guidance (FIFG) – a new financial instrument set up as part of the 1993 reforms (EC Commission, 1993). It reflects a growing concern within the EU of the severe problems being experienced by communities dependent on fishing and aquaculture. It is designed to operate alongside the structural funds in attempting to attain Objective 5a (see Table 14.1);

3 the European Investment Bank (EIB) – an investment bank which uses its own capital together with money borrowed on international capital markets to make loans in all parts of the EU (and, indeed, some outside the EU). A deliberately high proportion of EIB loans, however, are made to industrial, infrastructure

and environmental projects in the disadvantaged regions of the EU. In 1991, for example, the EIB made some ECU 14.4bn of loans inside the EU and, of these, no less than ECU 8.5bn were for regional development purposes; and finally

4 the European Coal and Steel Community (ECSC) – a body established in 1952 which continues to have a separate budget and policy existence within the EU. Although not strictly a regional policy instrument, the coal and steel areas are among some of the most disadvantaged regions of the EU. The ECSC makes loans to the coal, steel and associated industries for restructuring purposes (ECU 1.1bn in 1992). It also makes 'conversion loans' to other industries setting up in coal and steel areas (ECU 426m in 1992), together with a variety of types of 'redaptation' assistance designed to help ex-coal and steel workers to relocate, retrain and to migrate and re-house themselves.

COMPETITION POLICY REGULATIONS FOR STATE AIDS

The EU has adopted a number of competition policy regulations designed to control the activities of member state regional policies, particularly member state subsidies (EC Commission, 1988a) – see also Chapter 13. These regulations are designed to prevent member states from using their own regional subsidies to aggressively bid for inward investment projects from overseas (e.g., Japanese car assembly plants) or for firms from other EU countries. The regulations take the form of differentiated ceilings on the size of subsidies which can be offered, with poorer regions having less restrictive ceilings. Subsidies which are difficult to quantify (i.e., 'opaque' subsidies) are banned, as are subsidies which are paid on a continuing basis (rather than one-off grants).

RESEARCH AND ANALYSIS OF REGIONAL PROBLEMS IN THE EU

The EU underpins its regional policy with wide-ranging provision for research and analysis of regional problems. There is a substantial amount of in-house research undertaken at Brussels, quite a lot of which finds its way into the regular periodic reports on regional problems in the EU (EC Commission, 1991c). These periodic reports, in turn, form the basis of the EU's regional policy guidelines which serve as a framework when regional plans and CSFs are being drawn up. The EU also funds a large number of studies and consultancy reports from external researchers and organisations. Among the most important types of research undertaken are the regional impact assessment studies which are designed to identify, at an early stage, those EU policies likely to have adverse regional effects (see, for example, EC Commission, 1984).

CONCLUSIONS

The EU regional policy as it has now evolved is a rather complex one. Many of the developments contained in the key 1989 and 1993 reform packages are to be welcomed, particularly the large increase in the real value of the financial resources devoted to regional policy.

The regional policy of the EU will, however, continue to face problems in the years ahead. Five main difficulties can be highlighted. First, serious doubts remain on the ability of EU regional policy to solve regional problems. The experience of individual member states such as Britain suggests that many regional problems are highly intractable and require much larger budgets than that available to the EU. In addition, the SEM and EMU will pose new regional problems. Second, and closely associated with the funding problem, is the unusual nature of the EU's economic powers. In most federal systems such as the United States, the central government has wide fiscal powers which can be used to help to reduce regional disparities. Automatic stabilisers such as federal income taxation tend to damp down regional per capita income differences by taxing richer regions more heavily. In addition, in genuine federal states there is a powerful system of inter-personal transfers (e.g., unemployment benefits and other welfare payments) and inter-government transfers (e.g., grants from the federal government to state governments). Both sets of transfers tend to narrow regional disparities, yet the EU has virtually none of these systems in place.

Third, despite the provisions in the 1993 reforms, the ability of the EU to force member states to use EU regional policy money in an 'additional' manner cannot be guaranteed, particularly as we are entering a period of severe pressure on member states' budget deficits. Fourth, the 1993 reforms have failed to settle the issue of 'who does what' in regional policy. This goes to the heart of the current high-profile debate on subsidiarity. The struggle for power to control regional policy between the member states and the EU will continue until a final balance of authority is clearly set out. We are a long way from this stage.

Finally, an issue which will undoubtedly emerge into much sharper focus in the years ahead will be the relationship between regional policy and the external trade performance of the EU. With the EU facing severe competitive pressures from other parts of the world, it cannot be long before voices are raised questioning the effectiveness of EU regional policy. Some will see the disadvantaged regions as inherently poor locations for internationally competitive firms. Others will argue the contrary case. In the meantime, it is vital that the existing EU expenditures be very carefully spent if the policy is not to be discredited in the years ahead. In this respect it would be better to proceed with extreme caution in managing the sudden large increase in spending for the peripheral regions envisaged in the 1993 reforms. If certain peripheral regions are simply unable to efficiently absorb a sudden large increase in assistance, it would be safer for the spending to be phased in more slowly.

STATISTICAL APPENDIX

Key for abbreviations in Tables A1–A7:

B	Belgium
DK	Denmark
D	Germany
GR	Greece
E	Spain
F	France
IRL	Ireland
I	Italy
L	Luxembourg
NL	The Netherlands
P	Portugal
UK	United Kingdom
EU	European Union
USA	United States of America
J	Japan

Table A1 Unemployment rates (per cent of civilian labour force)

	B	DK	D	GR	E	F	IRI	I	L	NL	P	UK	EU	USA	J
1964	1.4	1.2	0.5	4.7	2.8	1.2	5.2	4.0	0.0	0.5	2.5	1.4	1.9	5.2	1.2
1965	1.6	0.9	0.4	4.8	2.6	1.5	5.0	5.0	0.0	0.6	2.5	1.2	2.0	4.5	1.2
1966	1.7	1.1	0.5	5.0	2.2	1.6	5.1	5.4	0.0	0.8	2.5	1.1	2.1	3.8	1.3
1967	2.4	1.0	1.4	5.4	3.0	2.1	5.5	5.0	0.0	1.7	2.5	2.0	2.6	3.8	1.3
1968	2.8	1.0	1.0	5.6	3.0	2.6	5.8	5.3	0.0	1.5	2.6	2.1	2.7	3.6	1.2
1969	2.2	0.9	0.6	5.3	2.5	2.3	5.5	5.3	0.0	1.1	2.6	2.0	2.4	3.5	1.1
1970	1.8	0.6	0.5	4.2	2.6	2.4	6.3	5.1	0.0	1.0	2.6	2.2	2.4	4.9	1.2
1961–70	2.0	1.0	0.7	5.0	2.7	2.0	5.5	5.0	0.0	1.0	2.5	1.7	2.3	4.2	1.2
1971	1.7	0.9	0.6	3.1	3.4	2.7	6.0	5.1	0.0	1.3	2.5	2.7	2.6	6.0	1.2
1972	2.2	0.8	0.8	2.1	2.9	2.8	6.7	6.0	0.0	2.3	2.5	3.1	2.9	5.6	1.4
1973	2.2	0.7	0.8	2.0	2.6	2.7	6.2	5.9	0.0	2.4	2.6	2.2	2.6	4.9	1.3
1974	2.3	2.8	1.8	2.1	3.1	2.8	5.8	5.0	0.0	2.9	1.7	2.0	2.8	5.6	1.4
1975	4.2	3.9	3.3	2.3	4.5	4.0	7.9	5.5	0.0	5.5	4.4	3.2	4.1	8.5	1.9
1976	5.5	5.1	3.3	1.9	4.9	4.4	9.8	6.2	0.0	5.8	6.2	4.8	4.7	7.7	2.0
1977	6.3	5.9	3.2	1.7	5.3	4.9	9.7	6.7	0.0	5.6	7.3	5.1	5.0	7.1	2.0
1978	6.8	6.7	3.1	1.8	7.1	5.1	9.0	6.7	1.2	5.6	7.9	5.0	5.3	6.1	2.3
1979	7.0	4.8	2.7	1.9	8.8	5.8	7.8	7.2	2.4	5.7	7.9	4.6	5.4	5.8	2.2

1980	7.4	5.2	2.7	2.8	11.6	6.2	8.0	7.1	2.4	6.4	7.6	5.6	6.0	7.1	2.0
1971–80	4.6	3.7	2.2	2.2	5.4	4.1	7.7	6.1	0.6	4.4	5.1	3.8	4.2	6.4	1.8
1981	9.5	8.3	3.9	4.0	14.4	7.3	10.8	7.4	2.4	8.9	7.3	8.9	7.7	7.6	2.2
1982	11.2	8.9	5.6	5.8	16.3	8.0	12.5	8.0	2.4	11.9	7.2	10.3	9.0	9.7	2.4
1983	12.5	9.2	6.9	7.9	17.7	8.2	15.2	8.9	3.5	12.1	7.8	11.0	9.9	9.6	2.7
1984	12.5	8.7	7.1	8.1	20.0	9.7	16.8	9.5	3.1	11.6	8.5	11.0	10.5	7.5	2.7
1985	11.8	7.2	7.1	7.8	21.1	10.1	18.2	10.1	2.9	10.5	8.6	11.4	10.8	7.2	2.6
1986	11.7	5.5	6.5	7.4	21.1	10.3	18.2	10.6	2.6	10.2	8.3	11.4	10.7	7.0	2.8
1987	11.3	5.6	6.3	7.4	20.5	10.4	18.0	10.8	2.5	10.0	6.8	10.4	10.4	6.2	2.8
1988	10.2	6.4	6.3	7.7	19.4	9.9	17.3	10.9	2.0	9.3	5.7	8.5	9.8	5.5	2.5
1989	8.6	7.7	5.6	7.5	17.1	9.4	15.7	10.9	1.8	8.5	5.0	7.1	9.0	5.3	2.3
1990	7.6	8.1	4.8	7.0	16.2	9.0	14.5	10.0	1.7	7.5	4.6	7.0	8.4	5.5	2.1
1981–90	10.7	7.6	6.0	7.1	18.4	9.2	15.7	9.7	2.5	10.1	7.0	9.7	9.6	7.1	2.5
1991	7.5	8.9	4.2	7.7	16.4	9.5	16.2	10.1	1.6	7.1	4.0	8.9	8.7	6.7	2.1
1992	8.2	9.5	4.5	8.7	18.2	10.0	17.8	10.3	1.9	7.2	3.9	10.2	9.4	7.4	2.2
1993	9.4	10.4	5.6	9.8	21.5	10.8	18.4	11.1	2.6	8.8	5.0	10.5	10.5	6.8	2.5
1994	10.3	9.9	6.9	10.1	23.3	11.5	17.8	12.0	3.0	10.2	6.5	9.9	11.3	6.3	3.1

Source: European Economy.

Table A2 Gross domestic product (ECU, bn)

	B	DK	D	GR	E	F	IRL	I	L	NL	P	UK	EU	USA	J
1964	14.3	8.5	98.2	4.9	19.3	86.2	2.5	58.1	0.6	16.9	3.1	87.4	400.0	607.2	76.7
1965	15.5	9.5	107.3	5.6	22.5	92.8	2.6	62.5	0.7	18.9	3.5	94.1	435.5	658.1	85.3
1966	16.7	10.4	114.1	6.2	26.0	100.5	2.8	67.7	0.7	20.6	3.8	100.2	469.7	720.9	99.1
1967	17.9	11.4	116.1	6.8	28.8	109.1	3.0	75.0	0.7	22.7	4.3	104.0	499.6	765.5	116.7
1968	19.9	12.2	129.6	7.6	29.1	122.7	3.0	84.1	0.8	26.0	4.9	101.9	541.8	865.0	143.0
1969	22.2	14.0	148.3	8.7	33.4	134.3	3.5	93.4	0.9	29.7	5.4	110.4	604.2	940.2	169.1
1970	24.7	15.5	180.5	9.7	37.2	139.8	4.0	105.1	1.1	33.3	6.1	121.2	678.1	989.6	199.3
1971	27.2	16.9	205.7	10.5	41.3	153.2	4.5	112.7	1.1	38.0	6.7	134.4	752.1	1048.1	221.8
1972	31.3	19.4	230.1	11.2	48.8	174.6	5.2	122.0	1.3	43.6	7.6	143.6	838.7	1076.8	272.0
1973	36.7	23.3	280.0	13.1	59.0	206.6	5.6	135.0	1.6	52.2	9.3	147.5	970.0	1096.4	337.7
1974	44.8	26.9	317.8	15.8	75.4	229.6	6.1	154.3	2.0	64.1	11.3	163.0	112.1	1215.0	395.2
1975	49.8	30.4	336.7	16.8	86.7	276.0	7.1	171.2	1.9	71.4	12.0	188.6	1248.5	1279.5	411.2
1976	59.7	37.2	398.0	20.2	98.1	318.2	7.8	188.0	2.3	86.7	13.9	201.1	1431.1	1583.4	502.9
1977	68.1	40.7	451.3	22.9	107.1	342.1	9.1	213.0	2.5	99.9	14.3	222.8	1593.9	1731.1	607.0
1978	74.6	44.4	502.2	24.8	116.8	380.3	10.6	234.7	2.8	109.7	14.1	253.3	1768.1	1749.9	765.3

Year															
1979	79.4	48.1	552.9	28.1	144.7	425.6	12.3	272.2	3.0	116.9	14.8	306.1	2004.2	1813.9	737.4
1980	85.0	47.8	583.2	28.8	154.3	478.5	14.5	326.0	3.3	124.1	18.1	386.4	2249.7	1945.1	762.4
1981	86.6	51.5	610.6	33.3	167.3	524.0	17.2	367.4	3.4	129.3	21.9	459.7	2472.2	2719.2	1051.3
1982	87.0	56.9	668.4	39.4	184.0	563.8	20.3	411.8	3.6	143.5	23.7	496.5	2698.8	3217.8	1111.1
1983	90.8	63.0	734.9	39.4	176.3	591.7	21.6	469.2	3.8	152.7	23.3	517.1	2883.9	3812.9	1333.2
1984	97.5	69.4	782.3	43.0	200.3	634.8	23.6	525.4	4.3	161.3	24.3	550.0	3116.6	4769.7	1606.4
1985	105.6	76.7	818.9	43.7	218.4	691.7	26.0	559.8	4.6	169.4	27.1	604.7	3346.4	5263.7	1774.6
1986	113.9	84.0	904.7	40.1	235.2	745.5	26.9	615.6	5.1	182.3	30.1	571.3	3554.5	4298.8	2028.0
1987	121.0	88.8	860.9	40.1	254.2	770.2	27.2	658.1	5.3	188.8	31.8	598.8	3745.1	3895.0	2091.4
1988	128.1	92.1	1010.4	45.2	291.8	815.1	29.2	710.2	5.8	195.9	35.3	707.0	4066.1	4104.9	2452.3
1989	139.0	95.3	1074.5	49.3	345.4	877.0	32.4	790.1	6.5	207.5	41.1	763.8	4422.0	4723.9	2607.6
1990	151.2	101.7	1181.8	52.4	387.3	940.9	35.1	861.1	7.1	223.3	47.0	769.6	4759.4	4291.4	2311.5
1991	158.8	104.6	1284.9	56.8	426.7	967.5	36.4	932.3	7.6	234.5	55.5	815.7	5081.3	4527.9	2707.6
1992	169.1	109.4	1383.1	60.1	444.1	1021.7	38.9	942.8	8.2	247.6	65.1	805.5	5295.5	4560.7	2831.1
1993	176.2	115.5	1462.5	62.8	408.3	1072.2	39.2	847.3	8.6	263.9	64.3	802.6	5323.3	5338.2	3619.4
1994	186.3	122.4	1509.9	65.2	403.2	1111.4	42.6	876.8	9.2	273.5	65.0	861.4	5526.8	5799.2	3993.7

Source: European Economy.

Table A3 Per capita gross domestic product (EU = 100)

	B	DK	D	GR	E	F	IRL	I	L	NL	P	UK	EU	USA	J
1964	110.2	130.1	122.8	41.9	44.4	129.3	62.3	71.4	138.5	101.2	26.8	117.3	100.0	229.4	56.9
1965	110.1	134.3	122.9	44.0	47.3	127.8	61.2	80.5	132.9	103.3	27.7	116.3	100.0	227.5	58.0
1966	109.8	136.5	121.0	45.4	50.6	128.2	60.1	81.0	129.6	103.7	28.5	115.1	100.0	230.1	62.3
1967	111.2	140.2	116.2	46.1	52.4	130.6	60.8	84.2	123.6	106.9	30.3	112.3	100.0	228.7	68.7
1968	113.8	138.4	119.9	47.9	48.7	135.3	57.3	87.1	129.4	112.7	32.1	101.6	100.0	237.3	77.2
1969	114.4	142.3	122.8	49.3	49.9	132.7	59.9	86.9	135.6	114.7	32.1	99.0	100.0	230.7	81.4
1970	114.2	140.1	132.8	48.5	49.4	122.8	60.1	87.2	141.7	114.0	32.2	97.2	100.0	215.3	85.0
1971	113.8	138.1	136.0	48.6	59.2	121.1	61.4	84.5	130.4	116.6	32.7	97.3	100.0	204.5	85.0
1972	118.0	141.9	136.5	46.2	51.8	123.6	63.0	82.1	135.2	119.7	33.5	93.7	100.0	187.7	92.9
1973	120.0	147.7	143.8	46.7	54.0	126.2	58.1	78.5	145.9	123.7	35.7	83.5	100.0	164.7	98.9
1974	129.9	148.8	143.3	49.1	59.9	122.1	54.2	78.1	160.2	132.0	37.6	80.9	100.0	158.5	100.1
1975	126.9	149.7	135.8	46.4	60.9	130.6	55.5	77.1	132.3	130.3	34.5	83.7	100.0	147.8	92.0
1976	133.0	160.0	141.3	48.3	58.0	126.7	54.8	74.9	136.7	141.9	31.5	78.0	100.0	154.7	104.9
1977	136.5	157.6	144.7	48.3	58.0	126.7	54.8	74.9	136.7	141.9	31.5	78.0	100.0	154.7	104.9
1978	135.1	154.8	145.8	46.9	56.6	126.8	57.1	74.4	137.8	140.1	27.7	80.3	100.0	140.0	118.6

Year														
1979	127.3	148.3	142.1	46.5	61.5	125.2	57.8	76.2	132.1	131.4	25.5	85.8	100.0	127.1	100.3
1980	121.8	131.5	133.6	42.1	58.3	125.3	60.0	81.5	126.8	123.7	27.5	96.8	100.0	120.5	92.1
1981	113.3	129.5	127.6	44.1	57.1	124.6	64.2	83.8	121.1	117.0	30.2	105.1	100.0	152.3	115.1
1982	104.4	131.6	128.3	47.6	57.3	122.4	68.9	86.1	114.9	118.6	30.0	104.3	100.0	163.7	111.0
1983	102.1	136.6	132.6	44.4	51.3	119.8	68.3	91.9	116.6	117.9	27.5	101.7	100.0	180.0	123.9
1984	101.7	139.5	131.4	44.7	53.8	118.5	68.7	95.3	119.7	114.9	26.6	100.1	100.0	206.8	137.5
1985	102.6	143.8	128.6	42.1	54.4	119.9	70.9	94.7	119.5	112.1	27.6	102.4	100.0	210.9	140.9
1986	104.5	148.3	134.0	36.4	55.1	121.4	68.6	98.2	125.2	113.3	28.9	91.0	100.0	160.9	151.0
1987	105.5	148.9	135.3	34.6	56.5	118.7	66.0	99.9	122.7	110.7	29.1	90.5	100.0	137.4	147.4
1988	102.7	142.7	130.7	35.9	59.8	115.5	65.6	99.6	122.5	105.5	29.9	98.5	100.0	132.5	159.0
1989	102.6	136.3	127.1	36.1	65.2	114.1	67.6	102.3	126.7	102.6	32.1	97.9	100.0	139.4	155.4
1990	104.1	135.7	128.2	35.4	68.2	113.8	68.8	104.2	127.2	102.5	34.4	92.0	100.0	117.8	128.4
1991	102.5	131.1	129.5	36.0	70.8	109.5	66.7	106.1	126.0	100.5	38.3	91.4	100.0	115.7	141.1
1992	104.9	131.8	132.8	36.4	71.0	110.9	68.4	103.3	129.6	101.6	43.4	86.7	100.0	111.2	141.8
1993	109.0	138.7	139.0	37.7	65.1	115.8	68.5	92.5	136.1	107.5	42.8	86.2	100.0	128.7	180.8
1994	111.2	141.8	137.6	37.7	62.1	115.5	71.8	92.5	139.7	106.9	41.8	87.2	100.0	133.9	192.4

Source: European Economy.

Table A4 Economic growth (per cent of change in gross domestic product per annum)

	B	DK	D	GR	E	F	IRL	I	L	NL	P	UK	EU	USA	J
1964	7.0	9.3	6.7	8.3	6.2	6.5	3.8	2.8	7.9	8.3	7.3	5.4	5.8	5.6	11.7
1965	3.6	4.6	5.4	9.4	6.3	4.8	1.9	3.3	1.9	5.2	7.6	2.5	4.3	5.6	5.8
1966	3.2	2.7	2.8	6.1	7.1	5.2	0.9	6.0	1.1	2.7	3.9	1.9	3.9	6.0	10.6
1967	3.9	3.4	-0.3	3.3	4.3	4.7	5.0	7.2	0.2	5.3	8.1	2.3	3.4	2.9	11.1
1968	4.2	4.0	5.5	6.7	6.8	4.3	8.2	6.5	4.2	6.4	9.2	4.1	5.3	4.0	12.9
1969	6.6	6.3	7.5	9.9	8.9	7.0	5.9	6.1	10.0	6.4	3.4	2.1	6.0	2.7	12.5
1970	6.4	2.0	5.0	8.0	4.1	5.7	2.7	5.3	1.7	5.7	7.6	2.3	4.7	-0.3	10.7
1961–70	4.9	4.5	4.4	7.6	7.3	5.6	4.2	5.7	3.5	5.1	6.4	2.9	4.8	3.8	10.5
1971	3.7	2.7	3.1	7.1	4.6	4.8	3.5	1.6	2.7	4.2	6.6	2.0	3.2	2.8	4.3
1972	5.3	5.3	4.3	8.9	8.0	4.4	6.5	2.7	6.6	3.3	8.0	3.5	4.3	4.7	8.2
1973	5.9	3.6	4.8	7.3	7.7	5.4	4.7	7.1	8.3	4.7	11.2	7.4	6.2	5.1	7.6
1974	4.1	-0.9	0.2	-3.6	5.3	3.1	4.3	5.4	4.2	4.0	1.1	-1.7	2.0	-0.7	-0.6
1975	-1.5	-0.7	-1.3	6.1	0.5	-0.3	5.7	-2.7	-6.6	-0.1	-4.3	-0.7	-0.9	-1.0	2.9
1976	5.6	6.5	5.3	6.4	3.3	4.2	1.4	6.6	2.5	5.1	6.9	2.7	4.7	4.8	4.2
1977	0.5	1.6	2.8	3.4	3.0	3.2	8.2	3.4	1.6	2.3	5.5	2.3	2.9	4.5	4.7
1978	2.7	1.5	3.0	6.7	1.4	3.4	7.2	3.7	4.1	2.5	2.8	3.5	3.2	4.8	4.9
1979	2.1	3.5	4.2	3.7	-0.1	3.2	3.1	6.0	2.3	2.4	5.6	2.8	3.5	2.5	5.5

1980	4.3	−0.4	1.0	1.8	1.2	1.6	3.1	4.2	0.8	0.9	4.6	−2.2	1.3	−0.4	3.6
1971–80	3.2	2.2	2.7	4.7	3.5	3.3	4.7	3.8	2.6	2.9	4.7	1.9	3.0	2.7	4.5
1981	−1.0	−0.9	0.1	0.1	−0.2	1.2	3.3	0.6	−0.6	−0.6	1.6	−1.3	0.1	2.2	3.6
1982	1.5	3.0	−0.9	0.4	1.2	2.5	2.3	0.2	1.1	−1.4	2.1	1.7	0.8	−2.2	3.2
1983	0.4	2.5	1.8	0.4	1.8	0.7	−0.2	1.0	3.0	1.4	−0.2	3.8	1.6	3.6	2.7
1984	2.2	4.4	2.8	2.8	1.8	1.3	4.4	2.7	6.2	3.1	−1.9	2.5	2.3	6.7	4.3
1985	0.8	4.3	2.0	3.1	2.3	1.9	3.1	2.6	2.9	2.6	2.8	3.5	2.5	3.1	5.0
1986	1.4	3.6	2.3	1.6	3.2	2.5	−0.4	2.9	4.8	2.8	4.1	4.3	2.9	2.8	2.6
1987	2.0	0.3	1.5	−0.5	5.6	2.3	4.5	3.1	2.9	1.2	5.3	4.8	2.9	3.1	4.1
1988	5.0	1.2	3.7	4.4	5.2	4.5	4.2	4.1	5.7	2.6	3.9	5.0	4.3	3.9	6.2
1989	3.6	0.6	3.6	3.5	4.7	4.3	6.2	2.9	6.7	4.7	5.2	2.2	3.5	2.7	4.7
1990	3.2	1.4	5.7	−1.1	3.6	2.5	9.0	2.1	3.2	4.1	4.4	0.4	3.0	0.8	4.8
1981–90	1.9	2.0	2.2	1.5	2.9	2.4	3.6	2.2	3.6	2.0	2.7	2.7	2.4	2.7	4.1
1991	1.8	1.0	4.5	3.3	2.2	0.7	2.6	1.2	3.1	2.1	2.1	−2.3	1.5	−1.1	4.0
1992	1.4	1.2	1.6	0.9	0.8	1.4	4.8	0.7	1.9	1.4	1.1	−0.5	1.0	2.6	1.3
1993	−1.3	1.1	−1.9	−0.2	−1.0	−0.7	2.5	−0.7	0.3	0.3	−1.2	1.9	−0.5	3.0	0.1
1994	1.3	3.8	0.7	0.7	1.1	1.6	4.2	1.5	1.6	1.3	1.1	2.5	1.5	3.7	0.8

Source: European Economy

Table A5 Gross domestic fixed capital formation (per cent change per annum)

	B	DK	D	GR	E	F	IRL	I	L	NL	P	UK	EU	USA	J
1964	14.7	23.5	11.2	20.7	15.0	10.5	10.8	-5.8	22.1	19.2	4.0	16.6	9.6	8.1	15.7
1965	4.1	4.7	4.7	12.8	16.6	7.0	10.5	-8.4	-13.9	5.3	10.3	5.2	4.0	8.6	4.6
1966	6.8	4.3	1.2	3.2	12.7	7.3	-3.0	4.3	-5.1	8.0	17.9	2.6	4.8	4.2	14.0
1967	2.7	5.4	-7.0	-1.6	6.0	6.0	6.8	11.7	-7.9	8.5	5.2	8.7	3.8	-1.6	18.1
1968	-1.3	1.9	3.3	21.4	9.4	5.5	13.2	10.8	-4.2	11.2	-9.3	6.3	6.3	5.8	20.5
1969	5.3	11.8	9.6	18.6	9.8	9.2	20.5	7.8	10.5	-2.2	8.1	-0.6	6.8	2.7	18.9
1970	8.4	2.2	8.9	-1.4	3.0	4.6	-3.3	3.0	7.5	7.5	11.4	2.5	5.0	-3.4	16.9
1961-70	5.8	7.0	4.2	9.3	11.2	7.8	9.6	5.1	3.4	6.7	6.9	5.2	6.0	3.9	15.7
1971	-1.9	1.9	5.9	14.0	-3.0	7.3	8.9	0.2	10.7	1.5	10.2	1.8	3.4	5.4	4.4
1972	3.4	9.3	2.7	15.4	14.2	6.0	7.8	1.3	7.0	-2.3	14.0	-0.2	3.9	8.9	9.7
1973	7.0	3.5	-0.3	7.7	13.0	8.5	16.2	8.8	11.8	4.2	10.3	6.5	6.1	7.0	11.6
1974	6.9	-8.9	-9.7	-25.6	6.2	1.3	-11.6	2.0	-7.0	-4.0	-6.1	-2.4	-2.2	-6.0	-8.3
1975	-1.9	-12.4	-5.4	0.2	-4.5	-6.4	-3.6	-7.3	-7.4	-4.4	-10.6	-2.0	-5.3	-10.9	-1.0
1976	4.0	17.1	3.6	6.8	-0.8	3.3	13.6	0.0	-4.2	-2.2	1.3	1.7	2.1	7.4	2.7
1977	0.0	-2.4	3.6	7.8	-0.9	-1.8	4.1	1.8	-0.1	9.7	11.5	-1.8	1.0	12.1	2.8
1978	2.8	1.1	4.1	6.0	-2.7	2.1	18.9	0.6	1.1	2.5	6.2	3.0	2.2	9.3	7.8
1979	-2.7	-0.4	6.7	8.8	-4.4	3.1	13.6	5.7	3.8	-1.7	-1.3	2.8	3.2	4.2	6.2

1980	4.6	-12.6	2.2	-6.5	0.7	2.6	-4.7	8.7	12.7	-0.9	8.5	-5.4	1.8	-6.7	0.0
1971-80	2.2	-0.8	1.2	2.8	1.6	2.5	5.9	2.1	2.6	0.2	4.1	0.4	1.6	2.8	3.4
1981	-16.1	-19.2	-5.0	-7.5	-3.3	-1.9	9.5	-3.1	-7.4	-10.0	5.5	-9.6	-5.0	0.6	2.4
1982	-1.7	7.1	-5.4	1.9	0.5	-1.4	-3.4	-4.7	-0.5	-4.3	2.3	5.4	-1.9	-7.2	-0.1
1983	-4.4	1.9	3.1	-1.3	-2.5	-3.6	-9.3	-0.6	-11.8	1.9	-7.1	5.0	0.0	5.8	-1.0
1984	1.7	12.9	0.1	-5.7	-5.8	-2.6	-2.5	3.6	0.1	5.2	-17.4	8.9	0.9	14.7	4.7
1985	0.7	12.6	-0.5	5.2	4.1	3.2	-7.7	0.6	-9.5	6.7	-3.5	4.2	2.1	5.5	5.3
1986	4.4	17.1	3.3	-6.2	9.9	4.5	-2.8	2.2	31.2	6.9	10.9	2.6	4.2	0.6	4.8
1987	5.6	-3.8	1.8	-5.1	14.0	4.8	-2.3	5.0	14.7	0.9	15.1	10.2	5.5	1.0	9.6
1988	15.4	-6.6	4.4	8.9	13.9	9.6	-1.6	6.9	14.1	4.5	15.0	13.5	8.7	3.7	11.9
1989	13.4	1.0	6.3	10.1	13.6	7.9	13.6	4.3	8.9	4.9	5.6	5.5	6.9	1.4	9.3
1990	8.5	-1.7	8.5	9.4	7.1	2.9	12.6	3.8	2.5	1.6	5.9	-3.4	3.8	-1.8	8.8
1981-90	2.4	1.6	1.6	0.4	4.9	2.3	0.3	1.7	3.5	1.7	2.7	4.1	2.4	2.3	5.5
1991	-1.7	-5.4	6.1	-4.4	1.7	-1.5	-7.3	0.6	9.8	0.4	2.4	-9.8	-0.4	-6.7	3.0
1992	1.0	-8.2	1.1	1.2	-3.9	-2.1	-1.9	-2.0	-2.1	1.1	5.4	-1.1	-1.0	-6.2	-1.0
1993	-7.0	-1.8	-6.9	-3.4	-10.3	-5.0	0.3	-11.1	4.0	-0.8	-3.9	0.8	-6.2	9.6	-1.3
1994	1.4	7.3	-0.3	1.9	-1.3	1.5	5.7	0.6	-1.8	-0.4	1.1	3.6	0.9	9.6	-0.9

Source: European Economy.

Table A6 Retail price inflation (per cent per annum)

	B	DK	D	GR	E	F	IRL	I	L	NL	P	UK	EU	USA	J
1964	4.2	4.0	2.2	2.2	6.7	3.4	7.0	4.9	3.0	6.8	0.8	3.6	3.9	1.6	4.1
1965	4.6	6.1	3.4	4.6	9.7	2.6	4.4	3.6	3.4	4.0	4.8	4.9	4.3	1.9	6.8
1966	4.1	6.5	3.4	3.5	7.3	3.2	3.9	2.9	3.4	5.4	5.5	4.0	4.0	2.9	4.6
1967	2.5	7.4	1.5	1.9	5.8	3.0	2.8	3.2	2.3	3.0	1.5	2.6	2.9	2.4	3.9
1968	2.9	7.1	1.6	0.7	5.1	5.0	4.8	1.5	2.5	2.6	4.3	4.7	3.4	4.3	5.1
1969	2.8	4.6	2.3	3.0	3.4	7.1	7.8	2.9	1.9	6.1	4.9	5.5	4.3	4.3	4.2
1970	2.5	6.6	3.9	3.1	6.6	5.0	12.4	5.0	4.3	4.4	3.2	5.9	5.0	4.6	7.2
1961–70	3.1	5.8	2.8	2.5	5.9	4.3	5.1	3.8	2.5	4.1	2.8	3.9	3.9	2.6	5.6
1971	5.3	8.3	5.6	2.9	7.8	6.0	9.4	5.5	4.7	7.9	7.0	8.7	6.6	4.7	6.8
1972	5.4	8.2	5.6	3.3	7.6	6.3	9.7	6.3	5.1	8.3	6.3	6.5	6.4	3.7	5.8
1973	6.1	11.7	6.7	15.0	11.4	7.4	11.6	13.9	4.9	8.5	8.9	8.4	9.2	5.6	10.8
1974	12.8	15.0	7.5	23.5	17.8	14.8	15.7	21.4	10.0	9.5	23.5	17.0	15.0	10.2	21.0
1975	12.3	9.9	6.0	12.7	15.5	11.8	18.0	16.5	10.2	10.1	16.0	23.5	13.9	8.1	11.2
1976	7.8	9.9	4.2	13.4	16.5	9.9	20.0	17.8	9.3	9.0	18.1	15.7	11.7	6.0	9.6
1977	7.2	10.6	3.4	11.9	23.7	9.4	14.1	17.6	5.7	6.1	27.3	14.7	11.8	7.0	7.4
1978	4.2	9.2	2.7	12.8	19.0	9.1	7.9	13.2	3.4	4.5	21.3	9.5	9.2	7.7	4.5
1979	3.9	10.4	4.2	16.5	16.5	10.7	14.9	14.5	4.9	4.3	25.2	13.9	10.7	8.9	3.6

1980	6.4	10.7	5.8	21.9	16.5	13.3	18.6	20.4	7.5	6.9	21.6	16.3	13.4	10.7	7.5
1971–80	7.1	10.4	5.2	13.2	15.1	9.8	13.9	14.6	6.5	7.5	17.3	13.3	10.7	7.2	8.7
1981	8.7	12.0	6.1	22.7	14.3	13.0	19.6	18.0	8.6	5.8	20.2	11.2	12.0	9.1	4.5
1982	7.8	10.2	4.9	20.7	14.5	11.5	14.9	17.0	10.6	5.5	20.3	8.7	10.7	5.9	2.7
1983	7.1	6.8	3.2	18.1	12.3	9.7	9.2	14.8	8.3	2.9	25.8	4.8	8.5	4.5	2.0
1984	5.7	6.4	2.4	17.9	11.0	7.7	7.3	12.1	6.5	2.2	28.5	5.0	7.2	3.9	2.5
1985	5.9	4.3	1.8	18.3	8.2	5.7	5.0	9.0	4.3	2.2	19.4	5.3	5.8	3.6	2.2
1986	0.7	2.9	−0.3	22.1	9.4	2.7	4.6	6.2	1.3	0.3	13.8	4.0	3.8	2.5	0.4
1987	1.9	4.6	0.7	15.7	5.7	3.2	2.6	5.3	1.7	0.2	10.0	4.3	3.6	4.1	0.2
1988	1.6	4.0	1.4	14.2	5.0	2.7	2.9	5.7	2.7	0.5	10.0	5.0	3.8	4.1	−0.1
1989	3.4	4.3	3.0	14.7	6.6	3.4	3.6	6.5	3.6	1.2	12.1	5.9	4.9	4.8	1.8
1990	3.6	2.7	2.8	19.2	6.5	2.9	1.6	5.9	3.6	2.2	12.6	5.5	4.7	5.0	2.6
1981–90	4.6	5.8	2.6	18.3	9.3	6.2	7.0	9.9	5.1	2.3	17.1	6.0	6.5	4.7	1.9
1991	2.5	2.2	3.8	18.5	6.3	3.0	2.3	6.9	2.9	3.4	11.1	7.4	5.4	4.1	2.5
1992	2.1	2.1	4.0	14.6	6.4	2.3	2.6	5.2	2.8	3.0	9.8	4.8	4.4	3.4	2.0
1993	2.8	1.7	3.3	13.7	5.1	2.2	2.0	5.1	3.6	2.1	6.8	3.5	3.8	2.6	1.1
1994	2.6	2.0	2.7	10.2	4.8	1.8	2.8	3.9	2.9	2.3	5.6	3.5	3.2	2.7	1.4

Source: European Economy.

Table A7 Current account (per cent of gross domestic product)

	B	DK	D	GR	E	F	IRL	I	L	NL	P	UK	EU	USA	J
1964	0.2	-2.2	0.2	-4.3	0.1	-0.3	-3.3	1.0	-0.1	-1.0	0.0	-1.3	-0.3	1.2	-0.5
1965	0.6	-1.8	-1.3	-5.8	-2.0	0.8	-4.2	3.4	0.7	0.1	-0.4	-0.4	0.0	0.9	1.1
1966	-0.3	-1.9	0.2	-2.0	-2.1	0.1	-1.5	3.0	1.7	-0.9	0.8	0.1	0.3	0.5	1.3
1967	0.8	-2.4	2.2	-2.2	-1.5	0.0	1.3	2.1	7.4	-0.3	3.6	-0.9	0.5	0.4	0.0
1968	0.9	-1.7	2.3	-3.6	-0.8	-0.5	-1.3	3.1	9.7	0.3	1.5	-0.8	0.7	0.2	0.8
1969	1.2	-2.8	1.4	-4.0	-1.1	-1.1	-4.6	2.5	14.0	0.2	3.6	0.6	0.5	0.2	1.3
1970	2.8	-3.9	0.6	-3.1	0.2	0.8	-3.9	0.8	15.5	-1.4	1.9	1.3	0.6	0.4	1.0
1964-70	0.6	-2.1	0.7	-3.1	-0.7	0.2	-2.2	1.6	5.6	0.0	-0.6	-0.1	0.3	0.6	0.2
1971	2.1	-2.1	0.4	-1.5	2.2	0.9	-3.7	1.4	6.6	-0.3	2.5	1.8	0.9	0.1	2.5
1972	3.6	-0.4	0.6	-1.2	1.5	1.0	-2.1	1.6	10.6	2.8	5.5	0.1	1.0	-0.3	2.2
1973	2.0	-1.7	1.5	-3.8	0.8	0.6	-3.3	-1.6	16.5	3.8	3.0	-1.9	0.3	0.6	0.0
1974	0.4	-3.1	2.7	-2.8	-3.5	-1.3	-9.4	-4.2	26.5	3.1	-6.2	-4.5	-0.9	0.5	-1.0
1975	-0.1	-1.5	1.2	-3.7	-2.9	0.8	-1.5	-0.2	17.0	2.5	-5.5	-2.0	0.0	1.3	-0.1
1976	0.3	-4.9	0.8	-1.9	-3.9	-0.9	-5.1	-1.2	21.6	2.9	-8.0	-1.6	-0.6	0.5	0.7
1977	-1.1	-4.0	0.8	-1.9	-1.7	-0.1	-5.2	1.1	21.7	0.8	-9.4	0.0	0.0	-0.5	1.5
1978	-0.3	-2.7	1.4	-1.3	1.0	1.4	-6.5	2.2	19.7	-0.9	-5.7	0.5	0.9	-0.5	1.7
1979	-2.9	-4.7	-0.5	-1.9	0.5	0.9	-12.8	1.6	21.7	-1.2	-1.7	0.2	0.0	0.0	-0.9

1980	-4.3	-3.7	-1.7	0.5	-2.4	-0.6	-11.3	-2.2	19.0	-1.4	-5.9	1.5	-1.2	0.4	-1.0
1971–80	-0.1	-2.9	0.7	-1.9	-0.8	0.3	-6.1	-0.1	18.1	1.2	-3.1	-0.6	0.0	0.2	0.6
1981	-3.8	-3.0	-0.6	-0.7	-2.7	-0.8	-14.1	-2.2	21.3	2.2	-12.2	2.5	-0.6	0.3	0.5
1982	-3.7	-4.2	0.8	-4.4	-2.5	-2.1	-10.1	-1.5	34.4	3.1	-13.5	1.5	-0.6	-0.1	0.7
1983	-0.8	-2.6	0.9	-5.0	-1.5	-0.8	-6.6	0.3	39.5	3.1	-8.3	0.8	0.1	-1.0	1.8
1984	-0.6	-3.3	1.4	-4.0	1.4	0.0	-5.6	-0.6	39.1	4.1	-3.4	-0.3	0.3	-2.5	2.8
1985	0.3	-4.6	2.4	-8.2	1.4	0.1	-3.8	-0.9	43.8	4.3	0.4	0.3	0.6	-2.9	3.6
1986	2.1	-5.4	4.3	-5.3	1.6	0.5	-3.3	0.5	38.8	3.1	2.4	-1.1	1.3	-3.3	4.3
1987	1.3	-2.9	4.1	-3.1	0.1	-0.2	-0.2	-0.2	30.3	1.9	-0.4	-2.2	0.7	-3.4	3.6
1988	1.7	-1.3	4.3	-2.0	-1.1	-0.3	0.0	-0.7	30.8	2.8	-4.4	-4.9	0.1	-2.4	2.8
1989	1.7	-1.5	4.8	-5.0	-3.2	-0.5	-1.7	-1.3	34.0	3.5	-2.3	-5.5	-0.2	-1.7	2.0
1990	0.9	0.5	3.6	-6.2	-3.7	-0.9	-0.7	-1.4	34.2	3.8	-2.5	-4.5	-0.4	-1.4	1.3
1981–90	-0.1	-2.8	2.6	-4.4	-1.0	-0.5	-4.6	-0.8	34.6	3.2	-4.4	-1.3	0.1	-1.9	2.4
1991	1.8	1.3	1.4	-5.1	-3.6	-0.5	2.0	-1.8	27.9	3.6	-2.9	-2.4	-0.6	0.2	2.5
1992	1.8	3.0	1.6	-4.3	-3.8	0.2	3.6	-2.2	30.0	3.2	-3.2	-2.4	-0.3	-0.9	3.3
1993	3.0	3.6	1.9	-3.6	-1.8	0.9	4.1	1.1	28.3	4.0	-3.5	-2.5	0.7	-1.7	3.1
1994	3.0	3.0	2.3	-3.8	-0.8	0.9	3.5	1.1	29.6	4.6	-3.6	-1.7	1.1	-1.7	2.9

Source: European Economy.

BIBLIOGRAPHY

Ackrill, R. W. (1992), 'The EU Budget and Agricultural Policy Reforms, with Special Reference to Cereals', unpublished PhD thesis, University of Nottingham

Ackrill, R. W., Rayner, A. J., Ingersent, K. A. and Hine, C. (1993), 'Reform of the Common Agricultural Policy and Budgetary Expenditures: The Cereals Sector', *Department of Economics Discussion Paper*, No. 93/3, University of Nottingham

Addison, J. and Siebert, W. (1993), *Social Engineering in the European Union: The Social Charter, Maastricht and Beyond*, IEA

Agra Europe, various issues

Alesina, A. (1989), 'Politics and Business Cycles in Industrial Democracies', *Economic Policy*, Vol. 8

Alesina, A. and Grilli, V. U. (1991), 'The European Central Bank: Reshaping Monetary Politics in Europe', *CEPR Discussion Paper Series*, No. 563, Centre for Economic Policy Research

Appleby, J. (1988), 'Why 1992 may be Disastrous for Health', *British Medical Journal* 296: 1620

Artis, M. (1989), 'The Call of a Common Currency', *The Social Market Foundation*, Paper No. 3

Artis, M. (1992), 'The Maastricht Road to Monetary Union', *Journal of Common Market Studies*, Vol. XXX

Artis, M. (1994), 'Stage Two: Feasible Transition to EMU', in D. Cobham (ed.), *European Monetary Upheavals*, Manchester University Press

Artus, J. R. and Young, J. H. (1979), 'Fixed and Flexible Exchange Rates: A Renewal of the Debate', *IMF Staff Papers*, Vol. 26

Backus, D. and Driffill, J. (1985), 'Inflation and Reputation', *American Economic Review*, Vol. 75

Balassa, B. (1961), *The Theory of Economic Integration*, Allen and Unwin

Baldwin, R. (1989), 'The Growth Effects of 1992', *Economic Policy*, Vol. 9

Bank of England (1990), 'The Exchange Rate Mechanism of the European Monetary System', *Bank of England Quarterly Bulletin*, Vol. 30, No. 4

Bank of England (1991), 'The Exchange Rate Mechanism of the

European Monetary System: A Review of the Literature', *Bank of England Quarterly Bulletin*, Vol. 31, No. 1

Bank of England (1992), 'The Maastricht Agreement on Economic and Monetary Union', *Bank of England Quarterly Bulletin*, Vol. 32, No. 1

Barber, L. (1993), 'Now Comes the Hard Part', *Financial Times Survey*

Barrell, R. (1992), *Economic Convergence and Monetary Union in Europe*, Sage

Barro, R. J. and Gordon, D. B. (1983), 'Rules, Discretion and Reputation in a Model of Monetary Policy', *Journal of Monetary Economics*, Vol. 12

Barro, R. J. and Sala-i-Martin, X. (1991), 'Convergence across States and Regions', *Brookings Papers*, No. 1

Barro, R. J. and Sala-i-Martin, X. (1992), 'Convergence', *Journal of Political Economy*, Vol. 100

Bayoumi, T. and Eichengreen, B. (1992), 'Shocking Aspects of European Monetary Unification', *CEPR Discussion Paper*, No. 643, Centre for Economic Policy Research

Beenstock, M., Capie, F. and Griffiths, B. (1984), 'Economic Recovery in the United Kingdom in the 1930s', in Bank of England Panel Paper No. 23, *The UK Recovery in the 1930s*

Begg, D. (1991), 'European Monetary Union – The Macro Issues', in *The Making of Monetary Union*, Centre for Economic Policy Research

Begg, D (1992), *Monitoring European Integration: The Making of Monetary Union*, Centre for Economic Policy Research

Begg, I. and Weale, M. (1990), 'Monetary Integration and the Balance of Payments', *Oxford Review of Economic Policy*, Vol. 6, No. 3

Booz, Allen and Hamilton (1989), *The Effects of the Internal Market on Greece, Ireland, Portugal and Spain*, EC Commission

Borts, G. H. (1960), 'The Equalization of Returns and Regional Economic Growth', *American Economic Review*, Vol. 50

Borts, G. H. and Stein, J. L. (1964), *Economic Growth in a Free Market*, Columbia University Press

Bos, M. and Nelson, H. (1988), 'Indirect Taxation and the Completion of the Internal Market of the EC', *Journal of Common Market Studies*, Vol. XXVII

Brittan, L. (1991), 'European Monetary Union: What Money for Europe?', *TSB Forum*

Brociner, A. (1991), 'Credibility, Fiscal Policy and EMU', *University of Leicester Discussion Paper*, No. 143

Brociner, A. and Levine, P. (1992a), 'EMU: A Survey', *Discussion Papers in European Economic Studies*, No. 92/3, Centre for European Economic Studies

Brociner, A. and Levine, P. (1992b), 'Fiscal Policy Coordination and EMU: A Dynamic Game Approach', *CEPR Discussion Paper*, No. 420, Centre for Economic Policy Research

Cantwell, J. (1989), *Technological Innovation and Multinational Corporations*, Basil Blackwell

Cantwell, J. (1992), 'The Relationship between International Trade and International Production', *Discussion Papers in International Investment and Business Studies*, No. 161, University of Reading

Cecchini, P. (1988), *The European Challenge: 1992 The Benefits of a Single Market*, Wildwood House

Centre for Economic Policy Research, (1992), 'Is Bigger Better? The Economics of EU Enlargement', *Monitoring European Integration*, No. 3

Centre for Economic Policy Research (1991), *The Road to EMU: Managing the Transition to a Single Currency*

Church, C. (1991), 'EFTA and the European Union', *PNL European Dossier*, No. 21

Cohen, D. and Wyplosz, C. (1990), 'Price and Trade Effects of Exchange Rate Fluctuations and the Design of Policy Coordination', *CEPR Discussion Paper*, Centre for Economic Policy Research

Collignon, S. (1994), *Europe's Monetary Future*, Pinter Publishers

Council of Ministers (1992), *Treaty on European Union*

Crafts, N. (1992), 'Productivity Growth Reconsidered', *Economic Policy*, Vol. 15

Culter, T., Haslem, C., Williams, J. and Williams, K. (1989), *1992 – The Struggle for Europe*, Berg

Currie, D. (1991), 'EMU: A Rocky Road from Maastricht', *International Economic Outlook*, December

Currie, D. (1992), 'European Monetary Union: Institutional Structure and Economic Performance', *The Economic Journal*, Vol. 102, No. 411

Davies, E., Kay, J. and Swales, C. (1989), *1992: Myths and Realities*, London Business School

Davies, G. (1989), 'Britain and the European Monetary Question', *Institute of Public Policy Research Economic Study*, No. 1

de Grauwe, P. (1988), 'Exchange Rate Variability and the Slowdown in Growth of International Trade', *IMF Staff Papers*, Vol. 35

de Grauwe, P. (1992), *The Economics of Monetary Integration*, Oxford University Press

de Grauwe, P. and Vanhaverbeke, W. (1991), 'Is Europe an Optimum Currency Area? Evidence from Regional Data', *CEPR Discussion Paper*, No. 555, Centre for Economic Policy Research

Delors, J. (1989), *Report on Economic and Monetary Union in the European Community*, Committee for the Study of Economic and Monetary Union, EC Commission

Demekas, D. G. (1988), 'The Effects of the Common Agricultural Policy of the European Union: A Survey of the Literature', *Journal of Common Market Studies*, Vol. XXVII

Demopoulos, G., Katsimbris, G. and Miller, S. (1987), 'Monetary Policy and Central Bank Financing of Government Budget Deficits', *European Economic Review*, Vol. 31

Dixon, R. J. and Thirlwall, A. P. (1975), 'A Model of Regional Growth Rate Differentials along Kaldorian Lines', *Oxford Economic Papers*, Vol. 27

Drazen, A. (1989), 'Monetary Policy, Capital Controls and Seigniorage in an Open Economy', in M. De Cecco and A. Giovannini, (ed.), *A European Central Bank? Perspectives on Monetary Unification after Ten Years of the EMS*, Cambridge University Press

Dunning, J. H. (1986), *Japanese Participation in British Industry*, Croom Helm

Dunning, J. H. (1988), *Explaining International Production*, Unwin Hyman

Dunning, J. H. (1990), *Transnational Corporations and the Growth of Services: Some Conceptual and Theoretical Issues*, UN Centre on Transnational Corporations

EC Commission (1983), *Britain in the Union, 1973–83: Ten Years in Europe*

EC Commission (1984), 'Study of the Regional Impact of the Community's External Trade Policy', *Regional Policy Series*, No. 24

EC Commission (1985), *Completing the Internal Market – White Paper from the Commission to the European Council*

EC Commission (1988a), 'Commission Communication on the Method of Application of Article 92(3)(a) and (c) to Regional Aid', *Official Journal*

EC Commission (1988b), *The Costs of Non-Europe*

EC Commission (1989a), 'First Survey on State Aids in the European Communities', Press Release

EC Commission (1989b), *Guide to the Reform of the Community's Structural Funds*

EC Commission (1990a), 'European Union Charter of the Fundamental Social Rights of Workers', *Social Europe*, No. 1

EC Commission (1990b), 'One Market, One Money – An Evaluation of the Potential Benefits and Costs of Forming an Economic and Monetary Union', *European Economy*, No. 44

EC Commission (1990c), 'The Impact of the Internal Market by Industrial Sector', *European Economy*, Special Edition

EC Commission (1991a), 'Developments in the Labour Market in the Union: Results of a Survey Covering Employers and Employees', *European Economy*, March

EC Commission (1991b), *Europe 2000: Outlook for the Development of the Community's Territory*

EC Commission (1991c), *The Regions in the 1990s: Fourth Periodic Report on the Social and Economic Situation and Development of the Regions of the Community*

EC Commission (1992a), *Third Survey on State Aids in the European Community in the Manufacturing and Certain Other Sectors*

EC Commission (1992b), 'Unemployment in the Regions of the Community in 1992', *Rapid Report 2*

EC Commission (1992c), 'First Report on the Application of the Union Charter of the Fundamental Social Rights of Workers', *Social Europe*, No. 1

EC Commission (1992d), *The Internal Market after 1992*

EC Commission (1993), *Community Structural Funds 1994–1999*

Eichengreen, B. (1990a), 'Costs and Benefits of European Monetary Unification', *CEPR Discussion Paper*, No. 435, Centre for Economic Policy Research

Eichengreen, B. (1990b), 'One Money for Europe? Lessons from the US Currency Union', *Economic Policy*, April

Eichengreen, B. (1992), *Golden Fetters: The Gold Standard and the Great Depression, 1919–39*, Oxford University Press

El-Agraa, A. (1983), *Britain within the European Union*, Macmillan

El-Agraa, A. (1994), *The Economics of the European Community*, Harvester Wheatsheaf

Emerson, M. (1988), *The Economics of 1992: the EC Commission's Assessment of the Economic Effects of Completing the Internal Market*, Oxford University Press

Emerson, M. (1992), *One Market, One Money: An Evaluation of the Potential Benefits and Costs of Forming an Economic and Monetary Union*, Oxford University Press

Emerson, M. and Huhne, C. (1991), *The ECU Report*, Pan Books

European Parliament (1991), 'A New Strategy for Social and Economic Cohesion after 1992', *Regional Policy and Transport Series*, No. 19

Export–Import Bank of Japan (1991), *Survey of Japanese Overseas Direct Investment 1990–93*, Research Institute of Overseas Investment, Export–Import Bank of Japan

Export–Import Bank of Japan (1992), *Results of FY1991 Foreign Direct Investment Survey*, Research Institute of Overseas Investment, Export–Import Bank of Japan

Feldstein, M. (1992), 'Europe's Monetary Union: The Case Against EMU', *The Economist*, June 13

Financial Times (1993), 'International Mergers and Acquisitions', *Financial Times*, September 17

Fourcans, A. (1992), 'One Currency for Europe: From Theory to Practice', *European Research*, Vol. 3, No. 3

Friedman, M. (1953), 'The Case for Flexible Exchange Rates', in *Essays in Positive Economics*, University of Chicago

Friedman, M. (1968), 'The Role of Monetary Policy', *American Economic Review*, Vol. 58

Friedman, M. (1975), 'Unemployment versus Inflation?', Occasional Paper 49, Institute of Economic Affairs

Gatsios, K. and Seabright, P. (1993), 'Regulation in the European Community', *Oxford Review of Economic Policy*, Vol. 5, No. 2

Gittelman, M. and Dunning, J. H. (1991), 'Japanese Multinationals in Europe and the United States: Some Comparisons and Contrasts', in M. W. Klein and P. J. J. Welfens (eds), *Multinational Enterprises in the New Europe and Global Trade*, Springer

Goodhart, C. A. E. (1991), 'An Assessment of EMU', *The Royal Bank of Scotland Review*, No. 171

Grahl, J. and Teague, P. (1990), *1992: The Big Market*, Lawrence and Wishart

Grilli, V. (1989), 'Seigniorage in Europe', in M. De Cecco and A. Giovannini (eds), *A European Central Bank? Perspectives on Monetary Unification after Ten Years of the EMS*, Cambridge University Press

Gros, D. (1989), 'Paradigms for the Monetary Union of Europe', *Journal of Common Market Studies*, Vol. XXVII, No. 3

Haaland, I. J. (1990), 'Assessing the Effects of EU Integration on EFTA Countries: The Position of Norway and Sweden', *Journal of Common Market Studies*, Vol. XXVII

Harden, I. (1990), 'EuroFed or "Monster Bank"?', *National Westminster Bank Quarterly Review*, August

Harris, P. and McDonald, F. (1993), *European Business and Marketing: Strategic Issues*, Paul Chapman Publishing

Healey, N. M. (1988), 'The Case for Britain Joining the European Monetary System', *Economic Affairs*, Vol. 8, No. 3, February/March

Healey, N. M. (1990), 'Taking the Plunge: Britain and the European Monetary System', *The Contemporary Review*, Vol. 257, No. 1499, December

Healey, N. M. (1991a), 'The European Road to Monetary Union', *Financial Review*, Spring

Healey, N. M. (1991b), 'EC92: The Coming of "Fortress Europe"?', *Business Quarterly*, Vol. 55, No. 4, Spring

Healey, N. M. (1991c), 'The End of Nation States?', *The Contemporary Review*, Vol. 259, No. 1510, November

Healey, N. M. (1992a), 'Sterling and the Exchange Rate Mechanism', *British Economy Survey*, Vol. 22, No. 1, Autumn

Healey, N. M. (1992b), 'From the Treaty of Rome to the Single Market', *Developments in Economics*, Vol. 8, Causeway Press

Healey, N. M. (1992c), 'European Monetary Integration' in A. Griffiths (ed.), *European Community Survey*, Longman

Healey, N. M. (1993a), 'Germany Policy Leadership and the Exchange Rate Mechanism: Anti-Inflation Anchor or Fault Line?', *Financial Review*, Summer

Healey, N. M. (1993b), 'The Exchange Rate Mechanism in Crisis', *British Economy Survey*, Vol. 23, No. 1, Autumn

Healey, N. M. (1993c), 'European Monetary Union', *Developments in Economics*, Vol. 9, Causeway Press

Healey, N. M. (1994), 'The Transition Economies of Central and Eastern Europe: A Political, Economic, Social and Technological Analysis', *The Columbia Journal of World Business*, Vol. XXIX, No. 1

Healey, N. M. and Levine, P. (1992a), 'The Economics of European Monetary Union', *The Economic Review*, Vol. 9, No. 4

Healey, N. M. and Levine, P. (1992b), 'Unpleasant Monetarist Arithmetic Revisited: Central Bank Independence, Fiscal Policy and European Monetary Union', *National Westminster Bank Quarterly Review*, August

Healey, N. M. and Levine, P. (1995), 'Should an Independent European Central Bank be Independent?', *Bulletin of European International Trade and Economic Issues*, Vol. 1

Healey N. M. , Levine, P. and Pearlman, J. (1994), 'The Political Economy of an Independent European Central Bank', *Current Politics and Economics of Europe*, Vol. 4

Heitger, B. and Stehn, J. (1990), 'Japanese Investment in the EC – Response to the Internal Market 1993?', *Journal of Common Market Studies*, Vol. XXIV

Hill, A. (1993), 'No Soft Touch for Business', *Financial Times*, January 15

Hirschman, A. O. (1958), *The Strategy of Economic Development*, Yale University Press

Holtham, G. (1989), 'Foreign Exchange Markets and Target Zones', *Oxford Review of Economic Policy*, Vol. 5, No. 3

Hughes, K. (1992), 'Competition and the Single Market', *Policy Studies*, Vol. 13, No. 3

ILO (1940), *Year Book of Labour Statistics, 1940*, International Labour Office

Ingersent, K. A., Rayner, A. J. and Hine, R. C. (1993), 'Agriculture in the Uruguay Round: The Blair House Agreement and Subsequent Developments', *CREDIT Research Paper*, No. 93/11, Department of Economics. University of Nottingham

Jackman, R. and Rubin, M. (1991), 'Should We Be Afraid of the Social Charter?', *Employment Institute Economic Report*, August

Jenkins, R. (1978), 'European Monetary Union', *Lloyds Bank Review*, No. 127

JETRO (1990), *Current Situation of Business Operations of Japanese-Manufacturing Enterprises in Europe*, JETRO International Economic and Trade Information Center

JETRO (1991), *7th Survey of European Operations of Japanese Companies in the Manufacturing Sector*, JETRO International Economic and Trade Information Center

Johnson, H. G. (1965), 'An Economic Theory of Protectionism, Tariff Bargaining and the Formation of Customs Unions', *Journal of Political Economy*, Vol. 73

Johnson, P. (1992), 'New Firms: The Key to Employment Creation?', in N. M. Healey (ed.), *Britain's Economic Miracle: Myth or Reality?*, Routledge

Journal of Common Market Studies, Special Issue, Vol. XXVIII, 1990 ('The European Union, EFTA and the New Europe')

Kaldor, N. (1970), 'The Case for Regional Policies', *Scottish Journal of Political Economy*, Vol. 17

Keynes, J. M. (1919), 'The Economic Consequences of the Peace', in *The Collected Writings of John Maynard Keynes. Volume IX: Essays in Persuasion*, Royal Economic Society/Macmillan.

Keynes, J. M. (1925), 'The Economic Consequences of Mr Churchill', in *The Collected Writings of John Maynard Keynes. Volume IX: Essays in Persuasion*, Royal Economic Society/Macmillan.

Kitson, M. and Solomou, S. (1990), *Protectionism and Economic Revival: The British Interwar Economy*, Cambridge University Press

Kotios, A. and Schafers, M. (1990), 'The Social Dimension and Cohesion: Complementary or Contradictory?', *Intereconomics*, May/June

Krugman, P. (1989), 'The Case for Stabilising Exchange Rates', *Oxford Review of Economic Policy*, Vol. 5, No. 3

Kydland, F. and Prescott, E. C. (1977), 'Rules Rather Than Discretion: The Inconsistency of Optimal Plans', *Journal of Political Economy*, Vol. 85

Labour Party (1989), *Meeting the Challenge in Europe*

Levine, P. (1992), 'Fiscal Policy Coordination under EMU and the Choice of Monetary Instrument', *Discussion Papers in European Economic Studies*, No. 92/8, Centre for European Economic Studies

Levine, P. and Pearlman, J. (1992), 'Fiscal and Monetary Policy under EMU: Credible Inflation Targets or Unpleasant Monetary Arithmetic?', *Discussion Papers in European Economic Studies*, No. 92/10, Centre for European Economic Studies

Levine, P. (1990) 'The European Road to Monetary Union', *European Research*, Vol. 1, Pt 6

Lintner, V. and Mazey, S. (1991), *The European Union: Economic and Political Aspects*, McGraw-Hill

Lomax, D. F. (1991), 'A European Central Bank and Economic and Monetary Union', *National Westminster Bank Quarterly Review*, May

Lucas, R. E. (1976), 'Econometric Policy Evaluation: A Critique', in K. Brunner and A. H. Meltzer (eds), *The Phillips Curve and Labour Markets*, Carnegie Rochester Conference Series on Public Policy, North-Holland.

MacDougall, D. (1977), *Public Finance in European Integration*, EC Commission

Markusen, J. R. (1987), 'Multinationals, Multiplant Economies and Gains from Trade', *Journal of International Economics*, Vol. 16

Masson, P. and Merlitz, J. (1990), 'Fiscal Policy Interdependence in a Monetary Union', *CEPR Discussion Paper*, Centre for Economic Policy Research

Masson, P. and Symansky, S. (1992), 'Evaluating the EMS and EMU Using Stochastic Simulations: Some Issues', Mimeo, International Monetary Fund

Masson, P., Symansky, S. and Meredith, G. (1990), 'Multimod Mark II: A Revised and Extended Model', *IMF Occasional Paper*, No. 71, July

Matthews, K. (1992), 'Britain's Economic Renaissance', in N. M. Healey (ed.), *Britain's Economic Miracle: Myth or Reality?*, Routledge

McDonald, F. and Dearden, S. (1994), *European Economic Integration*, second edition, Longman

McDonald, F. and Zis, G. (1989), 'The European Monetary System: Towards 1992 and Beyond', *Journal of Common Market Studies*, Vol. XXVIII

McKenzie, G. and Venables, A. (1991), *The Economics of the Single European Act*, Macmillan

McKenzie, G. and Venables, T. (1989), 'The Economics of 1992', *The Economic Review*, Vol. 6, No. 5

Meade, J. (1990), 'The EMU and the Control of Inflation', *Oxford Review of Economic Policy*, Vol. 6, No. 4

Michie, J. (1987), *Wages in the Business Cycle: An Empirical and Methodological Analysis*, Pinter Publishers

Michie, J. and Grieve-Smith, J. (1993), *Unemployment in Europe*, Academic Press

Minford, P. and Rastogi, A. (1990), 'The Price of EMU', in R. Dornbusch and R. Layard (eds) *Britain and EMU*, Centre for Economic Performance

Minford, P., Agenor, P. and Nowell, P. (1986), 'A New Classical Econometric Model of the World Economy', *Economic Modelling*, Vol. 3

Minford, P., Rastogi, A. and Hughes-Hallett, A. (1992), 'The Price of EMU Revisited', *CEPR Working Paper*, No. 656, Centre for Economic Policy Research

Morgan, E. J. (1993), 'Merger Appraisal under the EC Merger Control

Regulation', in M. Casson and J. Creedy (eds), *Economic Inequality and Industrial Concentration: Essays in Honour of Peter Hart*, Edward Elgar

Morsink, R. L. A. and Molle, W. T. M. (1991), 'Direct Investments and Monetary Integration', *European Economy*, Special Edition No. 1

Munday, M. (1990), *Japanese Manufacturing Investment in Wales*, University of Wales Press

Mundell, R. A. (1957), 'International Trade and Factor Mobility', *American Economic Review*, Vol. 47

Mundell, R. A. (1961), 'A Theory of Optimum Currency Areas', *American Economic Review*, Vol. 51

Myrdal, G. (1957), *Economic Theory and Underdeveloped Regions*, Duckworth.

National Farmers' Union (1990), *Farm Support Policies – The Reasons Why*, NFU

Neumann, M. (1990), 'Central Bank Independence as a Prerequisite of Price Stability', Mimeo, University of Bonn

Nevin, E. (1990), *The Economics of Europe*, Macmillan

Nicholson, F. and East, R. (1987), *From the Six to the Twelve: The Enlargement of the European Communities*, Longman

Nicolaides, P. and Thomsen, S. (1991), 'Can Protectionism Explain Foreign Direct Investment?', *Journal of Common Market Studies*, Vol. XXIX

Nicoll, W. and Salmon, T. C. (1994), *Understanding the New European Community*, Harvester Wheatsheaf

Norman, G. and Dunning, J. H. (1984), 'Intra-industry Foreign Direct Investment: Its Rationale and Trade Effects', *Weltwirtschaftliches Archiv*, No. 120

Organisation for Economic Cooperation and Development (1989), *Employment Outlook*, July, OECD

PA Cambridge Economic Consultants (1989), *The Regional Consequences of the Completion of the Internal Market for Financial Services*, Study for the EC Commission

Paterson, I. and Simpson, L. (1992), 'The Economics of Trade Union Power', in N. M. Healey (ed.), *Britain's Economic Miracle: Myth or Reality?*, Routledge

Perlman, M. (1991), 'In Search of Monetary Unions', *Financial Markets Group Special Paper*, No. 39, October

Perroux, F. (1950), 'Economic Space: Theory and Applications', *Quarterly Journal of Economics*, Vol. 64

Prescott, K. and Welford, R. (1992), *European Business: An Issue-based Approach*, Pitman

Preston, J. (1992), *Cases in European Business*, Pitman

Rayner A. J., Ingersent, K. A., Hine, R. C. and Ackrill, R. W. (1993), 'Does the CAP fit the GATT? A model of EU cereals', *CREDIT Research Paper*, No. 93/14, University of Nottingham

Rhodes, M. (1992), 'The Future of the "Social Dimension": Labour Market Regulation in Post–1992 Europe', *Journal of Common Market Studies*, March

Robinson, J. (1966), *The New Mercantilism, An Inaugural Lecture*, Cambridge University Press

Rogoff, K. (1985), 'The Optimal Degree of Commitment to an Intermediate Monetary Target', *Quarterly Journal of Economics*, Vol. 100

Rollo, J. and Smith, A. (1993), 'The Political Economy of Eastern Europe's Trade with the EU: Why So Sensitive?', *Economic Policy*, Vol. 16, April

Sapir, A., Buigues, P. and Jacquemin, A. (1993), 'European Competition Policy in Manufacturing and Services: A Two Speed Approach', *Oxford Review of Economic Policy*, Summer

Sargent, T. J. and Wallace, N. (1981), 'Some Unpleasant Monetarist Arithmetic', *Federal Reserve Bank of Minneapolis Quarterly Review*, Vol. 5, No. 3

Smith, S. (1988), 'Excise Duties and the Internal Market', *Journal of Common Market Studies*, Vol. 27, No. 2

Sumner, M. T. and Zis, G. (1982), 'On the Relative Bias of Flexible Exchange Rates', reprinted in M. T. Sumner and G. Zis (eds) (1993), *European Monetary Union: Progress and Prospects*, Macmillan

Swann, D. (1992), *The Single European Market and Beyond: A Study of the Wider Implications of the Single European Act*, Routledge

Temperton, P. (1993), *The European Currency Crisis: What Chance Now for a Single European Currency?*, Probus Publishing

Tharakan, P. K. M. (1991), 'The Political Economy of Anti-dumping Undertakings in the European Communities', *European Economic Review*, Vol. 35

The Economist (1989a), 'Sorry, I'll Read That Again', April 15

The Economist (1989b), 'The Passionate Dimension', April 8

The Economist (1989c), 'Set Up or Stay Out', February 18

The Economist (1989d), 'March in the EEC', April 1

The Economist (1989e), 'A Tilt in the Internal Balance', May 20

Thomsen, S. and Nicolaides, P. (1991), *The Evolution of Japanese Direct Investment in Europe: Death of a Transistor Salesman*, Harvester Wheatsheaf

Tsoukalis, L. (1991), *The European Union and its Mediterranean Enlargement*, Allen and Unwin

Ungerer, H. *et al.* (1986), 'The European Monetary System – Recent Developments', *Occasional Papers*, No. 48, International Monetary Fund

United Nations (1991), *World Investment Report 1991*, United Nations

van der Ploeg, F. (1989), 'Monetary Interdependence under Alternative Exchange Rate Regimes: A European Perspective', *CEPR Discussion Paper*, No. 358, Centre for Economic Policy Research

Vaubel, R. (1988), 'Monetary Integration Theory', in G. Zis (ed.), *International Economics*, Longman

Vickerman, R. W. (1992), *The Single European Market*, Harvester Wheatsheaf

Viner, J. (1950), *The Customs Union Issue*, Carnegie Endowment for International Peace

von Hagen, J. and Neumann, M. (1991), 'Real Exchange Rates Within and Between Currency Areas: How Far Away is EMU?', *Center for Global Business Discussion Paper*, No. 62, Indiana University

Walters, A. A. (1986), *Britain's Economic Renaissance*, Oxford University Press

BIBLIOGRAPHY

Whiteford, E. (1993), 'Social Policy After Maastricht', *European Law Review*, Vol. 18

Williamson, J. (1965), 'The Crawling Peg', *Essays in International Finance*, No. 50, Princeton University

Winters, L. A. (1987), 'Britain in Europe: A Survey of Quantitative Trade Studies', *Journal of Common Market Studies*, Vol. XXV

Yannopoulos, G. N. (1986), *Greece and the EEC*, Macmillan

INDEX

303

Printed in the United States
by Baker & Taylor Publisher Services